Letterland

Phonics Teacher's Guide

By Stamey Carter
and
Lyn Wendon
Originator of Letterland

Published by Letterland International Ltd,
Leatherhead, Surrey, KT22 9AD, UK

© Letterland International 2013
Reprinted 2018.
10 9 8 7 6 5 4 3 2

ISBN: 978-1-86209-961-6
Product Code: TE80

LETTERLAND® is a registered trademark of Lyn Wendon.

Written by: Stamey Carter, Lyn Wendon
Originator of Letterland: Lyn Wendon
Editor: Lisa Holt
Design: Lisa Holt, Sarah Edwards
Cover photograph: iStockphoto.com ©Mark Bowden

Adapted and extended from the 2003 edition of the Letterland Teacher's Guide by Gudrun Freese.

The author asserts the moral right to be identifi ed as the author of this work.

A catalogue record for this book is available from the British Library.

Welcome to Letterland

What is Letterland?

Letterland is a unique, phonics-based approach to teaching reading, writing and spelling to 3-8 year olds. Its characters make plain black letter shapes and their sounds easy and fun to remember. They give speedy access to all 44 sounds and their major spellings. They create fast, smooth transitions to blending plain letters to read, and segmenting spoken words to spell. The result? Young, confident and motivated readers and writers!

How does it work?

Hold your hand in front of your mouth and breathe onto it.

Sounds

Harry Hat Man makes the sound at the beginning of his name. Just whisper it – 'hhh...'.

Shapes

Hurry from the Hat Man's head down to his heel on the ground.

Go up and bend his knee over, so he'll hop while he makes his sound.

Actions

Actions for each letter of the alphabet create strong multisensory cues for quickly learning and recalling letter shapes and sounds.

Uppercase

When Harry Hat Man gets a chance to start an important word, he is so happy that he does a handstand with his hat still on.

Digraphs

Whenever Sammy Snake starts to hiss loudly behind Harry Hat Man, the Hat Man turns back and says 'sh!' because he hates noise.

Multisensory learning

Letterland activates every learning channel through simple phonics-related stories, actions, songs and activities.

1. Learn letter sounds

Once you have met the friendly Letterland characters, just start to say their names for the correct letter sound. Songs reinforce learning.

2. Learn letter shapes

Simple rhymes about the Letterland characters ensure correct letter formation, avoiding confusion over similar looking letters.

3. Word building

Blending and segmenting all through words is introduced very early on, covering blends, digraphs and trigraphs.

4. Advanced spelling

Phonics stories give children a friendly logic for remembering all 44 letter sounds and their major spellings.

Contents

Section 3: Blending with Adjacent Consonants 107-121

Section 4: Long Vowels...122-147

Section 5: Further Vowel Sounds and Spellings 148-177

Section 6: Appendix 178-225

The authors

Over the years Letterland has proven itself to be a powerful motivator, enabling children to enjoy learning to read, write and spell well. By drawing on visual, auditory, kinaesthetic and tactile learning channels with equal strength, Letterland is designed to impart essential phonic knowledge and skills in very natural ways, so that children develop into confident readers and writers from an early age.

I am therefore delighted to present this most up-to-date edition of Letterland which boasts three extremely powerful credentials. It is based on the latest and best research on how children learn. It meets the UK Government's core criteria for high quality phonics programmes. And happily it also matches the playful ways that children's minds work!

Lyn Wendon

Originator of Letterland

As educators and parents, we all want to prepare children for our fast-moving, technologically advancing world. But we also want them to be allowed to play, sing and laugh as children are wired to do.

Children's play is increasingly understood to be just as important to becoming complete, successful human beings as is the best academic training we can provide.

I love seeing children in Letterland classrooms developing both phonic skills and an enjoyment and confidence in *learning to read* that turns them into youngsters who love *reading to learn*.

Stamey Carter

Co-author

What's new?

This new edition of the Letterland Phonics Teacher's Guide includes many exciting new features with a greater emphasis on:

- Systematic decoding through the whole word, left to right
- Daily reviews of previously learned phonics (letter to sound/sound to letter)
- Blending and segmenting throughout the lessons after the first six letters
- A decodable story to go with each new sound and spelling learned
- New multisensory, phonics focused learning strategies
- Carefully sequenced teaching of 'tricky' words
- Assessment with optional quick weekly progress checks and in-depth assessments.

As always, children learn letter sounds and shapes faster with the Letterland characters. Then they immediately apply that knowledge to plain letters and to decoding words.

"Harry Hat   /**h**/
Man"

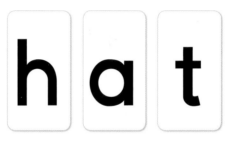

/**h**/ /**ă**/ /**t**/, **hat**

Teacher's Guide CD with:

- Assessment strand
- Fluency Lists
- Decodable Take-Home Booklets
- Learning activities

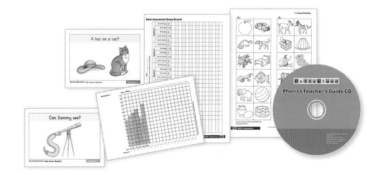

Now children have many more opportunities to practise their phonics in new decodable stories.

- **Phonics Readers** 83 short illustrated stories to accompany each new sound and spelling pattern taught.

✓ **Fully meets DfE core criteria for high quality phonics resources**

Teaching sections overview

This guide comprises of 103 lesson plans in five sections with a full assessment programme on the accompanying *Teacher's Guide CD*. In addition, an extensive Appendix offers details of all the learning strategies to help you teach your children. The sections are briefly described below. The following page lists the teaching focus and the assessment objectives of each section.

Section 1: Fast Track - Phonemic Awareness

The Fast Track provides a special group of strategies to give your children a quick and active start toward literacy. Children will be introduced to all 26 **a-z** letters and sounds (grapheme phoneme correspondences) in about three weeks. Special assessment options will help you see who needs more practice.

Section 2: a-z Word Building

After the Fast Track lessons, there is much more to learn about letters. In this section, each letter is the focus of a full lesson. Children will learn correct letter formation and how to recognise both upper and lowercase letter shapes. After the first six letters, they will begin to blend and segment sounds into CVC (consonant-vowel-consonant) words and start to read stories with the sounds they have just learned.

Section 3: Blending with Adjacent Consonants

In this section, children apply the sounds and the blending/segmenting techniques they learned in the previous section and read and spell words with adjacent consonants in words of four phonemes. They will also learn a steadily growing number of 'tricky' words.

Section 4: Long Vowels

In this section, children learn more about long vowels, allowing them to decode thousands of new words. They will continue to blend and segment and read longer, more complex stories.

Section 5: Further Vowel Sounds and Spellings

In this section, children will learn new sounds and new spelling patterns that make more and more words accessible. In addition they will learn more 'tricky' words and build fluency and comprehension by reading more challenging stories.

Appendix: Teaching and Learning Strategies

This section guides you through the steps for each of the important strategies regularly used in the lessons.

Activity Bank

The Activity Bank provides you with more phonics activities to add variety to daily lessons.

Teacher's Guide CD

This is an essential extension of your *Teacher's Guide*. It includes the Assessment Section and further useful resources. Full contents are listed on page 246.

Teaching focus and assessment objectives

Section 1: Fast Track - Phonemic Awareness

Teaching Focus:

- An alphabet immersion activity introducing all **a-z** shapes and their sounds
- Developing phonemic awareness of beginning sounds in words

Assessment Objective:

- Say the sound when shown the plain letter (21 consonants and 5 short vowels)
- Sort pictured words according to initial sound

Section 2: a-z Word Building

Teaching Focus:

- **a-z** letters in detail (uppercase/lowercase)
- First blending and segmenting (after six letters)
- Introducing long vowels while keeping the focus of Word Building on short vowels
- Common consonant digraphs: **ch ck sh th th ng**
- Introducing a limited number of 'tricky' words
- Practising decoding and reading 'tricky' words in brief engaging stories

Assessment Objective:

- Say the sound(s) when shown the plain letter(s) for 21 consonants, 5 short and long vowels, 5 consonant digraphs
- Write the letter(s) in response to the sound
- Recognise uppercase and lowercase letter forms
- Blend and segment VC and CVC words
- Spell regular VC and CVC words accurately
- Read 21 'tricky' words
- Read decodable text with adequate comprehension

Section 3: Blending with Adjacent Consonants

Teaching Focus:

- Initial adjacent consonants:
    sc sk sp st sm sn sw
    bl cl fl gl pl sl
    br cr dr fr gr pr tr
- Final adjacent consonants: **-st -sk -nd -nt -nk**
- Blending and segmenting words of four sounds

Assessment Objective:

- Read stories with adjacent consonant words
- Blend and segment CCVC and CVCC words
- Read 9 additional 'tricky' words (cumulative total: 30)
- Read decodable text containing adjacent consonants and 'tricky' words with accuracy, fluency and comprehension

Section 4: Long Vowels

Teaching Focus:

- **y** with long **i** sound (as in sk**y**)
  y with long **e** sound (as in bab**y**)
- Split digraphs: **a_e e_e i_e o_e u_e**
- Suffix: **ed** with three sounds /ed/ /d/ /t/
- Vowel digraphs: **ai ay ee ea oa ie ue**
- Long vowel spellings: **ind ild old**
- Blending and segmenting long vowel words
- Reading stories with long vowel words and also recognising 'tricky' words

Assessment Objective:

- Say the sound of split digraphs and long vowel digraphs when shown the plain letters
- Say three sounds for **y** and three for **-ed** when shown the plain letters
- Blend and segment words with long vowels
- Decode words with suffix **-ed**
- Read 17 new 'tricky' words (cumulative total: 47)
- Read decodable text containing long vowel words with accuracy, fluency and comprehension

Section 5: Further Vowel Sounds and Spellings

Teaching Focus:

- R-controlled vowels: **ar or er ir ur air ear**
- Long vowel patterns: **ow igh**
- Other vowel sounds: **oo oo u** (in push) **ou ow oi oy aw au ew**
- Reading stories with all the new sounds

Assessment Objective:

- Say the new sound when shown the letters
- Blend and segment words with the various vowel patterns and sounds
- Read 21 new 'tricky' words (cumulative total: 68)
- Apply the new sounds in reading with increasing accuracy, fluency and comprehension

Making the most of your Teacher's Guide

This *Teacher's Guide* will help you teach in ways that touch children's imagination while they accomplish important steps in literacy. Here are a few suggestions to help you make the most of it.

Prepare

To get a full understanding of Letterland teaching, read through the Appendix (pages 178-225) where all the strategies that you will be using regularly are explained.

Fast Track (optional)

Before you start, read through **Section 1: Fast Track - Phonemic Awareness** (pages 14-22), to become familiar with the strategies that most teachers will begin with.

Choosing the correct starting point

For most groups of children, the most appropriate place to start is **Section 1: Fast Track**. But groups that already know all the letter sounds well, may be able to start in **Section 2: a-z Word Building**. This allows the children to begin using the sounds to blend and segment words sooner.

To help you decide on a starting point, take a look at the Assessment Section on the *Teacher's Guide CD* which describes the assessments you can use.

Lesson scheduling

There are just over 100 lessons in this *Teacher's Guide*. Each lesson can be covered in one day or over several days depending on your schedule and the needs and attention level of your children. Lessons are designed to be taught in 20 to 30 minutes. (Additional time in another part of the day may be used for independent activities, re-reading stories, or small group work.)

The lessons have frequent changes in activity to help keep children involved, active and attentive. However, particularly at the beginning of the year, you may need to break the lessons into two or three shorter periods across the day with breaks for other types of activities scheduled between sessions.

Pacing your teaching

The 17 Fluency Lists described on the *Teacher's Guide CD* are for the practice and assessment of recently taught letter sounds, word decoding, 'tricky' words (common exceptions) and sentence reading. Using these with your children regularly will help you know when to spend more time revising some of the lessons and when they are ready to move on. Some children may need additional individual or small group practice to master the needed skills and to ensure continued progress.

Lesson charts

Lesson Charts are provided at the start of Sections 2-5. They are useful for planning your lessons and follow-up activities. The charts list the phonics taught in each lesson. Each 'tricky' word that is introduced is also listed by lesson.

The **100 high-frequency words list** on page 247 shows useful words in order of frequency. It indicates whether they are decodable words or irregular 'tricky' words.

A note on text conventions and abbreviations

Words that the teacher might say aloud are printed in blue without quotation marks.

Words that the children might say are printed in **"bold black with quotation marks"**.

Sounds of phonemes are enclosed by slashes /ĕ/, /d/.

Consonant phonemes that can be prolonged are sometimes repeated three times /fff/ /mmm/.

Abbreviations used: PCC - Picture Code Cards

BPCC - Big Picture Code Cards

TGCD - Teacher's Guide CD

Teacher's Guide CD

 Assessment It will be important to familiarise yourself with the Assessment Section on the *TGCD*. Feel free to use the assessments flexibly. They are provided to support your teaching and help ensure that each child is mastering the required knowledge and skills as the year progresses.

 Fluency Lists These can be used at the end of lessons. They are designed to help children build towards automatic word recognition of decodable words, to read previously taught 'tricky' words quickly and to read sentences with expression and fluency.

 Take-Home Booklets Print out and make a few copies of these decodable booklets or make one for each child to take home and read to their parents. The stories supplement the *Phonics Readers*.

 Learning activities These can be used to supplement lessons. With over 30 photocopiable pages of games and activities.

 NOTE: The full contents of the *Teacher's Guide CD* are listed on page 246.

Reading Direction

Letterland characters are designed to look or move in the Reading Direction so they can serve as signposts orienting the children's eyes to the right as they read. With this Reading Direction cue built into each Letterland pictogram children make fewer typical reversal errors.*

The pictograms also help with the correct sequence of handwriting strokes. For example, with Bouncy Ben, children start at the top of his big brown ears, then add the circle for his face, so he can look in the Reading Direction as he bounces along.

Simple built-in picture cues and logic like the above help children to tackle the common problem of reversing similarity shaped letters, such as **b** and **d**, **p** and **q**, and to learn to orient all the rest of the alphabet correctly.

It will help to make a Reading Direction sign similar to the one shown here to place above the area where you plan for children to do 'Live Reading' and 'Live Spelling' (page 198). It will help remind them to always blend and write words from left to right.

* 3 exceptions: Golden Girl, Quarrelsome Queen and Zig Zag Zebra. There are good reasons for these, explained in the lessons.

'Tricky' words

Some of the most frequently used words in English have very irregular spellings (**they, said, the, of, what**). Yet they are essential for good story telling. These words are sometimes called 'common exception words' or just 'sight words'. For children, the term 'tricky' word works well. They learn that some letters in 'tricky' words are decodable and some are not making their expected sounds.

Letterland slowly phases useful 'tricky' words into the *Phonics Readers* which accompany this *Teacher's Guide*. Each word is always introduced in the preceding lesson.

To introduce a 'tricky' word you can make a word card for it (e.g. **said**). The children can then help decide which letters are making their usual sounds and which letters are being 'tricky' (irregular). You then put a wavy line under the 'tricky' letters, acting as a reminder that those letters can't be sounded out but the rest can. For a full explanation of how to introduce 'tricky' words see the individual lessons and page 210.

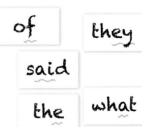

Building words at the front of the class

One activity that you will use often is forming words with *Picture Code Cards* for children to blend. At times you will also ask the children to come forward to help with building the words. You can do this by asking the children to hold the cards, by leaning the cards along a shelf, or using a pocket chart. The advantage of a pocket chart is that you can display all the cards you will need in the lower rows and then make the words in an upper row.

The other option is to use the new *Story Phonics* software. This allows you to build words on screen or on a white/smartboard in front of the class and switch easily between the plain letter and pictogram images.

Adapting Word Building for small groups

The lesson plans in this guide can be adapted for teaching small groups. In such a setting, if the teacher is sitting at a table with the children, words can be built, using the *Picture Code Cards,* directly on the table where the children can see them and even help build or change them.

In a small group, 'Live Reading' and 'Live Spelling' may need to be adapted. One innovative teacher used a child's toys to do 'Live Reading' by setting them up on a table and placing the *Picture Code Cards* in front of them. The child thoroughly enjoyed the process and when it came to 'Live Spelling', she was happy to place the *Picture Code Cards* in her toys arms herself.

Resources to support your teaching

Phonics Readers

This series consists of 20 books which are divided into four sets. Each book contains a selection of short stories, featuring the phonic elements listed below. In total there are 83 stories. See: www.letterland.com/Phonics-Readers

Set	Book	No. of stories	Focus elements		As in the word...
1	a	4	c, a, d, h, m, t, s, i, s		_c_at, _a_dd, _d_og, _h_en, _m_ap, _t_ap, _s_un, _it_, _is_
	b	4	i, i, n, g		_i_t, _i_ce, _n_et, _g_o
	c	4	o, o, p, s, s		_o_dd, _so_, _p_en, cat_s_, dog_s_
	d	4	e, e, ss, u		_e_gg, _he_, mi_ss_, _u_p
	e	4	u, k, ck, ng		_u_niform, _k_it, du_ck_, ri_ng_
2	a	4	sh, ch, th, th		_sh_op, _ch_ip, _th_at, _th_ing
	b	4	l, f, ff, ll, b		_l_eg, _f_an, pu_ff_, be_ll_, _b_at
	c	4	j, all, r, qu		_j_et, b_all_, _r_un, _qu_iz
	d	4	v, ve, o, w		_v_an, ha_ve_, s_o_n, _w_ig
	e	4	x, y, z		bo_x_, _y_es, _z_ip
3	a	5	sl, sp, st, sw, sk, sm, sn, cl, fl, pl, bl, gl, br, cr, dr, fr, gr, tr		_sl_ip, _sp_ot, _st_uck, _sw_im, _sk_ate, _sm_ash, _sn_ap, _cl_ock, _fl_ag, _pl_ug, _bl_ock, _gl_ad, _br_ick, _cr_ab, _dr_ip, _fr_og, _gr_in, _tr_ack
	b	4	cr, dr, fr, gr, nd, nk, nt, y		_cr_ab, _dr_ip, _fr_og, _gr_in, han_d_, ta_nk_, te_nt_, m_y_
	c	5	a_e, i_e, e_e, o_e, u_e, ed, ed, ed		m_a_k_e_, l_i_k_e_, th_e_s_e_, h_o_m_e_, c_u_b_e_, skat_ed_, smil_ed_, hop_ed_
	d	4	ed, ed, ed, y, ai, ay, ee		land_ed_, clapp_ed_, slamm_ed_, bab_y_, r_ai_n, s_ay_, b_ee_
	e	4	ea, oa, ie, ue		s_ea_, b_oa_t, t_ie_, bl_ue_
4	a	4	ild, ind, old, ar, or		m_ild_, k_ind_, c_old_, f_ar_m, f_or_
	b	3	ir, ur, er		g_ir_l, f_ur_, h_er_
	c	4	ow, igh		sh_ow_, n_igh_t
	d	4	oo, oo, u, aw, au, ew, ew		m_oo_n, b_oo_k, p_u_t, s_aw_, c_au_se, f_ew_, gr_ew_
	e	6	ou, ow, oi, oy, air, ear		_ou_t, h_ow_, c_oi_n, b_oy_, f_air_, y_ear_

ABC Trilogy

ABC book
This international best-selling picture book is the ideal introduction to the alphabet. Present each **a-z** character in depth to develop phonemic awareness and language skills. The 26 fascinating scenes with fun alliteration bring the world of Letterland to life.

Beyond ABC and Far Beyond ABC
You've met the Letterland alphabet characters in the best-selling *ABC* book. Now let's see what happens when letters come together to make new sounds in words. *Beyond ABC* and the award-winning *Far Beyond ABC* feature 42 engaging stories, rather than boring rules, to explain different spelling patterns. The story logic draws on children's thinking skills and imaginations, so they easily remember the phonic facts. With the help of all three books in the series the major sounds in the English language are covered!

Picture Code Cards

Picture Code Cards - Straight
These double-sided cards feature all the phonemes and spelling patterns in the *Teacher's Guide*. With plain black letters on one side and Letterland characters on the other, these cards are an important teaching tool for teaching blending and segmenting, finger-tracing, spelling, language development and role-play.

Big Picture Code Cards - Uppercase
These big double-sided cards feature plain letter shapes on one side and Letterland characters on the other. They are useful for finger-tracing letter shapes and for learning letter sounds and many lesson activities.

Vocabulary Cards
These big, double-sided cards help children to quickly develop vocabulary for reading and spelling. Use them for oral segmenting of initial sounds.

Software

Letter Sounds

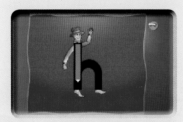

Letter Shapes

Living ABC software
Bring the alphabet letters to life in your classroom! In this award-winning software the **a-z** characters explain themselves and their sounds. Includes an animated alphabet song, handwriting song, character story and interactive scene for every letter. There are also assessed activities for letter shapes, sounds and regular word building that can be monitored in the Teacher Zone.

Story Phonics software
Letters really come to life in this new and exciting Letterland software. Use the software to listen to the sounds, build words on screen, blend and segment words, and share animated versions of the stories that explain all the key spelling patterns in this *Teacher's Guide*.

CDs

"Harry Hat Man whispers 'hhh...', whispers 'hhh...', whispers 'hhh...'. Harry Hat Man whispers 'hhh...'. He never talks out loud."

Alphabet Songs CD
Featuring a song for every letter of the alphabet, this CD is designed to help children learn letter sounds in a fun and entertaining way.

"Hurry from the Hat Man's head down to his heel on the ground. Go up and bend his knee over, so he'll hop while he makes his sound."

Handwriting Songs CD
This CD offers fun and easy to remember tips on forming the shape of every letter in the alphabet.

"The Cat belongs to the Hat Man. He lets her go where she pleases. But when she sits down beside him, she almost always sneezes. 'Ch, ch, ch!'"

Blends & Digraphs Songs CD
The *Blends & Digraphs CD* is a fun collection of **47** songs linked to the *Teacher's Guide* designed to consolidate the blends, digraphs and trigraph learning.

Magnetic Word Builder

This resource allows children to make new words and practise spelling with no mistakes to rub out! The board holds 52 magnetic letters making spelling a wide range of words possible, both in regular class work and in independent work. It also opens and closes without disturbing the child's work.

Posters

Action Tricks Poster

A great reference poster of the Action Tricks. Do the actions, make the letter sounds and learn the alphabet.

Class Train Frieze

Featuring the **a-z** Letterland characters and the Vowel Men, this bright frieze is perfect for a permanent display of alphabetic order in your primary classroom.

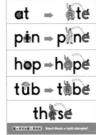
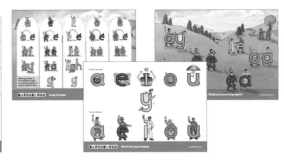

Vowel Scene Posters

This pack of five posters provides a great visual aid to the skills you'll be teaching as your children progress. They act as conceptual organisers and remind children at a glance of important phonics facts: short and long vowels, vowel digraphs, split digraphs, and **r**-controlled vowels.

My Alphabet Storybooks

Go on a reading adventure with your Letterland friends in this award-winning series of 26 books. Carefully designed imaginative stories allow you to share the reading experience with levelled sections for your child to read with minimal support.

Individual Activity Resources

A-Z Copymasters

These worksheets help children develop pencil control and vocabulary. Photocopy the worksheets that feature lower and uppercase letters and long vowels. Also includes two pages of instructions and teaching ideas.

Early Years Handwriting Copymasters

Photocopy the handwriting worksheets to motivate young children to form alphabet letter shapes correctly. Start with the pattern practice pages, then progress to full letters using the featured Letterland handwriting verses.

Blends & Digraphs Copymasters

Photocopy the worksheets to help children explore key spelling patterns taught in each lesson. Includes exercises on consonant blends, long vowel sounds and split digraphs.

Word Bank Copymasters

Photocopy these worksheets to consolidate the teaching of digraphs, consonant blends and trigraphs. Each page features phonemes, word examples and writing space, which is useful for vocabulary building.

Word Books (pack of 10)

This A5 word book helps children to create their own dictionary. Each page features high-frequency words and ruled lines to guide children's handwriting strokes while they add to their vocabulary.
One pack for ten children.

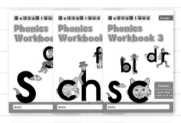

Phonics Workbooks (1-6)

This set of six full-colour workbooks help children move from letter sounds to blending them together to make words. The workbooks cover all the sounds and spelling patterns in the *Teacher's Guide.* Each workbook contains structured, decodable activities and guidance on blending and segmenting sounds, making them a valuable addition to the range for individual or group work. The workbooks correlate to the Teacher's Guide as follows:

Workbooks 1 & 2 - Section 2
Workbook 3 - Section 3
Workbook 4 - Section 4
Workbooks 5 and 6 - Section 5.

Resources Chart

This chart shows how each of the resources relates to the teaching progression. Choose the resources that best suit your teaching situation. For example, you may prefer to use the *Living ABC* and *Phonics Stories* software to introduce the Letterland stories and songs, rather than the Picture Books and CD's.

	Resource	Fast Track	Section 2	Section 3	Section 4	Section 5
Phonics Readers Set 1	Readers		✓			
Phonics Readers Set 2	Readers		✓			
Phonics Readers Set 3	Readers			✓	✓	
Phonics Readers Set 4	Readers					✓
ABC (paperback)	Picture Books		✓			
Beyond ABC (paperback)	Picture Books		✓		✓	✓
Far Beyond ABC (paperback)	Picture Books				✓	✓
Picture Code Cards - Straight	Cards	✓	✓	✓	✓	✓
Big Picture Code Cards - Uppercase	Cards		✓			
Vocabulary Cards	Cards	✓				
Living ABC software	Software		✓			
Story Phonics software	Software		✓	✓	✓	✓
Alphabet Songs CD	CDs		✓			
Handwriting Songs CD	CDs		✓			
Blends & Digraphs Songs CD	CDs		✓	✓	✓	✓
Magnetic Word Builder	Games and Fun		✓	✓	✓	✓
Action Tricks Poster	Posters and Friezes	✓	✓			
Class Train Frieze	Posters and Friezes		✓			
Vowel Scene Posters	Posters and Friezes		✓		✓	✓
A-Z Copymasters	Copymasters		✓			
Early Years Handwriting Copymasters	Copymasters		✓			
Blends & Digraphs Copymasters	Copymasters		✓	✓	✓	✓
Word Bank Copymasters	Copymasters		✓	✓	✓	✓
Word Books (pack of 10)	Workbooks		✓	✓	✓	✓
Workbooks (1-6)	Workbooks		✓	✓	✓	✓

Further Resources

Letterland offers many more resources to help children learn phonemic awareness, phonics, handwriting and develop a love of reading. See them all at www.letterland.com

Section 1 :
Fast Track - Phonemic Awareness

Research based

Research has well established that developing phonemic awareness is a crucial early step in learning to read. Children do not naturally attend to the individual sounds in words. They simply focus on the meaning of the words they speak and hear. Developing awareness of the separate phonemes (sounds) spoken in words is essential for making sense of written language. Children need to be able to isolate those sounds orally (become phonemically aware) before they can link them to letter shapes (phonics) and use them to crack the alphabetic code.

Letter shapes and sounds

It is now widely accepted that a rigorous and systematic phonics programme is required to help children master the alphabetic principal, leading to reading independence and helping to prevent reading problems. Teaching grapheme phoneme correspondences provides a "powerful tool for translating speech into print."[1] Research has shown that children learn letter sounds more easily when they are taught with pictures embedded with the shape of the letter to help them recall the sounds.[2]

With Letterland's Fast Track, children learn the 26 basic letter sounds within the first few weeks. This Letterland method has shown superior results in a controlled comparison and has been proven in practice by teachers all over the world. The Letterland children learned sounds and letter names faster and more completely even though letter names were not emphasised during the Fast Track.[3]

What is the Fast Track?

It is a rapid, lift-off strategy using an oral memory game for a first access to the alphabetic code. It provides:

- an oral multisensory activity right at the start of the year that develops children's attention spans, listening skills, fosters daily group cooperation and helps to close the gap between children with little or no previous literacy experience and those with a lot

- a 3-week 'alphabet immersion' experience, so every child has at least an acquaintance with all 26 lowercase letter shapes and their sounds, before going on to study them in depth

- a child strategy for discovering a letter's sound: The Sound Trick (page 181).
  Just START to say the character's name, and then STOP, e.g. "Annie Apple, /ǎ/, Zig Zag Zebra, /zzz/."

How do children see the Fast Track?

Simply as a game. Children give the Fast Track routine their full attention because they can play it like a game similar to the popular "I packed my suitcase and in it I put…" memory game. In that game each player adds an item to be remembered. One important difference: this Fast Track 'game' has visual props (the *Vocabulary Cards*) to help the children remember each alliterative word. So it is an easy way to develop awareness of initial sounds.

1 Ashby and Rayner, *Psychology of Reading*, page 73.
2 Ehri, L., Deffner, N. and Wilce, L. (1984). Pictorial mnemonics for phonics. *Journal of Educational Psychology*. 76, 880-893.
3 Felton, R. and Crawford, E. (2009). Mnemonics and multisensory strategies: *How important are these for teaching reading skills of at-risk students?* Paper presented at the annual Conference of the International Dyslexia Association, Lake Buena Vista, Florida.

Fast Track - An overview of the five simple steps

(These steps are explained in detail on pages 18-20.)

Assess Before and after using the Fast Track

5. Alphabet Line Children introduce themselves as the letters and name the objects that start with their sounds in a rap-like chant.

1. Quick Dash (After Day 1) Review of previously taught letters and sounds with the *Picture Code Cards*.

4. Live Word Sort Children role-play being the letters while their classmates deliver *Vocabulary Cards* to them to match their sound.

2. Introduce new letters Use both sides of the *Picture Code Cards* to introduce new letters.

3. Discover the sound Children learn how to segment the initial sound in spoken words. Then they learn an Action Trick to help them connect the letter shape and sound with a movement.

Fast Track objectives

Over the three weeks of Fast Track teaching children learn the following:

Recall routes to letter shapes
Plain letter shapes offer nothing familiar to a child. Children will quickly learn how to recall abstract letter shapes and sounds by drawing on their own memory bank of prior knowledge of the familiar human, animal and inanimate shapes that appear in the Letterland characters.

Character names
Children quickly learn the Letterland character names orally because they are both alliterative and descriptive. These character names then become the recall route for discovering and remembering each letter's sound.

Letter sounds
They add kinaesthetic learning by practising the sound together with a thematically linked action in response to the plain letter shape. This creates a strong grapheme/phoneme correspondence.

Phonemic awareness

The simple routines sharpen the children's visual discrimination and fine-tune their ears to the initial sounds in words – in other words it makes them phonemically aware! As one amazed teacher expressed it, "Once they know what to listen for, they begin to hear the sounds in all kinds of words."

Bouncy Ben's
Action Trick (see p.182)

Postponing Letter Names

You will notice that there is no use of the traditional letter names (aye, bee, cee, etc.) in the Fast Track. This is an important factor in the success of this 'lift off' strategy at the start of the year. Excluding letter names initially allows the children to focus exclusively on letter sounds so that typical confusions between letter sounds and letter names cannot occur.

Sticking to **sounds only** in the first month enables children to do particularly well at learning to blend and segment sounds – resulting in earlier and more confident reading. If possible, wait until your children are confident in sounding out new words, and only then introduce the traditional letter names.

At that point turn to the Activity Bank on page 239 for guidelines on helping children learn traditional letter names and incorporating them into the 'Quick Dash' and other routines. You may want to print out the *Alphabet Names Poster* (*TGCD*) with short rhymes about each letter's name.

If some of your children mention letter names, you could say, Those letter names will be useful later on, but for now we will only be using the sounds, because that's exactly what we need for reading stories and writing words.

Assessing children before and after the Fast Track

All Assessment Forms and instructions can be found on the *Teacher's Guide CD* (*TGCD*).

Begin by assessing all the children with form **1-A Letter Sounds**.
By reassessing at the end of Fast Track you will be able to see how much they have learned.
Keep a track of what your children are learning with the *Section 1 Assessments*.

Objectives	Assessments
Say the letter sound when shown the plain letter (21 consonants and 5 short vowels)	*1-A Letter Sounds*
Say the Letterland character name in response to the pictogram	*1-B Character Names*
Sort words according to initial sound	*1-C Sound Matching (Parts 1-5)* *1-D Initial Sounds*

Pacing the lessons

The Fast Track Lesson Plan (pages 18-21) describes the three to four week process for introducing all 26 Letterlanders and their letter sounds. You can vary the pace, depending on the knowledge your children already have and how quickly they pick up new information. Below are some suggestions to help you decide on how quickly to move along.

Faster pacing

If your children have been in a Letterland classroom before, you may be able to reintroduce three to five letters per day rather than just two. The key is making sure that children not only know the Letterland characters but also that:

1) they can respond to the **plain letters** with the sounds, and

2) they can match the *Vocabulary Card* words to the correct initial letter by identifying the initial sound.

More deliberate pacing

If your children are not familiar with Letterland and have little knowledge of letter sounds, it will be helpful to assess at least the more challenged children at three or four intervals during the Fast Track. These 'check-ups' will help you decide if you need to review before moving on or, alternatively, will indicate that you could move along faster. (See Fast Track assessments, page 22 and *TGCD*.)

Extra practice for small groups

If children in your class vary widely in their general knowledge at entrance and in the pace at which they can learn, the assessments will help you decide if you need to provide additional small group practice. This early support right from the start will be important. You will find a number of small group activities in Section 7: Activity Bank. Look for those activities that focus on **Letter Sounds** and **Initial Sounds in Words**.

Use the Steps 1-5 below every day to introduce new letters and to work towards the Fast Track objectives. The chart on page 22 provides a suggested schedule for teaching all the letters and sounds.

On Day 1, you must start at Step 2 as the children will not yet have the knowledge to complete Step 1.

Step 1 'Quick Dash'

Quick Dash is a review strategy that you will use each day, **beginning on Day 2** .

Hold up each *Picture Code Card* (PCC) that has been previously taught following these steps:

Teacher	Children
(Show the picture side. Wait for about 3 seconds for thinking time and then say...) Who is this?	**"Annie Apple"**
(Turn to the plain letter side.) What sound does she* make in words?	(Do her Action and say... /ă/)
(Show the next picture side, wait, then ask...) Who is this?	**"Bouncy Ben"**
(Turn to plain letter side.) His sound?*	(Do his Action and say... /b/)

* Using the pronouns 'him', 'her', 'he', 'she' etc. helps with language development, particularly for children learning English as an Additional Language.

- When you have taught beyond the first half of the alphabet you may want to just review 12-15 letters. Rotate the letters you review to keep them all fresh in the children's minds.

Sounds Race
- Next go back through the pack of *Picture Code Cards*. Now the goal is speed. Hold up each plain letter. Ask the children respond quickly with both sound and action.
- Repeat this Sounds Race once or twice, going a bit faster each time. The aim is to begin building instant connections between plain letters and their sounds.

Adjusting 'Quick Dash' timing
- **Waiting time for character names** Waiting three seconds or so, as suggested above, before children name the Letterlander gives those children who need it more time to remember the character name. Otherwise some children may give up trying to name the character and just allow their more advanced classmates to say it for them.
- **Adjusting waiting time** Allowing everyone the time needed to come up with the answer strengthens the connection between letter and character, and will eventually result in faster responses. When that happens you may want to reduce the wait time.
- **Letter sounds** Usually less waiting time is needed for letter sound responses because the character name will help recall the sound. Still you will want to observe your children to make sure everyone is able to respond.
- **More advanced children** You can adjust the speed of the Sounds Race to increase these children's faster response times.
  With the above suggestions you will be meeting the needs of all your children.

Step 2 Introduce new letters

- Introduce two letters very briefly in each lesson, using the *Picture Code Cards* (PCC). (Please note: fuller lessons on letters **a-z** follow in Section 2 of this guide.)
- Hold up the picture side and say, This is Annie Apple. This is how she looks in Letterland.
- Turn to the plain side. But most people only see her plain letter in words. That's because the Letterlanders like to hide behind their plain letters. They only show themselves to help children like you learn to read, write and spell.
- Let's learn some of the words Annie Apple likes to start. Display the three *Vocabulary Cards* and ask the children to name them: "**ant, apple and acrobat.**" Read out the sentence (under each picture) that links the word thematically to the Letterlander.
- Continue on to Step 3 with the first letter. Then come back and repeat Steps 2 and 3 with the second letter.

Picture Code Cards

Step 3 Discover the sound

- **On Day 1** teach children the Sound Trick (page 181). Then ask them to use it each day to discover the newly introduced letter sounds.

  Sound Trick Say the Letterlander's name, then just START to say it again but STOP after the first sound: "**Annie Apple, /ă/...**", "**Bouncy Ben, /b/...**".

- **IMPORTANT** Be sure to turn the *PCC* to the plain letter side when everyone says the letter sound. Always prompt children to give you only the letter sound (not the character name) when you show them the plain letter side.

- Action Trick Teach the Action Trick for the letter sound (page 182) e.g. Pretend you have an apple in your hand and bring it toward your mouth to take a bite as you say /ă/. Ask the children to do the action and say the sound in response to the letter. Sometimes you could ask the children to repeat the action and sound three times (or more) so you can observe more children and give them additional practice. Teach them to do the action and sound each time you show them the plain letter side.

Action Trick (see p.182)

A useful resource: headbands

As a part of the daily Fast Track lesson, you could give children headbands to hold the *Picture Code Cards* so their hands are free to receive the *Vocabulary Cards* and the other children can see which Letterlander they are role-playing. Headbands can be made from heavy paper. Make a small pocket (not so deep that it hides the letter, or alternatively make the pockets transparent) on the front to hold the *Picture Code Card*. The headbands can be fastened with paper clips to allow adjustment of the size.

Step 4 Oral live word sort

- Choose some children to wear *Picture Code Cards* (in headbands or plastic pockets on their chests) for the two letters taught that day and two to four of the letters already taught. (See chart page 22 for suggested letters). Ask these children to stand facing the rest of the class. Each one in turn says their Letterlander name and sound, e.g. "**Annie Apple, /ă/,**" etc.

- Hold up the picture side of a *Vocabulary Card* and ask the class to name the picture, e.g. "**ball**". Ask everyone to say the picture word again and think about which Letterlander's sound starts the word. Remind them not to say the answer yet but to pick out the Letterlander in their mind.*

- Ask one child to deliver the card to the Letterlander whose sound begins the word. Is that the one you were thinking of?

- Do the same with either 2 or 3 *Vocabulary Cards* for each Letterlander.

- With each child up front now holding two or three *Vocabulary Cards* they are ready for the next activity.
* If any children have difficulty matching the *Vocabulary Card* to the correct Letterlander, teach them to apply the same strategy they have learned with the Sound Trick: Say the word, start to say it again and stop, "ball, b..."

Step 5 Alphabet line

- The children already wearing the *Picture Code Card*s from the sorting activity above can stay up front to lead this next oral activity. Or ask each one to hand over their headband and *Vocabulary Cards* to another child to involve more children.
- The children now at the front have a chance to present themselves as the Letterlanders, holding up each *Vocabulary Card* in turn as they say:

  I'm Annie Apple, and I say /ǎ/ in words like ant, apple and acrobat.

  I'm Bouncy Ben, and I say /b/ in words like bed, blue and ball.

  I'm Clever Cat, and I say /c/ in words like car, cat, and cake.

Additional suggestions for alphabet line

- **Class repeats the chant** After the child says the chant, you could ask the whole class to repeat it. For a shyer child standing at the front, you could ask the whole class to say their **"I am..."** chant with them the first time.
- **Building towards rhythm and expression** At first you may need to help some children to say their chant by saying it with them. Explain that since you will be choosing different children to 'be' the letters on different days, they all need to be ready to step into any part. So they all need to listen well all the time. As children become familiar with the words and the routine over a few days, try to increase the pace so that it begins to sound like a lively rap.
- **ABC order or other order if preferred** As you work through the first six to eight letters, stick to your chosen order with your growing line. Ask each child to repeat their **"I am..."** sentence each day for all to hear. This sentence repetition builds phonemic awareness by regularly exposing your class to a lot of alliteration in each sentence – coming now from their own mouths.
- **How many letters?** As the children learn more letters, you may only want to practise the routine with the most recent four to eight. Occasionally, as suggested on the chart (page 22), you may want to review the whole alphabet and involve more children.
- **Fun photos** If possible, take some photos of the children in the Alphabet Line. You could photograph the same letters on different days with different children holding different *Vocabulary Cards* in front. You could also use the photos for review of letter sounds and key words. Children can try to remember the other key words that are not shown in a photo. You could align their photos to make a personalised phonemic awareness alphabet frieze.
- **Presentation** As a culminating activity for your Fast Track teaching, you may like to practise and present the whole Alphabet Line to parents or other classes.*
* They could involve the audience in saying the pictured words with them. If you have less than 26 children in your class, you might want to do **a-m** first while the rest of the class watches. Then do **m-z** letting some children have a second turn.

Fast Track extension idea

- **Word Hunt** Each day as you finish the lesson, review the two new letter sounds. Then suggest that children look for the letters all day in the classroom, around the school, and at home.

  Remember that Annie Apple and Bouncy Ben like to hide behind their plain letters in words. So today, all day long, be on the lookout for these two plain letters on signs, in books and on the television or computer screen. The Letterlanders don't like you to give away their hiding places by saying their name, so when you see one of these letters, just point to it and quietly say the sound. Do you think you can find some hidden Annie Apples and Bouncy Bens? And what will you do when you see them?

Moving on beyond Fast Track

- Not every child will learn every sound by the end of Fast Track. Children will also vary in their ability to match initial sounds in words to letters. The assessments will help you tell how much progress each child is making (see *TGCD*).

- Fast Track teaching should give everyone a boost in learning, but they will have many more opportunities to learn sounds and further develop phonemic awareness in Section 2. Numerous teachers have found by the end of Fast Track that *most* of their children, when randomly shown plain letters, will know from 18 to 26 letter sounds.

- **More practice** Those children who fall short of this number may need small group practice as you move the whole class into Section 2. Use some of the activities in Section 7: Activity Bank (see **Letter Sounds** and **Initial Sounds in Words**).

Teaching and assessment schedule

- **Using the chart** The schedule shown is meant only to suggest how you might schedule your Fast Track teaching. Make adjustments based on your class schedule, your children's prior knowledge, and their progress as you move through the alphabet.

- **Assessment scheduling** The different assessments are listed in the chart at the points where they may be most helpful. As the chart shows, rather than assess the first six letters, the day after the **e** and **f** are introduced, we suggest you wait two or three days to make sure children are retaining this learning.

- **Selecting Assessments** There is no need to give every assessment to every child at every suggested point. You may want to use the *Initial Sounds Assessment (1C, Parts 1-5)* with everyone since it can be done with whole class or small groups at the same time. Use the other individual assessments selectively. All assessments and full instructions for their use are provided on the *TGCD*.

Assessment Schedule

Day	New letters	Letters for Word Sort	Letters for Alphabet Line
Prior to or as you begin Fast Track, assess everyone with *Assessment 1-A*			
1	a, b	a, b	a, b
2	c, d	a, b, c, d	a, b, c, d
3	e, f	b, c, d, e, f	a, b, c, d, e, f
4	g, h	a, e, f, g, h	a, b, c, d, e, f, g, h
5	i, j	d, g, h, i, j	e, f, g, h, i, j
Assessment 1-C Part 1 (a, b, c, d, e, f), other assessments as needed			
6	k, l	h, i, j, k, l	g, h, i, j, k, l
7	m, n	e, k, l, m, n	a - n
8	o, p	i, m, n, o, p	k, l, m, n, o, p
Assessment 1-C Part 2 (g, h, i, j, k, l), other assessments as needed			
9	q, r	k, o, p, q, r	m, n, o, p, q, r
10	s, t	n, q, r, s, t,	o, p, q, r, s, t
11	u, v	l, s, t, u, v	q, r, s, t, u, v
Assessment 1-C Part 3 (m, n, o, p, q, r), other assessments as needed			
12	w, x	r, u, v, w, x	s, t, u, v, w, x
13	y, z	o, u, w, x, y, z	a - z
Assessment 1-C Part 4 (s, t, u, v, w) and Part 5 (x, y, z) *Assessment 1-A* Repeat Letter Sounds and other assessments as needed			

All assessment material including full instructions and Assessment forms are on the *TGCD* .

"Children learn best when they are enjoying themselves." Lyn Wendon

Section 2 :
a-z Word Building

Lesson	Lesson focus	Example word	Letterland Character
1	c	cat	Clever Cat
2	a	add	Annie Apple
3	a	apron	Mr A, the Apron Man
4	d	dog	Dippy Duck
5	h	hen	Harry Hat Man
6	m	map	Munching Mike
7	t	tap	Talking Tess
8	First blending	-	-
9	s	sun	Sammy Snake (Sleepy Sammy)
10	First segmenting	-	-
11	i, (s /z/)	it, (is)	Impy Ink
12	i	ice	Mr I, the Ice Cream Man
13	n	net	Noisy Nick
14	g	go	Golden Girl
15	Blending and segmenting	-	-
16	o	odd	Oscar Orange
17	o	so	Mr O, the Old Man
18	p	pen	Peter Puppy
19	s, s - adding s to words	cats, dogs	Sammy Snake - Sleepy Sammy
20	e	egg	Eddy Elephant
21	e	he	Mr E, the Easy Magic Man
22	ss	miss	Sammy and Sally Snake
23	u	up	Uppy Umbrella
24	u	uniform	Mr U, the Uniform Man
25	k	kit	Kicking King
26	ck	duck	Clever Cat and Kicking King
27	ng	ring	Noisy Nick and Golden Girl
28	sh	shop	Sammy Snake and Harry Hat Man
29	ch	chip	Clever Cat and Harry Hat Man
30	th	that	Talking Tess and Harry Hat Man
31	th	thing	Talking Tess and Harry Hat Man
32	l	leg	Lucy Lamp Light
33	f	fan	Firefighter Fred
34	ll, ff	puff, bell	Best Friends Frank and Linda
35	b	bat	Bouncy Ben
36	j	jet	Jumping Jim
37	all	ball	Giant All
38	r	run	Red Robot
39	qu	quiz	Quarrelsome Queen
40	v	van	Vicky Violet
41	ve	have	Vase e prop
42	o	son	Oscar's Bothersome Little Brother
43	w, (wh)	wig, (when)	Walter Walrus
44	x	box	Fix-it Max
45	y	yes	Yellow Yo-yo Man
46	z	zip	Zig Zag Zebra
	Review		

Lesson Chart

Story from *Phonics Readers*	'Tricky' word	Set/Book
Dad, a hat, a cat	a	1a
Sam		1a
Dad, Sam		1a
Is it him?		1a
Is it his?	Mr	1b
Nat		1b
Can Dan dig?		1b
Yes or no?		1b
Tom and Tim		1c
Go, go! No!	oh	1c
Go, pup, go!	the	1c
Ssss, zzzz	of	1c
Is Ed a hen?		1d
Pets	she	1d
Hiss, hiss!		1d
Us	to	1d
You	you	1e
Kicking King's maze	like, see	1e
Can he kick?		1e
Ding dong		1e
Shep		2a
Check on the chicks!		2a
Shep and me	my	2a
Lots of legs		2a
Is this her pet?	her	2b
Fred's fish		2b
Off we go!	for	2b
Ben and the cub	look	2b
Look at them go!		2c
Let's look		2c
Red Robot runs		2c
Look, quick!	was	2c
At the vet's	here	2d
Hugs	too	2d
Fun in the mud	come	2d
Wet	said	2d
Can you fix it, Max?	what	2e
Let's go and see Yo-yo Man	they	2e
Zig and zag		2e
Who said that?		2e

Further resources

ABC book & Living ABC software

Action Tricks Poster

Alphabet Songs CD and Handwriting Songs CD

Big Picture Code Cards - Uppercase

Blends & Digraphs CD

Magnetic Word Builder

Picture Code Cards

Beyond ABC

In the 46 lessons of this section, children take a giant step towards becoming readers and writers. They build on their alphabet knowledge, learn handwriting strokes and the uppercase letters. **After just six letters they begin to blend and segment words and read decodable stories.**

Contents

Letters **a-z short and long vowels, ck, s**/z/, **o**/ŭ/, double consonants **ff ll ss**

Digraphs **ch ng sh th th ve**

Objectives

By the end of this section, children should be able to:

- Say the sound when shown the plain letter(s) for 21 consonants, 5 short and 5 long vowels, 5 consonant digraphs
- Write the lowercase letter(s) in response to the sound
- Match uppercase to lowercase letters
- Write uppercase letters
- Blend and segment words of two or three sounds with VC or CVC pattern
- Spell regular CVC words accurately
- Read 21 'tricky' words
- Read decodable text with at least 90% accuracy and 80% comprehension.

Practise and apply

Letter sound associations Children continue practising **a-z** letter sounds to consolidate this knowledge and make their responses quicker and more automatic. Two activities to help accomplish this goal are the 'Quick Dash' begun in the previous section, and the new game 'Guess Who?'.

Letter formation Children learn and practise correct handwriting strokes while tracing letters with the *Handwriting Songs CDs*. They internalise these strokes with workbooks, copymasters and dictation activities.

Uppercase letters Each Letterlander does a special trick that changes their shape when they start an important word like a name or the beginning of a sentence. Learning the Uppercase Tricks helps children connect the often very different shapes of uppercase and lowercase letters.

Harry Hat Man

A-Z Copymasters

Digraphs Children learn early on the sounds of several commonly used digraphs to help them decode basic words (e.g. **th**em, wi**th**, **sh**e, mu**ch**, lo**ng**, ba**ck**, wi**ll**, o**ff**, le**ss**).

Blending sounds to read words Children use a multisensory strategy called the Roller Coaster Trick to help them blend sounds to read words (see page 188). They also develop their blending skills with activities such as 'Live Reading' and word building with *Picture Code Cards*. They apply blending in decodable stories right from the start.

Reading decodable stories As soon as children begin blending, they begin reading stories. The *Phonics Readers* provide an illustrated story for each lesson using only the sounds and 'tricky' words studied so far. Children re-read the stories to build fluency. Teachers guide retelling, discussion and dramatisation of the stories to develop comprehension.

Phonics Readers 1a

'Tricky' words Since many of the most common words in English have irregular spellings (e.g. **the, of, said, what**) children need to learn a few of these non-decodable words from the start in order to read even simple, brief stories. They learn to examine the words to decide which letters are not making the expected sound. Then with brief simple practice they work toward recognising these words instantly.

Segmenting and spelling Children begin segmenting words (breaking a spoken word into its constituent sounds, e.g. "**map**, /m/ /ă/ /p/") at the same time as they learn blending. Since segmenting is essentially the reverse of blending, the two phonemic abilities reinforce each other. They use a multisensory strategy called the Rubber Band Trick (see page 190) to slowly say the word to hear all the sounds. They use this new strategy with 'Live Spelling', and word building with the *Magnetic Word Builder* or *Story Phonics* software.

Teaching order

The teaching order for Section 2 is:

c ă ā d h m t s ĭ s/z/ ī n g ŏ ō p ĕ ē ss ŭ ū k ck ng sh ch th th l f ll ff b j r qu v ve o/ŭ/ w wh x y z

The logic for this order is based on three important considerations:

1) Letters and digraphs that occur most frequently in simple three letter words (CVC) are taught early on to allow children to begin blending and segmenting a variety of words right from the start.

2) Letters and sounds that are easily confused (e.g. **d** and **b**, /ă/ and /ĕ/) are widely separated in this sequence to allow children to master one before the other is introduced.

3) The first three letters introduced are **c**, **a**, and **d**. All begin with the same anticlockwise curved stroke. This grouping allows children to establish the circular motion, and it sets the pattern for consistent correct handwriting and orientation of letter **d**.

Teachers preferring a different teaching order (e.g. **s a t p i n**, etc.) should feel free to present it instead of **a-z** in the Fast Track. The resulting early acquaintance with all the letters will enable children to respond well to *any* early decodable texts.

'Tricky' words introduced in Section 2

a	come	for	her	here	like	look	Mr
my	of	oh	said	see	she	the	they
to	too	was	what	you			

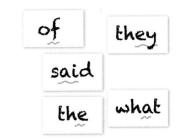

Lesson Plans in Section 2

Three basic types of lessons are used in Section 2. The activities in each type of lesson overlap somewhat, but the particular selection and sequence of activities varies with the purpose of the lesson.

1. New Letter/Sound Lessons

There are 26 lessons that teach a new letter and sound. Six more teach a second sound for a previously taught letter (e.g. long vowels). These lesson plans follow the steps below:

1. **Review** - 'Quick Dash' or 'Guess Who?' on alternating days

2. **Sound** Learn the Sound, Action and Song with the *Picture Code Cards* and *Alphabet Songs CD*

3. **Phonemic awareness and language development** Explore the letter sound in words with discussion, the *ABC* book or *Living ABC* software, and an optional game

4. **Shape** Teach correct letter formation with *Handwriting Songs CD* or *Living ABC* software and the Uppercase Trick with *Big Picture Code Cards - Uppercase*

5. **Individual activity** Encourage children to Picture Code (see page 193) the plain letter from the *TGCD*, or choose one of the many *Copymasters/Workbooks* to accompany the lesson.

Beginning with Lesson 8, the following additional activities are included in all three lesson types:

1. **Blending and segmenting** words with 'Live Reading' and 'Live Spelling', with *Picture Code Cards* or *Story Phonics* software and by writing words

2. **Reading and fluency** Practice Fluency List. Teach or revise 'tricky' words. Read decodable stories that correlate with the lesson. Children re-read previous stories to build decoding, fluency and comprehension.

2. Consonant Digraph Lessons
For lessons that teach a new consonant digraph (e.g. **ch**, **ng**, **th**) the order of activities varies but all include the following steps:

1. **Review** - 'Quick Dash' or 'Guess Who?'

2. **Introduce the new phoneme and story logic** Share the brief story logic that explains the sound using *Picture Code Cards* or *Story Phonics* software. The children role-play to internalise the letter/ sound connections and enhance their phonemic awareness . The aim is for instant plain letter recognition of the new phoneme's sound.

3. **Group activities** - Blending and Segmenting

4. **Individual activities**

5. **Reading and fluency**.

3. Review Lessons
There are five lessons that serve to consolidate previous learning.

Pacing the lessons
There are a total of 105 lessons in Sections 1-5. You may want to spend two or three days or more on some lessons and only one day on others. Pace your teaching based on the needs of your children. Spend more time on lessons they find challenging and less on the ones they find easier.

Scheduling lessons
Lessons are intended to be used flexibly. If you find children's attention flagging you may want divide the lesson into two sessions in the same day. Researchers have found that two shorter lessons in one day (15 to 20 minutes each) may actually be more effective than a single lesson. A good point to break the lesson would be before **Group activities**. Or you may choose to stop before **Reading and fluency** in some lessons and complete the lesson later. Either way it should be helpful to review just a bit from the earlier session before starting the additional activities.

Extra practice for small groups
Children in your class may vary widely in their general knowledge at entrance and in the pace at which they learn. The assessments for this and other sections will help you decide if additional small group practice is needed for some children. The value of early support can be pivotal for challenged children. You will find a number of small group activities in the Activity Bank. Look for those activities that focus on **Letter Sounds, Blending and Segmenting, Fluency and Comprehension**. The Assessment section on the *TGCD* also has some useful suggestions on choosing activities based on needs.

C c

You'll need

- ✓ *PCCs* for 'Quick Dash' plus **c**
- ✓ *ABC book*
- ✓ *Alphabet Songs CD* and *Handwriting Songs CD* or *Living ABC* software
- ✓ *BPCC - Uppercase* **C**

Optional

- ✓ Individual activities (p.228-238)
- ✓ Letters for Picture Coding (*TGCD*)

Note: As this is the first lesson, each section is explained in greater detail than subsequent lessons.

Review previously learned letters and sounds

'Quick Dash' (page 194). Review some letters from the Fast Track. *PCCs*: **a, b, h, m, o, r, t, w**

Show the picture side. Children name the character. Turn to the plain side, and ask, What is the letter sound? After going through the cards this way, go back through at a faster pace showing only the plain letter side. Children respond with the sounds.

Sound

Show the plain letter side of Clever Cat's *PCC*. Who is hiding behind this letter? Do you know? After children say, **"Clever Cat"**, show the picture side. Yes, and this is how Clever Cat looks when she is in Letterland.

Turn to the plain letter. This is how she looks in words. She loves to make her sound in words, but she doesn't miaow like ordinary cats. She's a Letterland cat so she whispers her own special sound instead. Let's use a Sound Trick to discover the sound she makes in words: Show the picture side of the *PCC* and ask for the character name. **"Clever Cat"**. Now just START to say her name again and STOP: Clever Cat, 'c...'. Emphasise whispering to avoid adding an unwanted 'uh' sound, /c/ not 'cuh'. Sound Trick (page 181).

To help children develop the link between the plain letter and the letter sound, ask them for the letter *sound* each time you push the plain letter side of the card forward, "/c/.../c/.../c/...". Praise correct answers with: Clever! or Correct!

Picture Code Cards

Action

Teach the Action Trick (page 182). Ask the children to do the action and make the sound in response to the plain letter side of the *PCC*.

Song

Sing Clever Cat's *Alphabet Song*. Show the picture side of her *PCC* when you sing her name. Turn to the plain letter every time you sing her sound (lyrics on *TGCD*) or use the animated version on the *Living ABC* software. Make sure the children drop into a whisper for her sound and make her action at the same time.

Action Trick (see p.182)

Phonemic awareness and language development

Alliteration

Read about Clever Cat in the *ABC* book or use the *Living ABC* software. Emphasise her sound as you read the text and explore the picture together, letting children identify things that begin with her sound. If you are using the *Living ABC* software, let Clever Cat introduce herself, then the children can interact with her by clicking on different items on the screen.

Clever Cat in ABC book

Ask questions and discuss

Ask some questions to encourage children to think in an alliterative way and to present some new and challenging language in a friendly context. Encourage discussion of each of these scenarios, and how Clever Cat always prefers the answers that start with her letter.

Can you imagine Clever Cat playing tennis or would she prefer **c**ard games? Do you think she might like to **c**onduct our next school **c**oncert? What instrument might she want to play: **c**astanets or drums? When she goes to stay in the **c**ountry in her **c**aravan, what do you think she likes to do: go for long walks or **c**limb **c**liffs? Praise answers with **C**ongratulations! or **C**lever!

Beginning sound games (Optional)

If children need more practice listening for the letter sound at the beginning of words, use a game in each lesson. Choose one from the Activity Bank (pages 232-238) the *Living ABC* software, or use the Alliteration Trick (page 184) and help children to think up their own alliterative information about Clever Cat.

For example:

Praise words
clever, correct, cool.

Book titles
The Hungry Caterpillar (Eric Carle),
Corduroy (Don Freeman).

Food and Drink
cake, cauliflower, carrots,
corn, cocoa, cucumber.

Hobbies
card games, cooking, computer
games, collecting coins.

Transport
camel, canoe, car,
caravan.

Names
Carla, Catherine, Colin, Connor.

Note: If children spot exceptions to the hard /c/ sound (nice, circle, Charlie, Cheryl), put a wavy line under the 'tricky' part and tell the children they will find out why later on.

Shape: c and C

Song

Sing or say the verse from the *Handwriting Songs CD* as you finger trace both sides of Clever Cat's *PCC* (more details, page 197).

Curve round Clever Cat's face to begin.
Then gently tickle her under her chin.

Write

Write a huge **c** on the board or project the Clever Cat handwriting screen of the *Living ABC* software for children to air-trace (page 199) as they sing. Follow up with a handwriting activity.

Uppercase

Introduce the concept of uppercase letters with the Uppercase Trick (page 186). First show the *Picture Code Card (PCC)*. Reveal the uppercase letter as you explain the trick:

Whenever Clever Cat starts important words, such as people's names, she takes a deep breath and gets bigger, like this!

Optional: You may also want to ask the children to look for Clever Cat's lowercase and uppercase letter on the Letterland *Class Train Freeze*.

Individual activities

Options for individual activity for learning the **a-z** letter shapes and sounds include:

A-Z Copymasters

These worksheets help children develop pencil control and vocabulary. The worksheets feature lower and uppercase letters.

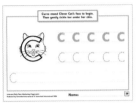

Early Years Handwriting Copymasters

The handwriting worksheets help to motivate young children to form alphabet letter shapes correctly.

Workbooks 1-6

The workbooks contain structured activities and are ideal for individual or group work. Workbooks 1 and 2 accompany Section 2 of the *Teacher's Guide*.

Picture coding

Ask the children to Picture Code Clever Cat (*TGCD*).

Provide time for Picture Coding Clever Cat's letter while everyone quietly repeats her little whispered sound. This drawing activity is a highly effective way of giving each child ownership of the letter shape, of its sound and its embedded character. Children enjoy it because they are in effect giving the plain letters life! Describe what you are doing as you model a simple Picture Coding to encourage children who lack confidence in their drawing.

Add simple details to plain black letter shapes on *TGCD*

Your *TGCD* includes large plain letters for you to copy for them to Picture Code. The support of having the letter shape provided for them at first helps build their confidence for drawing. Soon they will enjoy creating their own pictures of the Letterlanders from scratch. See page 193 for more ideas and examples of Picture Coding.

School/Home Link

Look at the *Take-Home Booklets* on the *TGCD*.

Focus on

You'll need

✓ *PCCs* for 'Guess Who?' plus **a**
✓ *ABC* book
✓ *BPCC* - Uppercase **A**
✓ *Living ABC* software or *Alphabet Songs CD* and *Handwriting Songs CD*

✓ *Vowel Scene Poster*

Optional

✓ Individual activities (p.228-238)
✓ Letters for Picture Coding (*TGCD*)

Review previously learned letters and sounds

'Guess Who?' (page 196)

Keep the *Picture Code Card (PCC)* out of sight and say the letter sound. Ask the children to repeat the sound. Ask, Who is it? Children name the Letterlander. Then show the picture side.

PCCs: **b, c, g, h, m, ŏ, r, t, w**

As children learn the Action Tricks and handwriting strokes, these can be included in your 'Guess Who?' activity. For convenient abbreviated instructions, see the Teacher Guide Cards on the *TGCD*.

Sound

Show the plain letter side of the *PCC* to see what Annie Apple looks like in words. Then the children can use the Sound Trick (page 181) to remind themselves of the sound she makes in words: **Annie Apple**, /ă/.

Picture Code Cards

Action

Teach the Action Trick (page 182). Ask the children to do the action and make the sound in response to the plain letter side of the *PCC*.

Song

Sing Annie Apple's *Alphabet Song*. Show the picture side of her *PCC* when you sing her name. Turn to the plain letter every time you sing her sound (lyrics on *TGCD*).

Action Trick (see p.182)

The Important Vowels

Annie Apple is one of five very special letters called 'vowels.' Point out Annie Apple and the other vowels on the *Vowel Scene Poster*. There are just a few of them but there is at least one of them in almost every word. And every Vowel Sound shares its letter with a Vowel Man. Annie Apple shares hers with Mr A. We'll learn more about Mr A and the other Vowel Men soon. Let's say Annie Apple's very important Vowel Sound three times: "/ă/ /ă/ /ă/." Also enjoy the Vowel Sounds Song.

'Short & Long Vowels' *Vowel Scene Posters*

Phonemic awareness and language development

Alliteration

Read about Annie Apple in the *ABC* book or use the *Living ABC* software. Emphasise her sound and explore the picture together.

Ask questions and discuss

For example: Is **A**nnie **A**pple the first letter in the **a**lphabet? Do you think she is **a**n **a**dventurous **a**pple? Which of these might she like to become (**a**ctress, teacher, **a**crobat, bus driver, **a**mbulance driver, **a**stronaut). **A**nnie has visited

Annie Apple in *ABC* book

Africa. Let's look for **A**frica in the **a**tlas. Praise words: **A**bsolutely! or **A**dmirable!

Beginning sound games

For children needing more practice in identifying beginning sounds, choose a game from the Activity Bank (pages 232-238), or the Alliteration Trick (page 184), or from the Annie Apple activities on the *Living ABC* software.

Shape: a and A

Song

Sing or say the verse from the *Handwriting Songs* as you trace both sides of Annie's *PCC* (lyrics on *TGCD*).

Write

Write a huge **a** on the board or project the Annie Apple scene of the *Living ABC* software for children to air-trace as they sing. Follow up with a handwriting activity.

Uppercase

Show the *BPCC* **A**. Annie Apple always hops up on a nice big apple stand to start important words like people's names or the first word in a sentence. Children can look for Annie Apple's two shapes on the *Class Train Freeze*. They can also quietly look for her letter around the classroom and school, on the way home and around the house. Tell the children when they see her letter to quietly say just her *sound* so as not to give away her hiding place.

Individual activity

- Use *A-Z Copymasters* or *Workbooks*.
- Ask the children to Picture Code Annie Apple, or paint her.

Add simple details to plain black letter

'Annie Apple', *A-Z Copymasters*

Lesson 3: Mr A, the Apron Man

A a

Focus on

You'll need

- ✓ *PCCs* for 'Quick Dash' plus **a**
- ✓ *BPCC - Uppercase* **A** (Mr A)
- ✓ *Vowel Scene Poster*
- ✓ *Alphabet Songs CD* or *Living ABC* software
- ✓ *A-Z Copymasters*

Optional

- ✓ Individual activities (p.228-238)
- ✓ Make *Vowel Flip-overs* for ă/ā (*TGCD*)

Review previously learned letters and sounds

'Quick Dash' (page 194) *PCCs*: ă, c, ĕ, g, ĭ, n, p, s

Sound

Show the plain letter side of the *PCC* to see what Mr A looks like in words. Do you remember that Annie Apple is a very special kind of letter called a vowel? Vowels are special because almost every single word needs at least one of them. But there is something else special about vowels like Annie Apple. She shares her letter shape with another Letterlander. Show the picture side. His name is Mr A. He came all the way from Asia to take care of Annie Apple and

Picture Code Cards

all the talking apples in the Letterland orchard. He uses the big pocket of his apron to carry apples. That's why he is called the Apron Man! He does not make a sound like Annie Apple in words. Instead he loves to say his name, 'A!' (ay) in words like apron, April, age and alien! Point out Mr A and Annie Apple on the *Vowel Scene Poster*.

'Short & Long Vowels'
Vowel Scene Posters

Action

Show his plain letter again. Mr A's letter shape is the same as Annie Apple's, but when Mr A appears in words, he says his name, 'A!' /ā/ and he shoots his hand up in the air to let everyone know he is there.

Teach the Action Trick (page 182). Ask the children to do the action and make the sound in response to the plain letter side of the *PCC*.

Song

Sing the Vowel Men's Song on the *Alphabet Songs CD*. Show the picture side of Mr A's *PCC* when you sing his name. Then at the end of the final line raise the plain letter side and call out his letter name, "a!" (lyrics on *TGCD*). You could stop after the first verse about Mr A, or perhaps play the whole song to begin to familiarise the children with all five of the Vowel Men.

Action Trick (see p.182)

Shape: a and A

Uppercase

Show the *BPCC - Uppercase* for Mr A. Mr A uses the same uppercase letter as Annie Apple to start an important word like someone's name. Listen, can you hear him at the beginning of names like **A**my, **A**idan, **A**va, **A**mos and **A**pril? Let's do his Action Trick again, as we say, "/ā/ /ā/ /ā/."

Shapes and Sounds for Annie Apple and Mr A

Although Mr A spells his name with an uppercase letter this doesn't mean that all capitals are long **a**'s. To head off this possible confusion, display the *PCCs* ă, ā, and the *BPCCs* Ă, Ā. Both Annie Apple and Mr A have a lowercase and an uppercase letter. So when we see a plain letter **a** we won't always know right away if Annie Apple or Mr A is hiding behind that letter. Write the following words on the board: **Age, age, Apron, apron, Apple, apple, Axe, axe.** Let's look at these words. I'll tell you the word and you decide if Annie Apple or Mr A is the one we hear at the beginning. Discuss each word and quickly Picture Code the **a** with a stick figure Mr A or a nice, round apple. So whichever shape you see, it could be Annie Apple saying /ă/, or Mr A saying /ā/.

For additional clarification of the two letter shapes, each with two sounds, use the pages in *A-Z Copymasters* that show Mr A in uppercase and lowercase along with the page that shows Annie Apple in both forms as well.

Phonemic awareness and language development

Games

Play the **Listen and Jump Game** for two sounds (page 232) with children jumping towards the Annie Apple or the Mr A *PCC*, depending on which sound they hear at the start of the words below. Or make *Vowel Flip-overs (TGCD)* to use with these words: **apple, apron, ache, ant, ate, acorn, acre, Africa, Asia, Antarctica, atlas, Amy, Alex.** (More games on *Living ABC* software.)

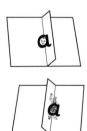

Note: For variant sounds made by the letter **a**, see our *Advanced Teacher's Guide* or website.

a as in f**a**ther is depicted in Letterland as a 'Yawning Apple', **a** as in Americ**a** is depicted as a 'Parachuted Apple'.

Lesson 4: Dippy Duck
D d

You'll need

- ✓ *PCCs* for 'Guess Who?' plus **d**
- ✓ *ABC* book
- ✓ *BPCC* **D**
- ✓ *Alphabet Songs CD* and *Handwriting Songs CD*

or *Living ABC* software
- ✓ *Dippy Duck's Day of Discovery*

Optional

- ✓ Individual activities (p.228-238)
- ✓ Letters for Picture Coding (*TGCD*)

Review previously learned letters and sounds

'Guess Who?' *PCCs*: ă, c, ĕ, g, ĭ, n, p, s

Sound

Show the plain letter side of the *PCC* to see what Dippy Duck looks like in words. Then the children can use the Sound Trick (page 181) to remind themselves of the sound she makes in words: **Dippy Duck, /d/.**

Picture Code Cards

Action

Teach the Action Trick (p.182). Ask the children to do the action and make the sound in response to the plain letter side of the *PCC*. Look at the plain letter and let children explain where her head would go, her feet, and her tail.

Song

Sing Dippy Duck's *Alphabet Song*. Show the picture side of her *PCC* when you sing her name. Turn to the plain letter every time you sing her sound (lyrics on *TGCD*).

Action Trick (see p.182)

Phonemic awareness and language development

Alliteration

Read about Dippy Duck in the *ABC* book or use the *Living ABC* software. Emphasise her sound and explore the picture together.

Ask questions and discuss

What would **D**ippy **D**uck like for **d**inner, green grass or **d**elicious **d**uckweed? **D**oes **D**ippy's **d**uck **d**oor into her **d**en look like our **d**oors or is it **d**ifferent? **D**o you think **D**ippy is better at **d**rawing **d**inosaurs or painting people? Praise words: **D**elightful! Well **d**one!

Beginning sound games

For more practice see Section 7: Activity Bank or use the activities on the *Living ABC* software.

Dippy Duck in *ABC* book

Shape: d and D

Song

Sing or say the verse from the *Handwriting Songs CD* as you trace both sides of Dippy's *PCC* (lyrics on *TGCD*).

Write

Write a huge **d** on the board or project the Dippy Duck scene of the *Living ABC* software for children to air-trace as they sing. Follow up with a handwriting activity.*

Uppercase

Show the *PCC* **d** and then *BPCC* **D** and introduce the Uppercase Trick. Dippy

Duck lives in a duck den at the edge of her duck pond. Her uppercase letter shape is the shape of her duck door. Dippy looks out of her duck door in the Reading Direction as she makes her usual sound, /**d**/.

Individual activity

- See page 12 for *Copymasters* or *Workbooks*.
- Ask the children to Picture Code Dippy Duck's lowercase letter shape.
- Make paper duck head finger puppets. Avoid b/d confusions with the activity on the *TGCD*. (There is also a poster available from Letterland to help children avoid the b/d confusions.)
- If available, read the rhyming story of *Dippy Duck's Day of Discovery* and leave the book where children can pore over the pictures later and hunt for Dippy Duck's little duckling in each scene.

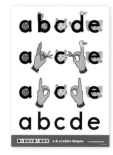

b and d Letter Shapes Alphabet Poster

Dippy Duck's Day of Discovery

Lesson 5: Harry Hat Man
H h

Focus on

You'll need

- ✓ *PCCs* for 'Quick Dash' plus **h**
- ✓ *ABC* book
- ✓ *Alphabet Songs CD* and *Handwriting Songs CD* or *Living ABC* software
- ✓ *BPCC - Uppercase* **H**

Optional

- ✓ Individual activities (p.228-238)
- ✓ Letters for Picture Coding (*TGCD*)

Review previously learned letters and sounds

'**Quick Dash**' (page 194) *PCCs*: ă, c, d, l, m, o, r, t, ŭ

Sound

Show the plain letter side of the *PCC* and ask the children who is hiding behind the letter. Show the picture side to confirm their answer. Turn back to the plain letter to show how he looks in words. Then children can do the Sound Trick (page 181) to remind themselves of the sound he makes in words: **Harry Hat Man**, /**hhh**/...

Picture Code Cards

Action

Teach the Action Trick (page 182). Ask the children to do the action and make the sound in response to the plain letter side of the *PCC*.

Song

Sing Harry Hat Man's *Alphabet Song*. Show the picture side of his *PCC* when you sing his name. Turn to the plain letter every time you sing his sound.

Action Trick (see p.182)

Phonemic awareness and language development

Alliteration

Read about Harry Hat Man in the *ABC* book or use the *Living ABC* software. Emphasise his sound and explore the picture together.

Harry Hat Man in *Living ABC* software

Ask questions and discuss

Have you noticed that Harry Hat Man doesn't wear shoes? It's because he hates noise – even the sound of his own footsteps! That's why you can hardly hear him in words. Do you think noise gives him a horrible headache? (Yes.) What do you think makes Harry Hat Man happiest: when you are noisy or when you are helpful? Can you think of some ways of being helpful that might make him happy?

Beginning sound games

Harry Hat Man Says... Play this game modelled on 'Simon Says' to practise Harry Hat Man's sound or anytime the children need to stand and stretch a bit. Tell the children you will pretend to be Harry Hat Man. Then give directions such as 'Harry Hat Man says put your hands on your... **head, hips, heels, hips, hands, hair, heart**' for them to follow. But if you name a body part that doesn't start with a /**h**/ sound then children should not follow it (e.g. knee, tum, feet, elbow). Soon children will be ready to play the role of Harry.

For more practice see Section 7: Activity Bank, or the *Living ABC* software.

Shape: h and H

Song

Sing or say the verse from the *Handwriting Songs CD* as you trace both sides of Harry's *PCC* (lyrics on *TGCD*), or watch and sing along to the *Living ABC* software.

Write

Write a huge **h** on the board or project the Harry Hat Man scene of the *Living ABC* software for children to air-trace as they sing. Follow up with a handwriting activity.*

Uppercase

Show the *PCC* **h** and then the *BPCC* **H** and introduce the Uppercase Trick. Whenever Harry Hat Man can do something as important as starting a name, or a sentence, he is so happy that he does a handstand with his hat on!

Individual activity

* See Letterland Resources (page 12) for *Copymasters* or *Workbooks*.
* Ask the children to Picture Code Harry Hat Man.

Picture code Harry Hat Man

Lesson 6: Munching Mike
M m

You'll need
✓ *PCCs* for 'Guess Who?' + **m**
✓ *ABC book*
✓ *BPCC - Uppercase* **M**
✓ *Alphabet Songs CD* and *Handwriting Songs CD*

or *Living ABC* software

Optional
✓ Individual activities (p.228-238)
✓ Letters for Picture Coding (*TGCD*)

Review previously learned letters and sounds
'Guess Who?' (page 196) *PCCs*: ă, d, h, j, k, ū, x, y

Picture Code Cards

Sound
Show the plain letter side of the *PCC* to see what Munching Mike looks like in words. Then the children can use the Sound Trick (page 181) to remind themselves of the sound he makes in words: **Munching Mike**, /**mmm**/.

Action
Teach the Action Trick (page 182). Ask the children to do the action and make the sound in response to the plain letter side of the *PCC*.

Song
Sing Munching Mike's *Alphabet Song*. Show the picture side of his *PCC* when you sing his name. Turn to the plain letter every time you sing his sound (lyrics on *TGCD*).

Action Trick (see p.182)

Phonemic awareness and language development

Alliteration
Read about Munching Mike in the *ABC* book or use the *Living ABC* software. Emphasise his sound and explore the picture together.

Ask questions and discuss
You have **m**any, **m**any of something in your body beginning with /**mmm**/ that help you to **m**ove. What are they? (**m**uscles.) Up in the sky, what would **M**unching **M**ike like to **m**unch if he could reach it? (**m**oon, **m**ilky way.) What school subject do you think **M**unching **M**ike might like **m**ost? (**m**aths.) Praise with: **M**arvellous! **M**agnificent! **Mmm**, you **m**ay be right!

Munching Mike in ABC book

Beginning sound games
For children who need more practice: Activity Bank, or *Living ABC* software.

Shape: m and M

Song
Sing or say the verse from the *Handwriting Songs* as you trace both sides of Mike's *PCC* (lyrics on *TGCD*).

Write
Write a huge **m** on the board or project the Munching Mike scene of the *Living ABC* software for children to air-trace **m** as they sing. Follow up with a handwriting activity.*

Uppercase
Show the *PCC* **m** and then *BPCC* **M** and introduce the Uppercase Trick. Munching Mike is just a little monster, so he calls his Mum to do the big job

of starting important words like names, because Mike's Mum is much bigger than he is.

Individual activity

* See Letterland Resources (page 10) for *Copymasters* or *Workbooks*
• Ask the children to Picture Code Munching Mike, or paint him with some mountains.

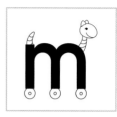
Picture code
Munching Mike

Lesson 7: Talking Tess
T t

Focus on **Tt**

You'll need
✓ *PCCs* for 'Quick Dash' + **t**
✓ *ABC* book
✓ *BPCC - Uppercase* **T**
✓ *Alphabet Songs CD* and *Handwriting Songs CD*

or *Living ABC* software

Optional
✓ Individual activities (p.228-238)
✓ Letters for Picture Coding (*TGCD*)

Review previously learned letters and sounds
'Quick Dash' (page 194) *PCCs*: **d, h, j, k, m, ū, x, y**

Sound

Show the plain letter side of the *PCC* to see what Talking Tess looks like in words. Then the children can use the Sound Trick (page 181) to remind themselves of the sound she makes in words: **Talking Tess**, /t/.

Picture Code Cards

Action
Teach the Action Trick (page 182). Ask the children to do the action and make the sound in response to the plain letter side of the *PCC*.

Song
Sing Talking Tess's *Alphabet Song*. Show the picture side of her *PCC* when you sing her name. Turn to the plain letter every time you sing her sound (lyrics on *TGCD*).

Phonemic awareness and language development

Action Trick (see p.182)

Alliteration
Read about Talking Tess in the *ABC* book or use the *Living ABC* software. Emphasise her sound and explore the picture together.

Ask questions and discuss
Talking **T**ess has a **t**elescope. Do you know what it's for? She also has a **t**ank of **t**en **t**adpoles. What happens to **t**adpoles' **t**ails when they get bigger? Is Talking Tess **t**aller than Munching Mike! Yes! Remember to make her look **t**aller when you write her letter. Start at the **t**op! Can you find some other **t**all letters on the Wall Frieze? Praise word: **T**errific!

Talking Tess in
ABC book

Beginning sound games
For children who need more practice: Activity Bank or the *Living ABC* software.

Shape: t and T

Song

Sing or say the verse from the *Handwriting Songs* as you trace both sides of Tess's *PCC* (lyrics on *TGCD*).

Write

Write a huge **t** on the board or project the Talking Tess scene of the *Living ABC* software for children to air-trace **t** as they sing. Follow up with a handwriting activity.*

Uppercase

Show the *PCC* **t** and then the *BPCC* **T** and introduce the Uppercase Trick. When Tess starts a name she takes a deep breath and grows so tall that her head disappears in the clouds! We still know it's Tess, though, because we can still see her arms.

Individual activity

* * See Letterland Resources (page 12) for *Copymasters* or *Workbooks*.
* • Ask the children to Picture Code Talking Tess (page193 and *TGCD*).

Note: Continue to look for similar activities for each letter as listed above for letter **t**. In subsequent lessons this space will be used for blending and segmenting activities.

Picture code - Add simple details to plain black letter

Lesson 8
First blending

You'll need

✓ To make a Reading Direction sign for your 'Live Reading' and 'Live Spelling' area (page 198)

✓ To make a card with the letter **a** on it
✓ *PCCs* for 'Quick Dash' plus Diana Duck
✓ *Phonics Readers 1a*

Review previously learned letters and sounds

'Quick Dash' *PCCs*: ă, c, d, h, m, t

First 'Live Reading'

> *PCCs*: h, ă, c, d, m, t   Words: **at, am, had, cat**

Reading Direction

Ask the two children showing the picture sides of *PCCs* **a** and **t** to line up in this order: **a t** (but don't say the word yet).

Let's pretend that these two children are Annie Apple and Talking Tess. Imagine that the wall behind them is a great big page in a book. All the Letterlanders like to build words so they can help you to read them. They always line up in the Reading Direction so we know where to start and which way to go.

Ask the two children to push their cards forward in turn and say their sounds as you touch each one on the shoulder, /ă//t/. Then they push their *PCCs* forward again and *all* the children say the sounds. (More details, page 201.)

Blending two sounds

To read this word, we hold Annie Apple's sound for a little longer /ăăă/. Do that as I put my hand over Annie's head, "/ăăă/."

This time we are going to hold Annie's /ă/ sound without stopping until my hand moves over Talking Tess and we *whisper* her quick little /t/ sound. Lead the class in saying /ăăăt/ as you move your hand over the two children without a pause between sounds. Repeat a bit faster.

What word did we make? Yes, **at**, as in, 'I am **at** school.' Ask several children to imagine they are somewhere else and say, "**I am at** _____."

Let two different children hold the **a** and **m** *PCC* picture sides to form the word **am**. Use the same steps to blend **am**. Then use it in a sentence.

Blending three sounds

Line up other children with *PCCs* to form **had**. They say their sounds in turn pushing *PCCs* forward. The class repeats the sounds.

Now we have a word with three sounds! Let's work on blending the first two sounds. Ask the child with **d** to take a step away from the other two letters.

Ask the children to prolong the whispered sound /hhh/ as you hold your hand over Harry Hat Man. Do the same with /ă/.

Now let's say the two sounds without stopping in between: "hhăăăă/..." Repeat a few times until the children are saying "hă."

Move the child with the Dippy Duck *PCC* back into the word. Ask the children to say /hă/ and /d/ separately first and then prolong /hăăă/ until they say the /d/ sound: **had**. Ask them to blend it two or three times.

The 'store and release' technique

Ask the children to form **cat** with *PCCs*.

There are some sounds that we can't hold out or stretch. Clever Cat's sound is a very quick, quiet sound. Say it with me, "/c/" (hard **c** sound).*

Clever Cat has a secret to help us read words that begin with quick sounds like hers. She says:

> I always sound better beside another letter,
>
> so don't make my sound all alone.
>
> Put a nice round apple right beside me,
>
> so I don't have to be on my own.

Reading Direction

Ask the *PCC* children to turn their cards around to reveal the plain letters. The whole class says the sound that each letter makes in words.

So let's make Clever Cat and Annie Apple's sounds together. First, get ready to say Clever Cat's sound, but don't say it yet. Then get ready to say Annie Apple's sound, but don't say it. Now, we are going to let both sounds burst out together! Are you ready? "/că/!"

Now blend all three sounds together: "/că/ /t/, **cat**."

*   Other 'stop' sounds that are difficult to blend include /**b**/ /**d**/ /**g**/ /**k**/ /**p**/ /**t**/.

Introduce the Roller Coaster Trick

> *PCCs*: **ă, c, d, d, h, m, t** Words: **hat, mat, ham, dad, had, cat**

Display the plain letter sides of the *PCCs* to form the word **hat** for all to see. Then introduce the kinaesthetic strategy of 'placing' the sounds along the arm to help develop good blending skills. (The **Roller Coaster Trick** is explained in detail on page 188.)

Now, here is another Letterland trick. We are going to pretend our arms are a steep part of a roller coaster and roll the sounds down it to read a word.

Show the class how to use their right hands to put the sounds on their left arms. (If you and the children all face in their Reading Direction, they will be able to copy your actions easily.) We are going to read the word that I have made.

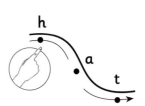

/hhh/   /ă/   /t/

- Touch your shoulder with your other hand and say the first sound, /**hhh**/.
- Next touch the crook or middle of your arm and say /**ă**/.
- Then touch your wrist and say the last sound /**t**/.
- Let's say those sounds as we touch again, /**hhh** / /**ă**/ /**t**/.

Combine two sounds, then add the third

Now we say the first two sounds without stopping like this. Place your hand on your shoulder and slide it to the crook of your arm as you say: /**hhhăăă**/.

Ask the children to do this twice without a pause in between the sounds.

Next we add the last sound, /**t**/. Ready... All put their hands on their shoulders and slide down the arm to their wrist saying, "/**hhhăăăt**/."

All repeat "/**hhhăăăt**/"as you do the Roller Coaster Trick again.

What's our word? '**hat**' Hat! Just like Harry Hat Man's hairy hat.

Change the *PCCs* to make the other words above. Guide the children in using the Roller Coaster Trick to read these words. They can take turns being the Blending Leader, who sounds out each word on their arm first. Then everyone repeats the blending on their own arms.

Note: Letting children serve as Blending Leaders has two purposes. One, they enjoy being the 'leader', and two, it allows you to see if that child is catching on to blending. If the child has difficulty you can just jump in and do it with them.

Reading and fluency

Now that children are blending words, each lesson will link to a decodable story in the *Phonics Readers*. These readers provide practice in blending words containing the new sounds or spelling by placing them in the context of a simple story. (More information and suggestions, page 217.)

First 'tricky' word

In preparation for the first story in *Phonics Readers 1a*, teach the irregular word **a**, using the steps below. Write the word **cat** on the board. Ask children to do the Roller Coaster Trick for the word. Add the word **a** in front of **cat**.

This says '**a cat**.' If you asked me what animal I saw on the way to school, I might say '**a cat**.' Ask the children to read the phrase.

'Tricky' word

Because we say this little word quickly, it doesn't sound like Annie Apple's /**ă**/ sound, does it? It sounds like 'uh' instead. Let's put a wavy line under that word. This will remind us that in this little one-letter word Annie Apple is not making her usual sound. Instead she says... "uh".

Make a 'Tricky' Word Card for the word **a** with a wavy line below it for future revision with other 'tricky' words.

Phonics Readers 1a: *Dad, a hat, a cat*

For the first reading, you may want to project the story. You may also want to cover each illustration and ask the children to read the caption first, using the Roller Coaster Trick to decode words. Before you reveal the picture, ask children to predict what they will see.

Phonics Readers 1a

Alternatively, you could ask the children to look at the pictures and describe what they see and how each picture relates to the one before it. Later let children read from their copies of the book. You can choral read it a few times.

Then let children read it with a partner.

More suggestions for using the *Phonics Readers* can be found in the Appendix, page 217.

Lesson 9: Sammy Snake
S s

You'll need
- ✓ *PCCs* for 'Guess Who?' plus **s**
- ✓ *ABC* book
- ✓ *BPCC - Uppercase* **S**
- ✓ *Alphabet Songs CD* and *Handwriting Songs CD*

or *Living ABC* software
- ✓ *Phonics Readers 1a*

Optional
- ✓ Individual activities (p.228-238)
- ✓ Letters for Picture Coding (*TGCD*)

Review previously learned letters and sounds
'Guess Who?' *PCCs*: ă, c, d, h, m, t

Sound
Show the plain letter side of the *PCC* to see what Sammy Snake looks like in words. Then the children can use the Sound Trick (page 181) to remind themselves of the sound he makes in words: **Sammy Snake**, /sss/.

Picture Code Cards

Action
Teach the Action Trick (page182). Ask the children to do the action and make the sound in response to the plain letter side of the *PCC*.

Song
Sing Sammy Snake's *Alphabet Song*. Show the picture side of his *PCC* when you sing his name. Turn to the plain letter every time you sing his sound (lyrics on T*GCD*).

Phonemic awareness and language development

Action Trick (see p.182)

Alliteration
Read about Sammy Snake in the *ABC* book or use the *Living ABC* software. Emphasise his sound and explore the picture together.

Ask questions and discuss
Sammy **S**nake loves to make his hi**ss**ing sound in words, like this: /**sss**/. Can you hear his hiss six times in this **s**entence? Li**sss**ten...and count with me.

"**S**ammy **S**nake loves to **s**it in the **s**un on the **s**and by the **s**ea."

What might **S**ammy like to eat - **s**ixty-**s**ix **s**izzling **s**ausages, or mouthfuls of mashed potatoes and macaroni? Which of these might he like to become one day? (a **s**ailor, or a **s**ausage-**s**eller or a dancer)? **Praise words: S**uper! **S**plendid!

Sammy Snake in ABC book

Shape: s and S

Song
Sing or say the verse from the *Handwriting Songs* as you trace both sides of Sammy's *PCC* (lyrics on *TGCD*).

Write
Write a huge **s** on the board or project the Sammy Snake scene of the *Living ABC* software for children to air-trace **s** as they sing. Follow up with a

handwriting activity.

Uppercase

Show the *PCC* **s** and then the *BPCC* **S** and introduce the **Uppercase Trick**. Whenever Sammy can do something as important as starting a name or sentence, he takes a deep breath and gets bigger. He says, 'Now I'm a **sss**uper-**sss**ized **sss**nake!'

Blending

Blending with Picture Code Cards

PCCs: **ă, d, h, m, s, t**   Words: **Sam, sad, hat, sat, mad, had**

Set out the words with the plain letter sides of your *PCCs*. Use the shelf under your whiteboard, a pocket chart to display the *PCCs*, or use the word building function in the *Story Phonics* software. Guide children in using the **Roller Coaster Trick** (page 188) to decode the words. After the first few words, let individual children be the Blending Leader for some words. Then you or a child can say a sentence containing the word to make sure everyone 'gets' the word and its meaning.

Reading and fluency

Phonics Readers 1a: *Sam*

You could cover the illustrations as children read the page so they can predict what they will see. Then show each illustration for children to check their predictions. Even this very simple story can be a source for discussion of cause and effect. Why is Sam sad on the first page and angry on the second? (That now it's too hot). Why is he happy on the third page and how does he feel on the last one? Later ask the children to re-read with partners using individual or shared copies of the book.

Phonics Readers 1a

First segmenting

You'll need

✓ *PCCs for 'Guess Who?'*

✓ *Phonics Readers 1a*
✓ *Magnetic Word Builders* or other letters

Review previously learned letters and sounds

'Guess Who?' (page 196) *PCCs*: ă, c, d, h, m, s, t

Stretch and segment

This lesson introduces segmenting the sounds in spoken words to build children's awareness of phonemes, an essential element of learning to read and a foundation for learning to spell. Segmenting is the reverse process of blending. In blending, children use the Roller Coaster Trick to blend the sounds so they can read words. In segmenting they say the words in slow-speak, prolonging the sounds while they use the kinaesthetic activity of stretching an imaginary rubber band with their hands. Stretch and segment is the name for this process and the Rubber Band Trick is the strategy the children will use to help them spell words.

Teaching segmentation

Introduce the lesson

Today we are going to learn a new trick that helps us hear all the sounds in our words. It is called the **Rubber Band Trick** (page 190). You can use this trick whenever you want to write a word. Put your two hands together and pretend that a strong rubber band is holding them together. Now, let's slowly stretch out our rubber band as we slow-speak the word: **sat**. Ready? **"Sssăăăt."** Repeat and make sure children are actually prolonging the sounds (except /**t**/) as they stretch their hands wider and wider.

Rubber Band Trick

PCCs: ă, c, d, h, m, s, t   Words: **sad, ham, at, had, sat**

Display the above *PCCs* for all to see. Children will help decide which letters are needed to spell the words.

Catch and stretch

Now we are going to listen for sounds and spell some words. First let me show you how to catch a word when I throw it. I am going to pretend to throw you an invisible ball with a word on it. The word is **sad**, meaning unhappy. Pretend for a moment that you are all **unhappy**. Let's see your sad faces... Now, as I throw my pretend ball, I'll say the word and as you catch it you repeat the word. Ready to catch it... **sad**. Children respond with a catching motion: **"sad."** Let's slow-speak the word **sad** as we stretch our rubber bands: **"sssssssaaaaaaaad."***

Segment the sounds

Slow-speak the word again, stopping on the first sound /**sss**/. So, who makes that sound? **"Sammy Snake."** Super! Place the Sammy Snake *PCC* in the first position (plain letter side).

Rubber Band Trick

Middle sound

Let's stretch **sad** again, but this time we'll listen for the second sound, /**ssssăăă-ă-ă-ă**/. Move your hands back and forth a bit midway through your stretching motion as you repeat the sound, /ă/ /ă/ /ă/. Ask the children to repeat the motions and sounds. Ask them who says /ă/ and then place the

Annie Apple *PCC* after Sammy Snake.

Last sound

We have only one more sound in our word **sad**. Let's stretch it one more time, "sssssaaad-d-d." Repeat the final /**d**/ sound as you move your hands slightly back and forth, this time at the widest position. Ask the children to repeat, "ssssaaaad-d-d". Ask, Whose sound? "**Dippy Duck's**." Definitely, so let's put Dippy Duck at the end of our word.

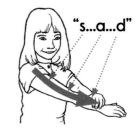

Check the spelling

Show children that they can check their spelling by using the reverse of segmenting which is blending. They can use the Roller Coaster Trick to decode the sounds and verify that they have spelled **sad** correctly.

Additional suggestions

Ask a child to come forward to be the Stretching Leader (page 191) for a word. Before everyone else stretches and segments the word, the Leader tries it (with your support, as needed). Then the rest of the class 'follows the leader' by stretching and segmenting together. This not only builds the leader's confidence but allows you to observe individual children's progress in segmentation.

Individual children to come forward to help place the letters on shelf or they can select the letters to show on screen in the word building section of the *Story Phonics* software. Ask everyone to check each others spelling by doing the Roller Coaster Trick.

Word building

You can use the Letterland *Magnetic Word Builders* or any set of separately cut-out letters or letter tiles. Each child can use their own set of letters or they can work in pairs.

Letters needed: **c, a, d, d, h, m, s, t**

Magnetic Word Builder

Words: **hat, Sam, dad, mat, had, cat**

Follow the steps below with as many of the words as you think are helpful. You can also let a child be the Stretching Leader, as described above, for some of the words in this activity. (For a more detailed explanation of the suggested steps see page 190.)

1. You say the word, use it in a sentence, repeat the word.
2. Children repeat the word.
3. Stretch the whole word with the children.
4. Segment out each sound with the children.
5. Children build the word.
6. Everyone uses the Roller Coaster Trick to check their spelling.

Reading and fluency

Phonics Readers 1a: *Dad, Sam*

Read with the children. Compare and contrast questions: What did Dad and Sam both do? What did they do differently? For comprehension, use the 'Story Stone' (page 221) or 'Plan and Play' (page 222).

Provide time for children to re-read this story and the previous one as a group and then with partners. (More suggestions in the Appendix).

Phonics Readers 1a

Lesson 11: Impy Ink and Sleepy Sammy Snake
I i and s as in his

You'll need

- ✓ PCCs for 'Quick Dash' plus **i** (Impy Ink), **s** (Sleepy Sammy)
- ✓ ABC book
- ✓ BPCC - Uppercase **I** (Impy Ink)
- ✓ Alphabet Songs CD and Handwriting Songs CD or Living ABC software

- ✓ Phonics Readers 1a
- ✓ Fluency List A (TGCD)
- ✓ Vowel Scene Posters, 'Short and Long Vowels'

Optional

- ✓ Individual activities (p.228-238)
- ✓ Letters for Picture Coding (TGCD)

Review previously learned letters and sounds

'Quick Dash' (page 194) PCCs: **ă, c, d, h, m,** n, **o, s, t, v**

Sound

Show the plain letter side of the PCC to see what Impy Ink looks like in words. Then the children can use the Sound Trick (page 181) to remind themselves of the sound he makes in words: **Impy Ink**, /i/.

Picture Code Cards

Action

Teach the Action Trick (page 182). Ask the children to do the action and make the sound in response to the plain letter side of the PCC.

Song

Sing Impy Ink's *Alphabet Song*. Show the picture side of his PCC when you sing his name. Turn to the plain letter every time you sing his sound (lyrics on *TGCD*). Also enjoy the Vowel Sounds Song.

Action Trick (see p.182)

The Important Vowels

Impy Ink is one of the very special letters called vowels. Refer to the *Vowel Scene Poster*. There are just a few of them but remember, one of them is in almost every word! And every Vowel Sound shares his letter with a Vowel Man. We'll learn more about Mr I soon. Let's say Impy Ink's very important vowel sound three times: "/ ĭ / / ĭ / / ĭ /."

'Short & Long Vowels'
Vowel Scene Posters

Phonemic awareness and language development

Alliteration

Read about Impy Ink in the *ABC* book or use the *Living ABC* software. Emphasise his sound and explore the picture together.

Ask questions and discuss

Impy Ink has an incredible imagination. He thinks of lots of interesting things. For example, why do you think he always puts a spot of ink above his head? (Perhaps this is Impy's way of helping children to recognise him in words, because his letter is so thin and little without the dot.) Praise words: Incredible! or Interesting!

Impy Ink in ABC book

Beginning sound games

For children needing more practice: Activity Bank, and *Living ABC* software.

Shape: i and I

Song

Sing the *Handwriting Song* as you trace both sides of the PCC (lyrics on *TGCD*).

Write

Write a huge **i** on the board or project the Impy Ink scene of the *Living ABC* software for children to air-trace as they sing. Follow up with a handwriting activity.

Uppercase

Show the *PCC* **i** and then the *BPCC* **I** and introduce the **Uppercase Trick**. When Impy takes a deep breath, his letter gets so tall and thin that you can't see his ink spot anymore. His uppercase letter looks like his incredible ink pen that writes in rainbow ink!

s /z/ Sleepy Sammy's Sound

Display the picture side of the Sleepy Sammy *PCC*. Sammy Snake is needed in so many words that sometimes he gets tired and has to take a quick snooze. Then, instead of his usual hissing sound, /**sss**/, you'll hear him snoozing, /**zzz**/, in words. Pretend you are snoozing and let's all make his sleepy sound, "**zzz**."

Picture Code Card

Blending

> *PCCs*: ă, ĭ, h, s/z/   Words: **is, his, has**

Make the word **is** with the picture side of Sleepy Sammy. Ask the children to use their arms to blend the word. Say a sentence with **is**. Ask several children to do the same. Follow the same steps with the words **his** and **has**.

Reading and fluency

Phonics Readers 1a: *Is it him*?

Read with the children. (Suggestions page 217.) Use this occasion to talk about question marks and exclamation marks.

Phonics Readers 1a

Fluency List A *(TGCD)*

Give children this list of sounds, words and sentences for practice in class and at home. (See page 214 for full explanation.)

Lesson 12: Mr I, the Ice Cream Man
I i

Focus on

You'll need

- ✓ *PCCs* for 'Guess Who?' plus Mr I
- ✓ *BPCC - Uppercase* **I** (Mr I)
- ✓ *Alphabet Songs CD* or *Living ABC* software
- ✓ *Phonics Readers 1b*

✓ Make a 'Tricky' Word Card: **Mr**

Optional

- ✓ Individual activities (p.228-238)
- ✓ Letters for Picture Coding *(TGCD)*
- ✓ *Alphabet Frieze* or *Vowel Scene Poster*

Review previously learned letters and sounds

'Guess Who?' *PCCs*: d, h, ĭ, m, s, t

Segment and spell

Ask everyone to say **hid** and then stretch and segment the sounds. As they segment out each sound, write the letters on the board until the whole word is written. (See page 206). Words to spell on the board: **hid, sit, had, him, mat**

Ask the children to re-read the list on the board each time you add a word.

Sound

Show the plain letter side of the *PCC* to see what Mr I looks like in words. Like the five other Vowel Sounds, Impy Ink shares his letter with a Vowel Man. Show the picture side. This is Mr I. Can you say his name? **"Mr I."** Everyone in Letterland likes Mr I because he sells ice cream! Like the other Vowel Men, Mr I says his name in words. You can hear him saying /ī/ at the start of words like ice cream, idea and island. Point out Mr I and Impy Ink on the *Vowel Scene Poster* or *Alphabet Frieze*.

Picture Code Cards

Action

When Mr I says his name he shoots his hand up in the air and says, / ī /. Show the plain letter. Children say his name and do his action.

'Short & Long Vowels'
Vowel Scene Posters

Song

Sing the Vowel Men's Song on the *Alphabet Songs CD*. Show the picture side of Mr I's *PCC* when you sing his name. Then at the end of the final line raise the plain letter side and call out his letter name, "i!" (lyrics on *TGCD*).

Review Mr A and Mr I and prepare the children to meet the other Vowel Men in later lessons.

Phonemic awareness and language development

Words with Mr I

Show the plain uppercase letter *BPCC*. We use this letter as a word every time we talk about ourselves. Say a sentence with the word **I**. Ask a few children to hold the **I** (plain side showing) and say a sentence with it.

Action Trick (see p.182)

Make the word **hi** with *PCCs* with the picture side for Mr I only. Ask the children to do the **Roller Coaster Trick**. Then place Mr I's picture side on a whiteboard shelf and write on the board above it for children to read: **"Hi, I am Mr I."**

Games

Place Impy Ink's picture side on the shelf. Above Impy Ink's picture write, **It is Impy Ink**. Children read it. Now listen for the first sound in this word as you say it after me, ice, "**ice**." Let a child come forward and point to Mr I to show that **ice** starts with his name. Then everyone reads Mr I's sentence, **"Hi, I am Mr I,"** as the child points to each word. Do the same with each of these words, reading Mr I's or Impy Ink's sentence to match the initial sound: is, **idea**, **ice**, internet, if, **iris**, inside, **ivy**.

Shape: i and I (Mr I)

Uppercase

Show the *BPCC - Uppercase* for Mr I. When Mr I starts an important word, he stands beside his long ink pen-like letter and his dot disappears!

Reading and fluency

'Tricky' word

Show everyone your card for **Mr**. Explain that it is a short way to spell the word 'Mister', as in Mr A, Mr E, Mr I and so on.

'Tricky' word

Phonics Readers 1b: *Is it his?*

Guide children in reading. Help them name the pictures on page 2 to choose those beginning with Mr I's *name*. (The horned animal is an ībex.) Do the same with Impy Ink on pages 3-4.

Phonics Readers 1b

Fluency List A *(TGCD)* Review and ask the children to partner read (page 215).

Lesson 13: Noisy Nick

N n

You'll need

- ✓ *PCCs* for 'Quick Dash' plus **n**
- ✓ *ABC* book
- ✓ *BPCC - Uppercase* **N**
- ✓ *Alphabet Songs CD* and *Handwriting Songs CD* or *Living ABC* software

- ✓ *Phonics Readers 1b*
- ✓ *Fluency List A (TGCD)*
- ✓ Whiteboard or other writing materials

Optional

- ✓ Individual activities (p.228-238)
- ✓ Letters for Picture Coding *(TGCD)*

Review previously learned letters and sounds

'Quick Dash' *PCCs*: ă, c, g, h, ĭ, m, s, s/z/, t, w

Sound

Show the plain letter side of the *PCC* to see what Noisy Nick looks like in words. Then the children can use the Sound Trick (page 181) to remind themselves of the sound he makes in words: **Noisy Nick**, /nnn/.

Picture Code Cards

Action

Teach the Action Trick (page 182). Ask the children to do the action and make the sound in response to the plain letter side of the *PCC*.

Song

Sing Nick's *Alphabet Song*. Show the picture side of his *PCC* when you sing his name. Turn to the plain letter every time you sing his sound (lyrics on *TGCD*).

Action Trick (see p.182)

Phonemic awareness and language development

Alliteration

Read about Noisy Nick in the *ABC* book or use the *Living ABC* software. Emphasise his sound and explore the picture together.

Ask questions and discuss

Do you know how **N**ick got his **n**ickname, **N**oisy **N**ick? He has a very **n**oisy hobby. He likes to make things with wood, so he is always banging **n**ails and making a **n**asty **n**oise! **N**ow... which parts of our bodies start with Nick's '**n**nn...' sound? (Eyes, **n**ose, mouth, **n**eck, ha**n**d, fi**n**gers, [finger] **n**ails) Praise word: **N**ice!

Noisy Nick in
ABC book

Beginning sound games

For more practice, see pages 232-238 and *Living ABC*.

Shape: n and N

Song

Sing or say the verse from the *Handwriting Songs* as you trace both sides of Nick's *PCC* (lyrics on *TGCD*).

Write

Write a huge **n** on the board or project the Noisy Nick scene of the *Living ABC* software for children to air-trace as they sing. Follow up with a handwriting activity.

Uppercase

Show the *PCC* **n** and then the *BPCC* **N** and introduce the Uppercase Trick. Nick starts important words by using three new nails. You can see them his name.

Blending

'Live Reading'

Line children up with *PCCs* to make the words below.

> *PCCs*: ǎ, c, ǐ, m, n, t   Words: **man, can, in, tin, tan**

Use all plain letter sides, but the picture side for Noisy Nick . The rest of the class use the Roller Coaster Trick to read the words (page 188) .

Segmenting

Written spelling

Provide each child with a whiteboard or other writing surface. Say a word, use it in a sentence and repeat it. Ask the children to repeat the word, stretch and segment and then write the word.

> Words: **in, is, it**

Reading and fluency

Phonics Readers 1b: *Nat*

Read the story with the children. Use your choice of suggestions from pages 217-224, or the *TGCD*.

Fluency List A *(TGCD)*

Continue to build reading fluency with this resource. Choose words and sentences from the list for dictation as well (page 214).

Phonics Readers 1b

Lesson 14: Golden Girl

G g

You'll need

- ✓ *PCCs* for 'Guess Who?' plus **g**
- ✓ *ABC* book
- ✓ *BPCC - Uppercase* **G**
- ✓ *Alphabet Songs CD* and *Handwriting Songs CD* or *Living ABC* software

- ✓ *Phonics Readers 1b*
- ✓ *Fluency List A (TGCD)*
- ✓ *Reading Racer* Chart *(TGCD)*

Optional

- ✓ Individual activities (p.228-238)
- ✓ *Letters for Picture Coding (TGCD)*

Review previously learned letters and sounds

'Guess Who?' *PCCs*: ǎ, d, h, ǐ, m, n, o, p, s, t

Sound

Show the plain letter side of the *PCC* to see what Golden Girl looks like in words. Then the children can use the Sound Trick (page 181) to remind themselves of the sound she makes in words: **Golden Girl**, /g/.

Picture Code Cards

Action

Teach the Action Trick (page 182). Ask the children to do the action and make the sound in response to the plain letter side of the *PCC*.

Song

Sing Golden Girl's *Alphabet Song*. Show the picture side of her *PCC* when you sing her name. Turn to the plain letter every time you sing her sound (*TGCD*).

Action Trick (see p.182)

Phonemic awareness and language development

Alliteration

Read about Golden Girl in the *ABC* book or use the *Living ABC* software. Emphasise her sound and explore the picture together.

Ask questions and discuss

Is **G**olden **G**irl facing the Reading Direction, like all the other Letterlanders? No! Do you know why? Let's do a little **g**uessing to find out. Listen carefully: do you **g**uess it's because she 'feels funny' or because she '**g**ets **g**iddy'? **G**ood! She **g**ets **g**iddy (or dizzy) from swinging on her swing. Praise words: **G**reat! or **G**ood!

Beginning sound games

For children needing more practice, pages 232-238 and *Living ABC* software.

Golden Girl in *ABC* book

Shape: g and G

Song

Sing or say the verse from the *Handwriting Songs* as you trace both sides of Golden Girl's *PCC* (lyrics on *TGCD*).

Write

Write a huge **g** on the board or project the Golden Girl scene of the *Living ABC* software for children to air-trace as they sing. Follow up with a handwriting activity.

Uppercase

Show the *PCC* **g** and then the *BPCC* **G** and introduce the Uppercase Trick. When Golden Girl is needed to start an important word, she gets out of her swing (where she isn't looking in the Reading Direction), and gets into her go-cart. She *has to* look where she is going in her go-cart so that she does not bump into the other Letterlanders!

Blending and segmenting

Blending with Picture Code Cards

Set out the words below. After children do the Roller Coaster Trick to blend each word, you or a child can make up a sentence with the word about Golden Girl or another Letterlander, e.g. "Golden Girl likes to **dig** in her garden."

> *PCCs*: ă, d, g, h, ĭ, m, n, s, t   Words: **dig, tag, sag, man, hid**

'Live Spelling' - Sound Pops

You may want to try this variation of 'Live Spelling' called Sound Pops (page 229) using the same *PCCs* and words you just used for blending. Distribute the *PCCs* and tell children to listen for their sounds as everyone uses slow-speak to segment the words. (More details on 'Live Spelling', see page 202). After everyone has stretched and segmented the three sounds say, Pop-up! The three children with letters in the word should quickly come to the front of the class and form the word. Everyone uses the Roller Coaster Trick to check the word. To involve more children, the three with *PCCs* then swap classmates.

Reading and fluency

Phonics Readers 1b: *Can Dan dig?*

Read the story with the children (ideas on page 217). Then ask them to re-read this story and previous ones with a partner when time permits.

Fluency List A *(TGCD)* You may want to time children on this list (page 214) and let them graph their scores on the *Reading Racer Chart (TGCD)* and page 217.

Phonics Readers 1b

Lesson 15
Blending and segmenting

You'll need

✓ *PCCs for 'Quick Dash' plus Diana Duck*

✓ *Phonics Readers 1b*

✓ *Fluency List B (TGCD)*

Optional

✓ Individual activities (p.228-238)

Review previously learned letters and sounds

'Quick Dash' *PCCs:* ă, c, d, g, h, ĭ, m, n, s, s/z/, t

'Live Reading'

Distribute *PCCs* from 'Quick Dash' plus a second **d**.

Words: **it, is, his, him, hit, hid, did, dig, an, can, man, and, in, tin**

Line children up to make the first word (**it**). The other children do the Roller Coaster Trick.

Then say, Sleepy Sammy, please take Talking Tess's place in the word. Tell children you want to see how quickly they can make the change and then do the **Roller Coaster Trick** for the new word (**is**). Praise for accuracy in reading the word and speed in changing the letters.

Segmenting

Whiteboard Spelling (page 206)

Use your classroom board and do this segmenting activity as a group.

Use some or all of the 'Live Reading' words above.

Say the word. Ask the children to repeat it and then stretch and segment it . Then ask them to tell you which letters (or Letterlanders) you need to write on the board to spell the word.

After everyone segments the next word, call on one child to tell you which letter needs to be changed to make the new word. Erase and replace letters to make the new word. You may want to let children help with writing some of the letters.

Reading and fluency

Phonics Readers 1b: *Yes or no?*

Read the story to the children. After each sentence is read and re-read by the class, ask everyone to indicate their answer with a smile for **yes** or a sad face for **no**. Later ask them to read the questions to a partner who answers with a thumb up or down.

Try to make time every day for children to re-read some of the previous stories in their *Phonics Readers*. This re-reading will build steadily towards fluency as the children process familiar words and sentences with increasing confidence.

Fluency List B *(TGCD)*

Give children this new list of sounds, words and sentences from Section 2 lessons 12-15. See page 214 for a full explanation.

Phonics Readers 1b

O o

Focus on

You'll need

✓ *PCCs* for 'Guess Who?' plus **o** (Oscar)
✓ *ABC* book
✓ *BPCC - Uppercase* **O**
✓ *Vowel Scene Poster*
✓ *Alphabet Songs CD* and *Handwriting Songs CD*

or *Living ABC* software
✓ *Phonics Readers 1c*
✓ *Magnetic Word Builder* or other letter sets

Optional

✓ Individual activities (p.228-238)
✓ Letters for Picture Coding (*TGCD*)

Review previously learned letters and sounds

'Guess Who?' *PCCs*: ă, d, g, h, ĭ, m, n, p, s, t

Sound

Show the plain letter side of the *PCC* to see what Oscar Orange looks like in words. Then the children can use the Sound Trick (page 181) to remind themselves of the sound he makes in words: **Oscar Orange**, /ŏ/.

Action

Teach the Action Trick (page 182). Ask the children to do the action and make the sound in response to the plain letter side of the *PCC*. Ask the children to look at each other's mouths as they say /ŏ/ to see that their mouths naturally make the letter shape **o**.

Song

Sing Oscar Orange's *Alphabet Song*. Show the picture side of his *PCC* when you sing his name. Turn to the plain letter every time you sing his sound (lyrics on *TGCD*). Also enjoy the Vowel Sounds Song with children representing each vowel with simple props and holding the relevant *PCC*.

The Important Vowels

Oscar Orange is one of the very special letters called vowels. Refer to the *Vowel Scene Poster*. Just like Annie Apple and Impy Ink, Oscar Orange shares his letter with a Vowel Man. We'll learn more about Mr O soon. Let's say Oscar Orange's very important Vowel Sound three times: "/ŏ/ / ŏ / /ŏ/."

Phonemic awareness and language development

Alliteration

Read about Oscar Orange in the *ABC* book or use the *Living ABC* software. Emphasise his sound and explore the picture together.

Ask questions and discuss

Which of these do you think **O**scar **O**range would prefer as a pet: **o**strich/horse; monkey/**o**ctopus? What do you think he would prefer to eat: scrambled eggs or an **o**melette? Play Oscar's favourite game, **O**scar's **O**pposites: Say a word and ask the children to give its **o**pposite, e.g. day/night; little/big; short/tall; up/down; gorgeous/ugly; **o**n/**o**ff; start/end.

Beginning sound games

For children needing more practice use the *Living ABC* software.

Shape: o and O

Song

Sing or say the verse from the *Handwriting Songs* as you trace both sides of

Picture Code Cards

Action Trick (see p.182)

'Short & Long Vowels' *Vowel Scene Posters*

Oscar Orange in *ABC* book

Oscar's *PCC* (lyrics on *TGCD*).

Write

Write a huge **o** on the board or project the Oscar Orange scene of the *Living ABC* software for children to air-trace as they sing. Follow up with a handwriting activity.

Uppercase

Show the *PCC* **o** and then the *BPCC* **O** and introduce the Uppercase Trick. When Oscar Orange is needed to start an important word, he takes a deep breath and gets bigger.

Blending

Blending with Picture Code Cards

Make the words below for children to use the Roller Coaster Trick to read.

PCCs: **d, g, h, m, n, o, t**   Words: **on, hot, nod, dog, not, Tom**

Segmenting

Spelling with Magnetic Word Builders

Call out the words for children to repeat, stretch and segment and build with their letters (page 207). Remind them to listen with care for the vowel sound.

Letters: **a, d, h, i, m, n, o, t**

Magnetic Word Builder

Words: **dot, nod, Tim, not, had, Tom**

Reading and fluency

Phonics Readers 1c: *Tom and Tim*

Read or project the book if possible. Show one page at a time. Before showing the third page, ask the children if they think Tim is a cat or a dog. Then before showing the final page, ask them to predict what will happen.

Fluency List B *(TGCD)*

Continue building fluency with this resource and choose words and sentences from the list for dictation as well.

Phonics Readers 1c

Lesson 17: Mr O, the Old Man

O o

Focus on

You'll need

- ✓ *PCCs* for 'Quick Dash' plus **Mr O**
- ✓ *BPCC* - Uppercase **O** (Mr O)
- ✓ *Vowel Scene Poster*: The Vowels
- ✓ *Alphabet Songs CD* or *Living ABC* software

- ✓ *Phonics Readers 1c*
- ✓ Make a 'Tricky' Word Card: **oh**

Optional

- ✓ Individual activities (p.228-238)
- ✓ Letters for Picture Coding (*TGCD*)

Review previously learned letters and sounds

'Quick Dash' *PCCs*: **ă, d, g, ĭ, l, n, ŏ, r, s, s/z/, v, z**

Sound

Show the plain letter side of the *PCC* to see what Mr O looks like in words. Just like the other five vowels, Oscar Orange shares his letter with a Vowel Man.

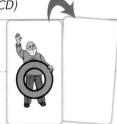

Picture Code Cards

Show the picture side. This is Mr O. Can you say his name? "**Mr O**." Mr O, the Old Man, is the **o**ldest Vowel Man in Letterland. He brings in whole boat-loads of oranges from **o**ver the **o**cean. (He also brings over special talking oranges that he pops in words like **on**, **off** and **orange**.) But when you hear /ō/ in a word it will be Mr O himself appearing in that word. Can you hear his name 'O' in words like **old**, **ocean** and **over**? Point out Mr O and Oscar Orange on the *Vowel Scene Poster*.

Action

Show his plain letter again. When Mr O appears in words, he says his name, '**O**' (oh) and he shoots his hand up in the air to let everyone know he is there. Teach the Action Trick (page 182). Ask the children to do the action and make the sound in response to the plain letter side of the *PCC*.

Action Trick (see p.182)

Song

Sing the Vowel Men's Song on the *Alphabet Songs CD*. Show the picture side of Mr O's *PCC* when you sing his name. Then at the end of the final line raise the plain letter side and call out his letter name, "o!" (lyrics on *TGCD*).

Perhaps play the whole song to gradually begin to familiarise the children with all five of the Vowel Men.

Shape

Uppercase

Show the *BPCC - Uppercase* for Mr O. To start an important word, Mr O takes a deep breath and both he and his letter get bigger!

Phonemic awareness and language development

Game

Display Mr O and Oscar Orange *PCCs* on opposite sides of the room. Play the Listen and Jump Game (page 232). Children jump towards either card, depending on which sound they hear at the start of these words: **ocean**, on, **open**, **old**, office, **only**, ostrich, octopus.

Blending

Whiteboard Reading (page 205)

Words: **go, no, so**

Show the plain lowercase Mr O *PCC*. There are three very useful little words where Mr O loves to say his name. Make **go** with *PCCs*. Children use the Roller Coaster Trick for the word. Write **go** on the board and use it in a sentence. Do the same with **so** and **no**.

Ask the children to read **go**, **so** and **no** on the board as you point to each **o**. What do you notice about Mr O in every one of these words? Is he at the beginning or the end? Yes, he is at the end **so**... he can **go**... and shout out his name in the Reading Direction and, as there is **no**... other letter in the way, he won't be shouting in anyone else's ear. Let's watch out for Mr O's favourite little words because you will find him right there, shouting out "**O**" at the end of **go**, **so** or **no**.

Segmenting

Written spelling

Erase the words **go**, **so** and **no**. Give children whiteboards or other writing materials. Call out each word for children to stretch, segment and then write.

Reading and fluency

'Tricky' word

Show the card you have made for **oh**. Let children create their own explanation of why Harry Hat Man is silent in this word and mark it as shown.

Phonics Readers 1c: *Go, go! No!*

Children practise reading Mr O's three little words in this story.

'Tricky' word

Phonics Readers 1c

Lesson 18: Peter Puppy
P p

Focus on **Pp**

You'll need

✓ *PCCs for 'Guess Who?' plus* **p**
✓ *ABC book*
✓ *BPCC - Uppercase* **P**
✓ *Alphabet Songs CD* and *Handwriting Songs CD* or *Living ABC* software

✓ *Phonics Readers 1c*
✓ *Reading Racer Charts (TGCD)*
✓ Make a 'Tricky' Word Card: **the**

Optional

✓ Individual activities (p.228-238)
✓ Letters for Picture Coding (*TGCD*)

Review previously learned letters and sounds

'Guess Who?' *PCCs*: ă, d, ĕ, g, h, ĭ, n, o, p, s, t, ŭ

Sound

Show the plain letter side of the *PCC* to see what Peter Puppy looks like in words. Then the children can use the Sound Trick (page 181) to remind themselves of the sound he makes in words: **Peter Puppy**, /**p**/.

Picture Code Cards

Action

Teach the Action Trick (page 182). Ask the children to do the action and make the sound in response to the plain letter side of the *PCC*.

Song

Sing Peter Puppy's *Alphabet Song*. Show the picture side of his *PCC* when you sing his name. Turn to the plain letter every time you sing his sound (lyrics on *TGCD*).

Phonemic awareness and language development

Action Trick (see p.182)

Alliteration

Read about Peter Puppy in the *ABC* book or use the *Living ABC* software. Emphasise his sound and explore the picture together.

Ask questions and discuss

Can you finish this sentence? **P**eter **P**uppy **p**ut his **p**aw in his **p**ocket and **p**ulled out …? (a **p**encil, a **p**ony, **p**izza, a **p**ear, **p**aint, **p**aper, **p**enguin, etc. Accept all ideas with p, saying, 'It's **p**ossible. All sorts of things are **p**ossible in Letterland!') **P**eter **P**uppy always feels **p**leased and **p**roud when **p**eople are **p**olite. What **p**olite things can we say to make him **p**roud of us? (**p**lease and thank you). Remember Oscar's Opposites? So what's the opposite of **p**ush? (**p**ull) Praise word: **P**erfect!

Peter Puppy in
ABC book

Beginning sound games

For children needing more practice, try the *Living ABC* software, or activities from the Appendix.

Shape: p and P

Song

Sing or say the verse from the *Handwriting Songs* as you trace both sides of Peter's *PCC* (lyrics on *TGCD*).

Write

Write a huge **p** on the board or project the Peter Puppy scene of the *Living ABC* software for children to air-trace as they sing. Follow up with a handwriting activity.

Uppercase

Show the *PCC* **p** and then the *BPCC* **P** and introduce the Uppercase Trick. When Peter Puppy gets to start an important word he is so pleased that he pops up on to the line so that everyone can see him better. He wishes his ears would pop up too, but, sadly, they still droop.

Blending and segmenting

'Live Spelling'

Distribute the *PCCs* below and follow the usual stretch and segment steps to 'Live Spell' the words below (page 202). After checking the first word, **hop**, with the Roller Coaster Trick, ask the children in the word to **hop** in place. Then they stay in place as the class stretches and segments **top**. The class now decides who needs to sit down and who needs to take their place. Children may come up with ways to act out the meanings of the other words.

> *PCCs*: **ă, d, h, ĭ, n, o, p, s, t**   Words: **hop, top, pot, pit, pin, pan, sip, dip**

Reading and fluency

'Tricky' word

Show children the word card you have made for **the**. Use the word in a few brief oral sentences. Ask the children which letters need a wavy line below to show they are not saying their usual sounds (all of them). (Note: the **th** digraph will become decodable after Lesson 30, Section 2).

'Tricky' word

Phonics Readers 1c: *Go, pup, go!*

Read with the children. (More suggestions, page 217.)

Phonics Readers 1c

Fluency List B *(TGCD)*

You may want to time children on this list (see page 214) and let them graph their scores on the *Reading Racer Chart* (*TGCD*).

Adding s to words

You'll need

✓ PCCs for 'Quick Dash'
✓ Whiteboard or other writing materials
✓ Phonics Readers 1c

✓ Fluency List C (TGCD)

Optional

✓ Individual activities (p.228-238)

Review previously learned letters and sounds

'Quick Dash' PCCs: ă, c, d, g, h, ĭ, m, n, o, p, s, s/z/, t

Adding s to words

Display the picture sides of the Sammy Snake (s) and Sleepy Sammy (s/z/) PCCs. When we say 'cat' we are talking about one cat. What if we want to talk about more than one cat? I might want to say, "I saw three _____." Children finish the sentence with "**cats.**"

Yes, and when we say **cats**, what is the last sound you hear in **catsss**? "/**sss**/"

Picture Code Cards

Blending with the Picture Code Cards

Words: **cat, cats, map, maps, dog, dogs, dot, dots, pan, pans, hop, hops, dig, digs**

Make the word **cat** for the children to see. They can use the Roller Coaster Trick to read the word.

Which Sammy sound?

Super, so do we need to add Sammy Snake or Sleepy Sammy to the end of this word? "**Sammy Snake.**" Right!

Add the Sammy Snake PCC to make the word **cats**. All say, "**cats.**"

When we add one letter or more on to the end of a word, we call that a suffix. The suffix at the end of **cats** is **s**. We can take it off and we still have a base word, "cat."

If we see just one **s** on the end of word it might be a suffix. We can use the **Roller Coaster Trick** to blend the base word and say it, like "**cat.**" Then we can say it again and add the suffix, "**cats**". Now we have made the word plural. Say, "plural". A word that means more than one is a plural word - like **cats**.

As you work with the words, ask the children to pick out the base words and suffixes. Encorage them to use the terms suffix, base word and plural. Separate the suffix and ask the children to read just the base word, and then the base word and suffix together.

Make the other base words and then let children decide if wide-wake or Sleepy Sammy Snake is needed:

maps (**s**), **dogs** (**s/z/**), **dots** (**s**), **pans** (**s/z/**).

Adding s to verbs

Make the word **hop** for children to blend. We might say, "I hop all around." But what if we wanted to say the same about Harry Hat Man, we would say, "Harry Hat Man _____." Children say, "**Harry Hat Man hops.**"

So what is the last sound in **hopsss**? "**Sss.**" So who do we add? "**Sammy Snake.**"

Follow similar steps with **dig**/**digs** with the spoken sentences "We **dig** in the garden" and "Golden Girl **digs** (**s/z/**) in the garden."

Segmenting and spelling

Provide whiteboards or other writing materials for the following activity.

Words to spell: **lips, tags, nods, pots**

The first word we are going to spell is **lips**. Can you hear the /**sss**/ on the end? Yes, we can, but it will help us hear the other sounds better if we stretch the word *without* the /**sss**/ suffix on the end. What word do we have if we take the suffix off **lips**? "**Lip**." Yes, **lip**, so let's stretch and segment just the word **lip** first.

Guide children in hearing the sounds and writing the word **lip**. Now what do we do to make this word say "**lips?**" Yes, add the letter **s**.

Follow similar steps with each word. Also discuss whether Sammy is making his usual /**sss**/ sound or his sleepy /**zzz**/ sound.

First spell just the base word.

Then add the suffix.

Reading and fluency

'Tricky' word

Teach the word **of** with the card you have made.

'Tricky' word

Phonics Readers 1c: *Sssss, zzzz*

Guide the children in reading and discussing the story.

After reading the story you might ask the children to write all the words they can find that end with the letter **s** in the story. Then they could write beside each word an **s** or **z** to show which sound the **s** makes.

They could also circle the suffixes on their list. Call their attention to the word **has**. It ends with **s** but it is not a suffix. How do we know? If we take off the **s** we don't have a base word.

Phonics Readers 1c

Fluency List C *(TGCD)*

Give children this list of sounds, words and sentences for practice in class and at home. It includes words from Section 2, Lessons 16-19 and a few from previous lessons. (See page 214 for full explanation.)

Lesson 20: Eddy Elephant
E e

Focus on **E e**

You'll need
- ✓ *PCCs for 'Guess Who?' plus **e** (Eddy)*
- ✓ *ABC book*
- ✓ *BPCC - Uppercase **E** (Eddy Elephant)*
- ✓ *Alphabet Songs CD and Handwriting Songs CD or Living ABC software*
- ✓ *Phonics Readers 1d*
- ✓ *Fluency List C (TGCD)*
- ✓ *Vowel Scene Poster*

Optional
- ✓ Individual activities (p.228-238)
- ✓ Letters for Picture Coding *(TGCD)*

Review previously learned letters and sounds
'Guess Who?' *PCCs:* ă, g, ĭ, k, m, n, o, p, s, s/z/, t, ŭ, y

Sound

Show the plain letter side of the *PCC* to see what Eddy Elephant looks like in words. Then the children can use the Sound Trick (page 181) to remind themselves of the sound he makes in words: **Eddy Elephant**, /ĕ/.

Picture Code Cards

Action

Teach the **Action Trick** (page 182). Ask the children to do the action and make the sound in response to the plain letter side of the *PCC*.

Song

Sing Eddy Elephant's *Alphabet Song*. Show the picture side of his *PCC* when you sing his name. Turn to the plain letter every time you sing his sound (lyrics on *TGCD*). Also enjoy the Vowel Sounds Song with children playing the role of each vowel with simple costumes or props, and holding the *PCC*.

Action Trick (see p.182)

The Important Vowels

Eddy Elephant is one of the five very special letters called vowels. **Refer to the** *Vowel Scene Poster*. Just like all the other vowels, Eddy Elephant shares his letter with a Vowel Man, Mr E. We'll learn more about Mr E soon. Let's say Eddy Elephant's very important vowel sound three times. **Push the plain letter forward three times as children say:** "/ĕ/ / ĕ / /ĕ/."

'Short & Long Vowels'
Vowel Scene Posters

Phonemic awareness and language development

Alliteration

Read about Eddy Elephant in the *ABC* book or use the *Living ABC* software. Emphasise his sound and explore the picture together.

Ask questions and discuss

Do you think **E**ddy does **e**xercises **e**very day? He must be very **e**nergetic. Could **E**ddy fit into an **e**mpty **e**nvelope? Can you think of a part of your body that starts with **E**ddy's sound? (**e**lbow) **E**ddy sometimes goes to schools and encourages everyone to make an **e**xtra special **e**ffort to make his sound just right and to get a good **e**ducation. Let's make his sound again, "/ĕ/ / ĕ / /ĕ/." Praise word: **E**xcellent!

Beginning sound games For more practice try the *Living ABC* software.

Eddy Elephant in
ABC book

Shape: e and E

Song

Sing or say the verse from the *Handwriting Songs* as you trace Eddy's *PCC*.

Write

Write a huge **e** on the board or project the Eddy Elephant scene of the *Living ABC* software for children to air-trace as they sing. Follow up with a handwriting activity.

Uppercase

Show the *PCC* **e** and then the *BPCC* **E** and introduce the **Uppercase Trick**. Eddy Elephant is very proud of his 'elephant on end' trick. He sits down and points everything - his trunk and all his feet - in the Reading Direction whenever he gets a chance to start an important word.

Blending

'Live Reading' (page 201)

Line children up with *PCCs* to make the words below. Use plain letters except for Eddy Elephant who holds up his picture side. Before making the final word **yes**, ask the children to remind themselves of Yellow Yo-yo Man's sound by using the **Sound Trick**, "Yellow Yo-yo Man, /y/."

PCCs: ĕ, g, m, n, p, s, s/z/, t, y

Words: **pet, pens, ten, nets, met, get, yes**

Reading and fluency

Phonics Readers 1d: *Is Ed a hen?*
Read the story with the children. Children can point to **yes** or **no** in answer to the questions. On question 2, you may want to discuss the meaning of the word **pet** and whether Eddy Elephant is a pet or not? Respond to either opinion with, 'You could be right.'

Phonics Readers 1d

Fluency List C *(TGCD)*
Ask the children to partner read. Dictate some of the review words or a sentence to children (page 215)

Lesson 21: Mr E, the Easy Magic Man
E e

Focus on

You'll need

✓ *PCCs for 'Quick Dash' plus* **Mr E**
✓ *BPCC - Uppercase* **E** (Mr E)
✓ *Vowel Scene Poster: The Vowels*
✓ *Alphabet Songs CD or Living ABC software*
✓ *Phonics Readers 1d*
✓ Make a 'Tricky' Word Card: **she**
✓ *Fluency List C (TGCD)*

Optional

✓ Individual activities (p.228-238)
✓ Letters for Picture Coding *(TGCD)*
✓ Make *Vowel Flip-overs* for ĕ/ē *(TGCD)*

Review previously learned letters and sounds

'Quick Dash' *PCCs*: ă, ĕ, g, ĭ, k, n, o, p, s, t, ŭ, y

Sound and shape

Show the plain letter side of the *PCC* to see what Mr E looks like in words. Just like the other five vowels, Eddy Elephant shares his letter with a Vowel Man. Show the picture side. This is Mr E. He is the Easy Magic Man and the man who has Eddy Elephant for a pet. Mr E does a lot of magic tricks in words. His tricks make it eeeasy for us to read. That's why he is called the Easy Magic Man! He loves to say his name, 'E!' /ē/ in words like **e**agle, **e**ating, **e**ven and **e**ek! Point out Mr E and Eddy Elephant on the *Vowel Scene Poster*.

Revise other Vowel Men briefly with the help of the *Vowel Scene Poster*.

Picture Code Cards

Action

Show his plain letter again. Mr E's letter shape is the same as Eddy Elephant's, but when Mr E appears in words, he says his name, 'E!' (ee) and he shoots his hand up in the air to let everyone know he is there. Teach the **Action Trick** (page 182). Ask the children to do the action and make the sound in response to the plain letter side of the *PCC*.

Action Trick (see p.182)

Uppercase

Show the *BPCC - Uppercase* for Mr E. Mr E uses the same uppercase letter as Eddy Elephant, so you will sometimes hear him instead of Eddy Elephant at the beginning of a sentence or a person's name. Let's do his Action Trick again, as we say, "/ē/ /ē/ /ē/."

Song

Sing along with the Vowel Men Song. You may want to provide simple costumes or props (see photo) and ask the children to represent the Vowel Men as everyone sings. As his verse is sung, each Vowel Man steps forward, vigorously raises his hand and shouts out his name.

Phonemic awareness and language development

Games

Play the Listen and Jump Game (page 232) with children jumping towards the Eddy Elephant or the Mr E *PCC*, depending on which sound they hear at the start of the words below. Or make *Vowel Flip-overs* (*TGCD*) and use them with these words: **eagle**, egg, **easy**, **eat**, echo, **eager**, everybody, effort, **each**.

Children can also work on distinguishing short and long **e** on the *Living ABC* software in the Vowel Men section.

Blending

Mr E's little words

Write **he** on the board and Picture Code **e** with a stick figure of Mr E. There are four little words where Mr E appears most often, and calls out his name. So let's learn them right away. Guide children in blending **he** with the **Roller Coaster Trick** and then use it in a brief sentence. Do the same with **me**, **be** and **we**.

Reading and fluency

'Tricky' word

'Tricky' word

Show your word card for **she**. This word is **she**. (Use it in a sentence.) Sammy Snake and Harry Hat Man are not making their usual sounds in this little word, so we'll put a wavy line below the **sh**. We'll learn why soon, but for now let's just remember this word is **she** with Mr E saying his name at the end.

Note: This word will become fully decodable after Lesson 28, Section 2.

Phonics Readers 1d: *Pets*

Read the story with the children. Then ask partners to re-read to each other.

Phonics Readers 1d

Fluency List C *(TGCD)*

Ask the children to practise fluency with a partner (page 215).

ss as in miss

You'll need

✓ PCCs for 'Guess Who?' plus **ss**
✓ Phonics Readers 1d

✓ Reading Racer Charts (TGCD)

Optional

✓ Individual activities (p.228-238)

Review previously learned letters and sounds

'Guess Who?' *PCCs:* ă, d, ě, g, h, ĭ, ŏ, p, t.

Blending: Vowels-go-round

Choose four children to be the short vowel characters Annie Apple, Eddy Elephant, Impy Ink and Oscar Orange. Hand them the short vowel *PCCs* for **ă, ě, ĭ, ŏ**. Hand out additional *PCCs:* **d, g, h, p, t**

Consonants stand in place

The **p** and **t** letter children stand at the front of the class, leaving a space for a third child to stand in between them.

Try each vowel in the middle

The vowel children stand to the left side so they can see the words and take turns to appear in the middle of the word.

Real or nonsense

The class blends each word and decides if it is a real word or not with a vote.

Make a list of real words and another of nonsense words on the board. Ask the class to read either list each time a word is added to it.

Repeat with **d_g** and **h_t**.

....

Sammy Snake and his sister Sally

PCCs: ă, ě, h, ĭ, k, m, p, s/z/, ss

Set out the word **hiss** with plain letters, except for the picture side showing Sammy Snake and Sally Snake.

Did you know that Sammy Snake's best friend is his sister Sally Snake? When you hear /**sss**/ on the end of words you will often find both Sally and Sammy Snake there making their hissing sound together at exactly the same time! We call them Best Friends on the End. And you can be sure they are saying Sammy's wide awake /**sss**/ sound because he never falls asleep when he has Sally to play with beside him.

Picture Code Cards

Blending

Blending with Picture Code Cards

Words: **hiss, miss, mess, kiss**

Ask the children to blend the word **hiss** using the Roller Coaster Trick. Then make the rest of the words above. After making the word **kiss**, leave it on display as you continue below.

Suffix -es

What if Munching Mike gave his Mum not one kiss but two...how do we say it...? **"Kisses."** Yes, we have the word kiss, but how do we make it say kiss**es**? Let's listen to that last part kiss...**es**. Place the picture side of **ě** and **s**/z/ *PCCs* to make the word **kisses** and ask the children to read it. Yes, sometimes to make a word plural – that means more than one, right? — we have to add the suffix **es** to the base word. Have you noticed that when we say this plural ending quickly it sounds more like /iz/? If so, you have discovered one more place where Sammy likes to have a quick snooze! Let's read some more plural words.

> Words with **es**: **kiss, kisses, hiss, hisses, pass, passes**

Reading and fluency

Phonics Readers 1d: *Hiss, hiss!*
Read the story with the children. After reading the story a few times, ask the children to find all the words that end with **ss** to check if the sound really is /**s**/ in all of them rather than /**z**/. Ask them why Sammy never makes his sleepy /**z**/ sound when he is at the end of a word with his sister.

Hiss, hiss!

Focus on: ss as in *hiss*

Phonics Readers 1d

Fluency List C *(TGCD)*
Time children on this list (page 214) and let them graph their scores on the *Reading Racer* Chart *(TGCD)*. They compare to their current rate to their earlier ones to check their own progress.

Lesson 23: Uppy Umbrella
U u

Focus on Ŭŭ

You'll need
- ✓ *PCCs* for 'Quick Dash' plus **u** (Uppy)
- ✓ *ABC book*
- ✓ *BPCC - Uppercase* **U**
- ✓ *Vowel Scene Poster: The Vowels*
- ✓ *Alphabet Songs CD* and *Handwriting Songs CD* or *Living ABC* software

- ✓ *Phonics Readers 1d*
- ✓ Make a 'Tricky' Word Card: **to**
- ✓ *Fluency List D (TGCD)*

Optional
- ✓ Individual activities (p.228-238)
- ✓ Letters for Picture Coding *(TGCD)*
- ✓ Make *Vowel Flip-overs* for ŭ/ū *(TGCD)*

Review previously learned letters and sounds

'Quick Dash' *PCCs*: ă, d, ě, g, ĭ, m, n, o, p, s, s/z/, t, ŭ

Sound
Show the plain letter side of the *PCC* to see what Uppy Umbrella looks like in words. Then the children can use the **Sound Trick** (page 181) to remind themselves of the sound she makes in words: **Uppy Umbrella**, /ŭ/.

Picture Code Cards

Action
Teach the **Action Trick** (page 182). Ask the children to do the action and make the sound in response to the plain letter side of the *PCC*.

Song
Sing Uppy Umbrella's *Alphabet Song*. Show the picture side of his *PCC* when you sing his name. Turn to the plain letter every time you sing his sound (lyrics on *TGCD*). Also enjoy the Vowel Sounds Song with five children role playing the vowels.

Action Trick (see p.182)

The Important Vowels

Uppy Umbrella is one of the five very special vowel letters. Refer to the *Vowels Poster*. Why are vowels so important? It's because one of them has to be in almost every word. Tell your partner which vowel letters are in your name. Just like the other vowels, Uppy Umbrella shares her letter with a Vowel Man, Mr U. We'll learn about Mr U soon. Let's say Uppy Umbrella's vowel sound three times, "/ŭ/ / ŭ / /ŭ/."

'Short & Long Vowels'
Vowel Scene Posters

Phonemic awareness and language development

Alliteraton

Read about Uppy Umbrella in the *ABC* book or use the *Living ABC* software. Emphasise her sound and explore the picture together.

Ask questions and discuss

Do you think **U**ppy **U**mbrella sleeps downstairs or **u**pstairs? Where do you sleep? Can you think of some creatures that live **u**nderwater? Do you think **U**ppy likes being **u**pside down? What is the opposite of over? (under). **U**ppy **U**mbrella does something that other **u**mbrellas don't do. What **u**nusual thing does **U**ppy **U**mbrella do? (She talks!)

Uppy Umbrella in
ABC book

Beginning sound games

See pages 232-238, and *Living ABC* software.

Shape: u and U

Song

Sing or say the verse from the *Handwriting Songs* as you trace both sides of Uppy's *PCC* (lyrics on *TGCD*).

Write

Write a huge **u** on the board or project the Uppy Umbrella scene of the *Living ABC* software for children to air-trace as they sing. Follow up with a handwriting activity.

Uppercase

Show the *PCC* **u** and then the *BPCC* **U** and introduce the Uppercase Trick. When Uppy Umbrella starts an important word she just takes a deep breath and gets bigger.

Blending and segmenting

Blending with Picture Code Cards

Set the words below for children to blend.

PCCs: ă, c, g, h, n, p, s, t, ŭ, ss

Words: **up, cut, hug, sun, pass, passes**

'Live Spelling'

Distribute the *PCCs* below. Line up five children to the left with the five vowel *PCCs*. These are the five very important vowels and we should find that we need one of them in each of the words we are going to spell.

PCCs: ă, d, ě, g, ĭ, m, m, n, o, p, s, s/z/, t, ŭ, ss

Words: **mum, gap, met, tops, dug, pins, ten, pass, passes**

Did we need a vowel in every word? "**Yes.**" Yes we did!

'Tricky' word

Reading and fluency

'Tricky' word

Teach the word **to** with the card you have made.

Phonics Readers 1d: *Us*

Read the story with the children.

Fluency List D *(TGCD)*

Practise this new list with the children (page 214).

Phonics Readers 1d

Lesson 24: Mr U, the Uniform Man

U u

You'll need

- ✓ PCCs for 'Guess Who?' plus **Mr U**
- ✓ *BPCC - Uppercase* **U** (Mr U)
- ✓ *Vowel Scene Poster: The Vowels*
- ✓ *Alphabet Songs CD* or *Living ABC* software
- ✓ *Phonics Readers 1e*

- ✓ *Fluency List D (TGCD)*
- ✓ Make a 'Tricky' Word Card: **you**

Optional

- ✓ Individual activities (p.228-238)
- ✓ Letters for Picture Coding *(TGCD)*

Review previously learned letters and sounds

'Guess Who?' *PCCs*: ă, c, d, ĕ, f, h, k, l, ĭ, n, o, ŭ, y

Sound and shape

Show the plain letter side of the *PCC* to see what Mr U looks like in words. Just like the other five vowels, Uppy Umbrella shares her letter with a Vowel Man. Show the picture side. This is Mr U. He has the important job of looking after all the umbrellas in Letterland. In fact, Uppy Umbrella is one of Mr U's special talking umbrellas. You can tell Mr U has an important job because he is wearing a uniform. What do you think he says in words? His name, of course: 'U' (you) in words like **u**niform, **U**nited Kingdom and **u**nicorn. Point out Mr U and Uppy Umbrella on the *Vowel Scene Poster*. Revise the other Vowel Men briefly with the help of the *Vowel Scene Poster*.

Picture Code Cards

Action

Show his plain letter again. Mr U's letter shape is the same as Uppy Umbrella's, but when Mr U appears in words he says his name, /ū/, and he shoots his hand up in the air to let everyone know he is there. Teach the Action Trick (page 182). Ask the children to do the action and make the sound in response to the plain letter side of the *PCC*.

Song

You may want to provide simple costumes or props and ask the children to represent the Vowel Men as everyone sings. As his verse is sung, each Vowel Man steps forward, vigorously raises his hand and shouts his name at the end of his song.

Action Trick (see p.182)

Uppercase

Show the *BPCC - Uppercase* for Mr U. When Mr U starts an important word, his uppercase letter looks almost like his lowercase letter but it is bigger.

Phonemic awareness and language development

Games

Play the **Listen and Jump Game for two sounds** (page 232) with children jumping towards the Uppy Umbrella or towards the Mr U *PCC*, depending on which sound they hear at the start of the words below. Or make *Vowel Flip-overs* (*TGCD*) and use them with these words: us, **uniform**, **united**, umbrella, **use**, **useful**, up, under.

Reading and fluency

'Tricky' word

Mr U's useful word. Show children the word card **you** and ask them to say the word. Use **you** in a few brief sentences. Then ask the children to repeat **you** a few times as you push the card forward. Talk to them about the sounds they hear in the word: Yo-yo Man is making his sound (which is also the start of Mr U's name). And at exactly the same time Mr U is saying his name. But that middle letter is the tricky bit in this word because it isn't making any sound at all. Draw a wavy line below the silent **o** to show it is not behaving either like Oscar Orange or old Mr O.

'Tricky' word

Phonics Readers 1e: *You*

This story uses the word **you** in all four pages and allows children to imagine themselves in the story. Ask the children to read the first page to a partner first and then read it with the whole class. After reading the final page, ask the children to tell you which pet they would choose. (See further suggestions, pages 217-224.)

As time allows during the day, ask the children to re-read their favourite stories with a partner. You could ask them to write down the titles of their favourites and compile a list or a graph of the most popular stories in the classroom.

Phonics Readers 1e

Fluency List D *(TGCD)*

To ensure children are not memorising try reading the Word Section in different directions: 1) rows from left to right; 2) columns from top to bottom; or 3) columns from bottom to top (page 214).

Lesson 25: Kicking King
K k

Focus on

You'll need

✓ *PCCs* for 'Quick Dash' plus **k**
✓ *ABC* book
✓ *BPCC - Uppercase* **K**
✓ *Alphabet Songs CD* and *Handwriting Songs CD* or *Living ABC* software

✓ *Phonics Readers 1e*
✓ Make a 'Tricky' Word Card: **like**

Optional

✓ Individual activities (p.228-238)
✓ Letters for Picture Coding (*TGCD*)
✓ Magnetic Word Builder

Review previously learned letters and sounds

'Quick Dash' *PCCs*: ă, b, ĭ, j, n, r, s, s/z/, t, v, w, y, z, ss

Sound

Show the plain letter side of the *PCC* to see what Kicking King looks like in words. Then the children can use the Sound Trick (page 181) to remind

Picture Code Cards

themselves of the sound he makes in words: **Kicking King**, /**k**/. Clever Cat enjoys sharing the same sound as Kicking King. But she prefers to appear at the *beginning* of words. Kicking King often prefers to say their sound at the *end* of words – where there is plenty of room to kick!

Action

Teach the Action Trick (page 182). Ask the children to do the action and make the sound in response to the plain letter side of the *PCC*.

Song

Sing Kicking King's *Alphabet Song*. Show the picture side of his *PCC* when you sing his name. Turn to the plain letter every time you sing his sound (lyrics on *TGCD)*.

Phonemic awareness and language development

Alliteration

Read about Kicking King in the *ABC* book or use the *Living ABC* software. Emphasise his sound and explore the picture together.

Ask questions and discuss

Not every country has a **k**ing. Does our country have a **k**ing? Do you think **K**icking **K**ing is a nasty **k**ing or a **k**ind king? **K**icking **K**ing loves to practise his **k**icks in words. Can you hear him **k**icking in these words? (**k**itchen, bedroom, **k**ettle, chair, **k**eys, **k**eep, goal, **k**etchup) How many times can you hear **K**icking **K**ing's sound in his name? **K**icking **K**ing (slow-speak it to discover that his sound is heard three times).

Beginning sound games

Pages 232-238 and the *Living ABC* software.

Shape: k and K

Song

Sing or say the verse from the *Handwriting Songs* as you trace both sides of Kicking King's *PCC* (lyrics on *TGCD)*.

Write

Write a huge **k** on the board or project the Kicking King scene of the *Living ABC* software for children to air-trace as they sing. Follow up with a handwriting activity.

Uppercase

Show the *PCC* **k** and then the *BPCC* **K** and introduce the Uppercase Trick. When Kicking King starts an important word, he takes a deep breath. Then, amazingly, his arm and kicking leg get longer!

Blending

Blending with Picture Code Cards

Build the words below.

PCCs: ĭ, **k**, **n**, **t**, **ss**   Words: **kit**, **kin**, **kiss**.

Spelling with Magnetic Word Builders

Use the *Magnetic Word Builder* or other letter sets to build:

Letters: **a, e, g, i, k, m, n, o, p, p, s, t, u**

Words: **kin**, **gums**, **net**, **Kim**, **pop**, **taps**

Spelling tip: Which to use, **c** or **k**? Always choose **k** before **e, i** or **y**.

Action Trick (see p.182)

Kicking King in *ABC* book

Magnetic Word Builder

Reading and fluency

'Tricky' word

Teach the word **like**.* Mark it as shown.

* **like** is a 'tricky' word now, but it becomes a decodable word after Lesson 57.

Phonics Readers 1e: *Kicking King's maze*

Children help Kicking King find his ball by tracing a path through the maze in this special activity.

Fluency List D *(TGCD)*

Children read their lists with partners (page 214).

'Tricky' word

Phonics Readers 1e

Lesson 26: Blending

ck as in duck

You'll need

- ✓ *PCCs for 'Guess Who?'* plus **ck**
- ✓ *Phonics Readers 1e*
- ✓ *Reading Racer Charts (TGCD)*
- ✓ Prepare two Kicking King crowns

✓ Soft ball

Optional

- ✓ Individual activities (p.228-238)
- ✓ Letters for Picture Coding *(TGCD)*

Review previously learned letters and sounds

'Guess Who?' *PCCs:* ă, b, c, ě, ĭ, k, o, p, s, t, ŭ, v

Clever Cat or Kicking King?

As you know, Clever Cat and Kicking King make the same sound. But how can we know which letter to use in a word? In fact Kicking King usually finds it too crowded at the start of words. He prefers, when he can, to be at the end of words where there is more space to kick. So Clever Cat proudly begins far more words than Kicking King. (The proof is in the dictionary – have a look!)

Blending

You will need a ball that can be safely kicked in the classroom e.g. a beach ball, a balloon, or balled-up newspaper.

'Live Reading'

Distribute the *PCCs*. Help children form the word **cat** and then ask the class to do the Roller Coaster Trick.

PCCs: ă, c, ě, ĭ, k, o, p, s, t, ŭ, ck

> Words: **cat, pack, peck, pick, kick, sick, sock**

Temporarily replace the Clever Cat child with the Kicking King child. Let Kicking King hold the ball and demonstrate your point. Kicking King doesn't start many words because there is no room to kick. As you can see if he tried to kick in the Reading Direction – well, there is just not room.

Help children form the word **pack** using the **ck** *PCC* at the end held by two children. The one representing **k** on the end holds the ball.

Same sound

When Kicking King and Clever Cat are next to each other, they say their sound at exactly the same time. So it sounds like one sound.

Ask the children in the word to say their sounds in order (Clever Cat and Kicking King say /k/ together. Then ask the class to use the Roller Coaster Trick to blend **pack**.

Story logic

We know that Kicking Kick likes to be on the end of words because then he has plenty of room to kick in the Reading Direction. And we can guess that Clever Cat likes to watch him kick, because in lots of words we will see her sitting just behind him when he is at the end.

Role-play the story

Ask Kicking King to kick the ball and Clever Cat to praise him with a pat on the back and perhaps clapping. Use different children for **ck** in making each word below and let them role-play as above. Ask the class to blend each word.

When you make the word **kick**, point out: One of the most exciting things about all the Letterlanders is that they can be in more than one place at a time! So it is no problem for Kicking King to be in the same word twice – just like in his own name, **Kicking King**. Write it on the board and let children notice again that he actually appears in it three times!

Reading and fluency

Phonics Readers 1e: *Can he kick?*

Read the story with the children. Then they can choose a character and pretend to be that character. They tell, in the first person, what they were doing and what they saw. Further suggestions, pages 217-224.

Phonics Readers 1e

Fluency List D *(TGCD)*

Time children and ask them to graph the results (page 214).

Assessment - Refer to your TGCD

Use the Section 2, Part 1 assessments a few days to two weeks after completing Section 2, Lesson 26.

All assessment material including full instructions and Assessment forms are on the *TGCD* .

ng as in ring

You'll need

✓ PCCs for 'Quick Dash' plus **m**, **ng** and **ing**
✓ Blends & Digraphs CD
✓ Phonics Readers 1e

✓ Fluency List E (TGCD)

Optional

✓ Individual activities (p.228-238)
✓ Letters for Picture Coding (TGCD)

Review previously learned letters and sounds

'Quick Dash' PCCs: ă, d, h, ĭ, k, o, p, s, s/s/, ŭ, ck

When you show the picture side of the **ck** PCC, call on a child to share the story logic that explains why these two letters say /**k**/ at the end of words.

Noisy Nick and Golden Girl

This is the first digraph with its own new sound that you will teach. Show the -**ng** PCC and tell this story: Today we are going to learn something new about Noisy Nick and Golden Girl. They really like being together in a word, so whenever they find themselves next to each other, they make a special singing sound. We can hear their singing sound if we stretch the end of the word si**nnnggg**.... (prolong the /**ng**/ sound). Then ask the children to do it with you. Golden Girl thinks that when she and Noisy Nick make this sound together, they sound like singing bells. She has even written a song about their /**ng**/ sound. We'll sing it in a minute. Meanwhile from now on let's look out for these two friends and expect that special si**ng**ing /**ng**/ sound when you see them next to each other in a word. Can you hear them saying that /**ng**/ sound two times in the word si**ng**ing?

Picture Code Cards

Song

The Letterland Bells - *Blends & Digraphs Songs CD*. You may want to read the lyrics to children first (*TGCD*). Then ask them to sing along and afterwards recall the /**ng**/ words (i**ng**, a**ng**, o**ng**, u**ng** and ri**ng**).

Blends & Digraphs Songs CD

Blending

'Live Reading'

Distribute the PCCs and line children up to make the first word. Ask two children to hold the **ng** PCC together and both say their sound at the same time. Do the same with the **ck** PCC.

Use the terms 'base word' and 'suffix' as you add **s** to some of the words below.

PCCs from 'Quick Dash' plus **ng**

> Words: **king, sing, song, songs, hang, pack, duck, ducks**

Suffix -ing

Blending with Picture Code Cards

Show the plain letter side of the **ing** PCC. This is a new **suffix** for us. We can add it on the end of lots of words. Now, what was that other suffix we used that makes words like **duck** mean more than one?... Yes, **s** can be a suffix. We add it on the end of base words.

This new suffix says /**ing**/. Push the card forward a few times as children

Picture Code Cards

repeat, **ing**... **ing**... If we turn it over who do you think we will see? After children make comments, show the picture side.

Here's an **i** with Noisy Nick with Golden Girl making their singing sound. Let's make some base words and then add this suffix /**ing**/.

Set out these words. As children blend the base word (e.g. "/**p**/ /**a**/ /**ck**/, **pack**") and then add the suffix (**packing**), ask them to use the terms 'base word' and 'suffix'.

PCCs from 'Quick Dash' plus **m**, **ss**, **ing**

Words: **packing, hanging, singing, missing, kicking**

Reading and fluency

Phonics Readers 1e: *Ding dong*
Tell the children that Peter Puppy is having a party for his pals in this story.

Fluency List E *(TGCD)*
Practise this new list with children.

Phonics Readers 1e

Lesson 28: Sammy Snake and Harry Hat Man

sh as in shop

Focus on

You'll need

✓ *PCCs* for 'Guess Who?' plus **sh** and **ee**
✓ *Beyond ABC*
✓ *Blends & Digraphs CD*
✓ *Phonics Readers 2a*
✓ Make a snake headband and a hat

✓ Make a 'Tricky' Word Card: **see**
✓ *Magnetic Word Builder* or similar

Optional

✓ Individual activities (p.228-238)
✓ Letters for Picture Coding *(TGCD)*

Review previously learned letters and sounds

'Guess Who?' *PCCs*: ă, d, ĕ, h, ĭ, o, p, ŭ, w, ck, ng, ss

Word building

Letters: **c, g, g, i, i, k, k, n, n, o, p, p, s, u**

Words: **sick, pick, picking, ping-pong, kicks, king, sing, songs**

Use Letterland *Magnetic Word Builder* or similar letter sets for each child (page 207).

Call out the first word, say a sentence and say the word again. Children repeat the word, stretch and segment it and build it with their own letters.

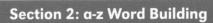

Magnetic Word Builder

Provide a correct model for children to check their spelling by writing on the board or using your own set of letters. All blend the corrected word.

Children leave the letters in place, as you call out the next word. They stretch and segment it, then decide which letters they need to replace.

Sammy Snake and Harry Hat Man

Role-play

(Props: Harry Hat Man's hat and a Sammy Snake headband or toy snake.) Choose two children to be Sammy Snake and Harry Hat Man. Sammy stands a few paces to Harry's right as they stand facing the class.

What sound does Sammy Snake usually make in words? Yes, he likes to hiss /sss/ very loudly. How does the Hat Man feel about noise? That's right, he hates it! So what do you think happens when Sammy comes slithering and sliding up behind Harry Hat Man in a word? What do you think Harry does? He turns his head and says /sh/ to hush Sammy up.

Ask all the children to do the **sh** action with one finger raised to the lips as they say the sound. You could pair them all up to role-play Sammy Snake and Harry Hat Man.

Show the picture side of the **sh** PCC and ask a child to re-tell what is happening.

Push the plain letter side forward several times for children to repeat, "/**sh**/ /**sh**/ /**sh**/" with the action.

Picture Code Cards

Phonemic awareness and language development

Explore the **sh** scene in the *Story Phonics* software and/or *Far Beyond ABC* book. Listen to or watch the animated story of Sammy and Harry and ask the children to hunt for items in the scene that include the /**sh**/ sound. (The full list is at the end of the book).

Song

Sing along with the **sh** song (lyrics on *TGCD*) on the *Blends & Digraphs Songs* CD or the *Story Phonics* software.

sh in Beyond ABC book

Blending

Blending with Picture Code Cards

Make the words below for children to blend. With the words **dishes** and **ashes** ask the children to talk about base words and suffixes.

PCCs: **ă, d, ě, h, ĭ, ŏ, p, ŭ, sh**

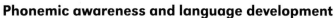

Words: **ship, shop, shed, hush, dish, dishes, ash, ashes**

Reading and fluency

'Tricky' word

Teach the 'tricky' word **see*** with the *PCCs* for **s** and **ee**. Tell children that Mr E has a twin brother they will learn more about later. Show them the word card **see** and say, For now, just remember that whenever we see two of the same letter in a row, the second one will be silent. So in this word we hear just Mr E saying his name, but when we write the word we need to add his brother.

*   The word **see** becomes decodable after Lesson 64.

'Tricky' word

Shep

Phonics Readers 2a

Phonics Readers 2a: *Shep*

Read with the children. Ask them to re-read it with partners. More suggestions, pages 217-224.

ch as in chip

You'll need

- ✓ *PCCs for 'Quick Dash' plus* **ch**
- ✓ A hat and cat ears headband
- ✓ *Beyond ABC or Story Phonics* software
- ✓ *Blends & Digraphs Songs CD*

- ✓ *Phonics Readers 2a*

Optional

- ✓ Individual activities (p.228-238)
- ✓ Letters for Picture Coding (*TGCD*)

Review previously learned letters and sounds

'Quick Dash' *PCCs*: ă, ĕ, h, ĭ, m, n, o, p, s, s/z/, ŭ, ck, ng, sh

'Live spelling' (page 202)

Use the words below as a review of recently learned digraphs and other letters sounds. Do fewer words or use the *PCCs* for some words if time is short or attention is flagging.

PCCs: ă, ĕ, h, ĭ, m, n, o, p, ŭ, ck, ng, sh

Words: **ship, shop, shock, mash, neck, hung, hang, shin**

Clever Cat and Harry Hat Man

Show the **ch** *PCC* picture side and ask, What does Clever Cat seem to be doing? Yes, she's sneezing! Let's find out why.

Show the **ch** pages in the *Beyond ABC* book or *Story Phonics* software which explain her sneezes.

Picture Code Cards

Role-play

Pair up all the children to role-play this story logic. Each Clever Cat and Harry Hat Man pair stands a bit apart, filling the room with their own /h/ and /c/ single letter sounds. On a signal from you, each pair comes together. Clever Cat sniffs at Harry's imaginary hat and says /**ch**/ as she covers her sneeze. Harry Hat Man just looks startled. Try it again reversing roles.

Push the plain letters forward a few times as everyone does the sneeze catching action and says "/**ch**/ /**ch**/..." (This should be a whispered sound so make sure no one adds an "uh" sound!)

ch in Beyond ABC book

Phonemic Awareness and Language Development

Show the scene in *Beyond ABC* again and ask the children to name as many things as they can see with the /**ch**/ sound (complete list on final page).

Song

Play the **ch** song on the *Blends & Digraphs CD* and sing along (lyrics on *TGCD*). You may want to let several pairs of children at a time role-play the song as everyone else sings.

Blends & Digraphs Songs CD

Blending

Blending with Picture Code Cards

Make the words below with *PCCs* and guide children in using the **Roller Coaster Trick** to blend them (page 188).

PCCs: ă, c, h, ĕ, ĭ, m, n, o, p, s, s/z/ t, ŭ, ch, ck

Words: **chins, chicks, chop, check, chap, much, such**

Blending with tch

Some words that end with the /ch/ are spelled a bit differently. Let's stretch and segment the word **catch**. "/c/ /ă/ /ch/". Temporarily spell the word this way: cach. That's how it sounds but in quite a few words when we hear /ch/ at the end, Talking Tess is going to be right there, too. Change the word to **catch**. She doesn't make a sound. For once she's not talking at all! I wonder... do you think she could be quietly reminding Clever Cat to "catch" her sneeze so she doesn't spread any germs, or maybe she is just silently trying to toss a tissue to Clever Cat? Let's read some other words with this silent Talking Tess.

Words: **catch, hatch, match, witch, fetch**

Reading and fluency

Phonics Readers 2a

Phonics Readers 2a: *Check on the chicks!*

In this story Firefighter Fred is helping out at Forest Farm. It is a good story for using the strategy of covering each picture until after children read the sentence. Then they predict what they will see. See further suggestions for sharing, pages 217-224.

Comprehension

This could be a fun story to use with the Plan and Play strategy on page 222. In this strategy children read the story several times and discuss how to role-play it. They can even add more dialogue if they think it helps tell the story. 'Characters' could include Fred and several chicks. Children may think of a way to play the role of logs that Fred is chopping as well.

Discussion

Use this story to talk about the functions of farms. Why are there chicks here and bales of hay, etc.

Fluency List E *(TGCD)*

Ask the children to practise reading the list to gain fluency (page 214). You might also dictate some of these review words and sentences for them to write.

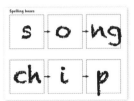

Lesson 30: Talking Tess and Harry Hat Man
th as in that

You'll need

- ✓ *PCCs* for 'Guess Who?' plus **th**
- ✓ Toy telephone or headset and a hairy hat
- ✓ *Beyond ABC*
- ✓ 'Tricky' Word Cards: **the, my**
- ✓ Spelling Boxes *(TGCD)*

- ✓ *Phonics Readers 2a*
- ✓ *Reading Racer Charts (TGCD)*

Optional

- ✓ Individual activities (p.228-238)
- ✓ Letters for Picture Coding *(TGCD)*

Review previously learned letters and sounds

'Guess Who?' *PCCs*: ă, ě, ĭ, m, n, p, s, t, ck, ch, ng, sh

Spelling Boxes

Use the *Spelling Boxes (TGCD)* or ask the children to spell words on whiteboards (see page 205). If using *Spelling Boxes*, remind children that each box is for one sound. For example, if they hear /**ch**/ at the beginning of a word both letters **c** and **h** would go in one box. You can draw *Spelling Boxes* on the board or project a copy to provide a model for children to check their spelling.

Children stretch and segment words and write them. After every three words, they read their words to a partner and then erase them.

Group 1: **song, chip, cash**

Group 2: **pick, king, shed**

Group 3: **shut, check, hang**

s	o	ng
ch	i	p

Spelling boxes

Talking Tess and Harry Hat Man

Show the picture side of both **th** *PCCs* and ask them to talk about what they see. Read the first paragraph of the **th** page from *Beyond ABC* to find the explanation of what is happening with Harry Hat Man and Talking Tess.

These two make two sounds when they are together. You will be introducing the 'voiced' sound first.

Role-play

Ask two children to play the roles of Talking Tess and Harry Hat Man. They stand apart at first each making their own sounds /**t**/ and /**h**/.

The rest of the class begins to make thunder sounds. Harry Hat Man looks up and covers his ears. Talking Tess hurries over to him. On your signal, the thunder is silenced so that everyone can hear Talking Tess as she pats Harry Hat Man on the shoulder and says, **"There, there it's only the thunder."**

If children are having difficulty pronouncing the two sounds of **th**, teach them to put their **th**umbs up to their mouths and wet their thumbs four times as they say Tess's sentence above. If they don't stick out their tongues just a little bit, they may end up sounding like Dippy Duck ('dere, dere') or Firefighter Fred ('funder') instead of like Tess and Harry Hat Man!

The voiced th

Ask everyone to repeat what Talking Tess said. Then ask them to say the word **there**. Let's stretch out that first sound in **there** so we can hear it better, /**th**.../. Show the **th** *PCC* with Harry pointing upwards. Turn to the plain letter. Ask the children to repeat the sound a few times as you push the *PCC* forward, "/**th**/, /**th**/..."

th in *Beyond ABC* book

Picture Code Cards

Blending

Blending with Picture Code Cards

There are several words that we use all the time that begin with this sound. Make a word below and ask the children to blend it. Then say a sentence with the word. Do the same with each word.

PCCs: ǎ, ě, ǐ, m, n, s, t, th

Words: **this, then, them, that**

Reading and fluency

'Tricky' word

Show the 'Tricky' Word Card you have made for the word **the** (first shown Lesson 18, Section 2). Point out that you had made a wavy line below **th**, but now we all know why these two letters say /th/. You can erase the wavy line below **th** or make a new card with a wavy line only below the **e**.

'Tricky' word

Phonics Readers 2a: *Shep and me*

This story is a sequel to a previous story about a boy and his dog. See suggestions for sharing, pages 217-224. Children could find all the words with **th** and read them again. If they have personal dictionaries, or the Letterland *Word Bank Copymasters* ask them to enter these useful **th** words.

Phonics Readers 2a

Fluency List E *(TGCD)*

Pair children to time them and graph the scores (page 214).

Lesson 31: Talking Tess and Harry Hat Man
th as in thing

Focus on **th**

You'll need

✓ *PCCs for 'Quick Dash' plus* **th**
✓ *Beyond ABC*
✓ *Blends & Digraphs Songs CD*
✓ *Phonics Readers 2a*

✓ *Fluency List F (TGCD)*

Optional

✓ Individual activities (p.228-238)
✓ Letters for Picture Coding (T*GCD*)

Review previously learned letters and sounds

'Quick Dash' *PCCs*: ǎ, ě, ǐ, l, o, ǔ, ck, ch, ng, sh, ss, th

'Live Spelling'

Distribute the *PCCs*. Have individual children hold the digraph cards rather than pairs for today's activity.

PCCs: ǎ, d, ě, ǐ, k, m, n, o, s, s/z/ t, ǔ, ch, ck, ng, sh, ss, th

Words: **this, then, much, tack, song, kiss, dish, match, matches**

Use Sound Pops 'Live Spelling' as detailed on page 229. Briefly, you say the word. Children repeat it and stretch and segment. Then whoever hears their sound in the word lines up to form it.

Everyone uses the **Roller Coaster Trick** to check the spelling and make corrections if needed.

Talking Tess and Harry Hat Man

Show the picture side of the unvoiced **th** *PCCs* with Harry and Tess's hands over their ears. Ask the children to recall and repeat what Talking Tess says to Harry Hat Man, **"There, there, it's only the thunder."**

Picture Code Cards

We know one sound for these letters already. We can hear it at the beginning of the words **there** and **the**. What sound is that? /**th**/. But the word **thunder** begins with a sound that is different. Stretch out the first part of **thunder** with me in a whisper, /**th**.../. You need to stick out your tongues just a little bit, but only *whisper* this sound.

Show the unvoiced **th** *PCC*. Turn to the plain letter side for children to repeat the sound a few times as you push the *PCC* forward, "/**th**/ /**th**/..."

Phonemic awareness and language development

Show children the **th** picture in the *Beyond ABC* book. Read the second paragraph and find things that have the unvoiced /**th**/ sound (full list at the back).

Blends & Digraphs Songs CD

Song

Sing along to the **th** song from the *Blends & Digraphs Songs CD* (lyrics on *TGCD*). You could also ask the children to role-play the story while they sing.

Blending

Blending with Picture Code Cards

Each of these words will have the whispered sound of **th** as in the word **thunder**. What is that sound? "/**th**/." Set out each word and ask the children to blend them. Then say a sentence using each word.

Words: **thin, thick, thing, maths**

Reading and fluency

Phonics Readers 2a: *Lots of legs*

After reading this story with the class, partners can re-read it to each other.

Ask partners to call out the **th** words for each other to spell with magnetic letters or on whiteboards.

Phonics Readers 2a

Fluency List F *(TGCD)*

Introduce this new list in this way: read one line to the children and then ask them to echo you by reading it together. Later ask partners to read it together (more on page 214).

Focus on **L l**

You'll need

- ✓ PCCs for 'Guess Who?' plus **l**
- ✓ ABC book
- ✓ BPCC - Uppercase **L**
- ✓ Alphabet Songs CD and Handwriting Songs CD or Living ABC software
- ✓ Phonics Readers 2b
- ✓ Make a 'Tricky' Word Card: **her**

Optional

- ✓ Individual activities (p.228-238)
- ✓ Letters for Picture Coding (TGCD)

Review previously learned letters and sounds

'Guess Who' PCCs: ă, d, ě, h, ĭ, n, o, p, s, t, ŭ, ng, ck, sh

Sound

Show the plain letter side of the PCC to see what Lucy Lamp Light looks like in words. Then the children can use the Sound Trick (page 181) to remind themselves of the sound she makes in words: **Lucy Lamp Light**, /lll/.

Picture Code Cards

Action

Teach the Action Trick (page 182). Ask the children to do the action and make the sound in response to the plain letter side of the PCC.

Song (lyrics on TGCD)

Sing Lucy Lamp Light's Alphabet Song. Show the picture side of her PCC when you sing her name. Turn to the plain letter every time you sing her sound.

Action Trick (see p.182)

Phonemic awareness and language development

Alliteration

Read about Lucy Lamp Light in the ABC book or use the Living ABC software. Emphasise her sound and explore the picture together.

Ask questions and discuss

What do we call Lucy Lamp Light's long house with a lovely light on top? (lighthouse) How many times can you hear her sound at the start of these words, 'little lambs leaping down the lane'? (four). When we go to the library does the librarian lend us books or give us books? (lend) There are 26 of these in the alphabet. What are they? (letters). A place that starts with Lucy's sound? (Letterland). Praise word: Lovely!

Lucy Lamp Light in ABC book

Beginning sound games

See pages 232-238, and the Living ABC software.

Shape: l and L

Song

Sing or say the verse from the Handwriting Songs as you trace both sides of Lucy's PCC (lyrics on TGCD).

Write

Write a huge **l** on the board or project the Lucy Lamp Light scene of the Living ABC software for children to air-trace as they sing. Follow up with a handwriting activity.

Uppercase

Show the PCC **l** and then the BPCC **L** and introduce the Uppercase Trick. Whenever Lucy Lamp Light starts important words, she takes a deep

breath and gets bigger. In her case, however, her legs also grow longer – so long, in fact, that she has to kneel down with her legs on the line!

Blending

'Live Reading'

Let's make some words with Lucy Lamp Light's /lll/ sound. Children use the **Roller Coaster Trick** to blend each word. For the final compound word **laptop**, first make two separate words. Then put them together for them to read the whole word. Ask them to use the term 'compound word' as they talk about this word and its meaning. (More on compound words on page 214.)

PCCs: ă, d, ĕ, ĭ, l, o, p, p, t, ng, sh

Words: **lap, lid, let, long, lash, laptop**

Reading and fluency

'Tricky' word

'Tricky' word

Show the word **her*** on the card you have made. This word is **her**. We might use it in talking about some of Lucy Lamp Light's things like her lighthouse or her lemon lollipops. Let children help decide which letters in **her** need a wavy line below them to show that they are not making their usual sounds.

Ask the children to think of some other things that Lucy would like because they begin with her sound (e.g. "**her l**izard, **her l**aptop, **her l**amp"). Point to the word card each time they say "**her**". Push the card forward several times as children repeat the word, "**her, her, her...**". Revise other 'tricky' words.

* The word **her** is a 'tricky' word now, but becomes decodable after Lesson 75, Section 5.

Phonics Readers 2b: *Is this her pet?*

To answer the questions on pages 1, 2 and 3. Children can work with a partner (page 216.)

Phonics Readers 2b

Fluency List F *(TGCD)*

Children continue to practise this review list (page 214).

Lesson 33: Firefighter Fred
F f

Focus on

You'll need

- ✓ *PCCs* for 'Quick Dash' plus **f**
- ✓ *ABC* book
- ✓ *BPCC - Uppercase* **F**
- ✓ *Alphabet Songs CD* and *Handwriting Songs CD* or *Living ABC* software

- ✓ *Phonics Readers 2b*
- ✓ Make a 'Tricky' Word Card: **of**

Optional

- ✓ Individual activities (p.228-238)
- ✓ Letters for Picture Coding (*TGCD*)

Review previously learned letters and sounds

'Quick Dash' *PCCs*: ă, ĕ, ĭ, l, n, o, s, s/z/, ŭ, ng, ss, sh, th, th

Sound

Show the plain letter side of the *PCC* to see what Firefighter Fred looks like in words. Then the children can use the Sound Trick (page 181) to remind themselves of the sound he makes in words: **Firefighter Fred**, /fff/.

Action

Teach the Action Trick (page 182). Ask the children to do the action and make the sound in response to the plain letter side of the *PCC*.

Song

Sing Firefighter Fred's *Alphabet Song*. Show the picture side of his *PCC* when you sing his name. Turn to the plain letter every time you sing his sound and make sure everyone whispers the sound (lyrics on *TGCD*).

Picture Code Cards

Action Trick (see p.182)

Phonemic awareness and language development

Alliteration

Read about Firefighter Fred in the *ABC* book or use the *Living ABC* software. Emphasise his sound and explore the picture together.

Ask questions and discuss

What **f**ive things have you all got in your hands right now, just like **F**irefighter **F**red? (**f**ive **f**ingers!) What comes out of his **f**ire hose? (**f**oam) Which **f**ood do you think **F**irefighter **F**red would pre**f**er, bread and butter or **f**resh **f**ruit?) (**f**resh **f**ruit) **F**irefighter **F**red is **f**amous for putting out **f**ires **f**ast in Letterland. Praise words: **F**abulous! **F**ast work! and **F**antastic!

Beginning sound games

See pages 232-238 and *Living ABC* software.

Firefighter Fred in *ABC* book

Shape: f and F

Song

Sing or say the verse from the *Handwriting Songs* as you trace both sides of Fred's *PCC* (lyrics on *TGCD*).

Write

Write a huge **f** on the board or project the Firefighter Fred scene of the *Living ABC* software for children to air-trace as they sing. Follow up with a handwriting activity.

Uppercase

Show the *PCC* **f** and then the *BPCC* **F** and introduce the Uppercase Trick. Whenever Firefighter Fred can do something as important as starting a name or sentence, he takes a deep breath and becomes a bit bigger. His letter gets sharper as well.

Blending

Blending with Picture Code Cards
Set out the words below for all to see.

PCCs for 'Quick Dash' plus: **d, ĕ, f, ĭ, l, n, g, s, t, ŭ, ng, sh, ss**

Words: **fish, fat, fog, fun, less, lungs, selfish, until**

Blending two syllables
Make the word **selfish** with a space between the syllables (i.e. **sel fish**). Ask the children to use the Roller Coaster Trick to blend the sounds within each syllable ("/s/ /ĕ/ /l/, **sel**", "/f/ /ĭ/ /sh/, **fish**"). Then put the syllables together and ask them to read ("**selfish**"). Do the same with **until** (**un til**).

Reading and fluency

'Tricky' word
Show children the word card **of**. This is one of the nine most used words in the English language! The word is **of**. Use it in a sentence or two. Ask the children to stretch and segment the word to discover that when we say it quickly /ŭv/ (which we usually do) neither letter is making its usual sound. Make a wavy line below both letters.

'Tricky' word

Ask the children to come up with some things that Firefighter Fred might like to have lots of because they begin with his sound (e.g. "lots **of f**ish, lots **of f**lowers, lots **of f**riends"). Point to the word card each time they say "**of**".

Phonics Readers 2b: *Fred's fish*
Guide children in reading the story.

Fluency List F *(TGCD)*
Children continue to build fluency with partners (page 214).

Phonics Readers 2b

Lesson 34: Best friends on the end
ff as in puff, ll as in bell

You'll need
- ✓ PCCs for 'Guess Who?' plus **ff** and **ll**
- ✓ Phonics Readers 2b
- ✓ Reading Racer Charts *(TGCD)*
- ✓ Magnetic Word Builder or other letters set

- ✓ Make a 'Tricky' Word Card: **for**

Optional
- ✓ Individual activities (p.228-238)
- ✓ Letters for Picture Coding *(TGCD)*

Review previously learned letters and sounds
'Guess Who?' *PCCs:* **ă, b, c, d, ĕ, h, ĭ, o, p, t, ŭ, ch, ss, sh**

Word building
Letters: **a, c, e, f, g, h, i, k, l, n, o, p, s, t, t**

Words: **fit, lit, let, then, that, long, thin, shack, chop, fish**

Use Letterland *Magnetic Word Builder* or other sets of individual letters for each child to review recent learning (see page 207 for details).

Magnetic Word Builder

Best friends on the end

PCCs for 'Guess Who?' plus **ff**

Words: **off, huff, puff, cuff, hiss, mess, pass**

Firefighter Fred and Firefighter Frank

Picture Code Cards

Make the word **off** using the **ff** card. Just like with **ss**, we only hear one sound when we see the same letter twice in a row in a word.

Blend the two sounds in **off** with the children. Point to the **ff** as you say, Firefighter Fred never sets **off** to fight a fire without his best friend Firefighter Frank. They like to be together at the end of words because they have lots of room to spray their foam onto a fire. When the fire bell rings they say, "**Off** to the fire!" Can you say that just like the firefighters? "**Off to the fire!**" Just like Sammy and Sally Snake, we call Firefighter Fred and Firefighter Frank 'Best Friends on the end!'

Make the words above with **ff** for the children to blend. Ask the children a question or two about each word, such as these: Who are the best friends? How many sounds do the two letters make? What part of the word do these two like to be in? Why do they like to be together at the end of a word? Make the **ss** words for review.

Lucy Lamp Light and Linda Lamp Light

Picture Code Cards

Show the picture side of the **ll** *PCC*. Here are two more best friends on the end. Lucy Lamp Light's best friend is Linda Lamp Light. Lucy often gets lonely at the end of words, especially short little words (one syllable, short vowel followed by one consonant sound on the end). So she calls her best friend Linda to join her.

Make the words below with **ll** for children to blend. Ask similar questions about Linda and Lucy to those above about the firefighters.

PCCs for 'Quick Dash' plus **ll**

Words: **bell, tell, hill, pill, doll, dull, shell, chill**

Reading and fluency

'Tricky' word

'Tricky' word

Teach the 'tricky' word **for*** with the word card you have prepared. Let children help decide which letters need a wavy line below them because they are not making their usual sound (**or**). Write these phrases on the board for children to read: a bell **for** you, a doll **for** me, a hug **for** mum.

* The word **for** is a useful 'tricky' word now, but it will be fully decodable once you have taught Lesson 71, Section 5.

Phonics Readers 2b: *Off we go!*

Phonics Readers 2b

Guide children in reading the story. (See more ideas, page 217). You might let each child choose one of the **ll** or **ff** words to Picture Code.

Fluency List F *(TGCD)*

You may want to pair children up and time them (twice each) on this list (see page 214) as they begin a new list in the next lesson.

B b

You'll need

- ✓ PCCs for 'Quick Dash' plus **b**
- ✓ ABC book
- ✓ BPCC - Uppercase **B**
- ✓ Alphabet Songs CD and Handwriting Songs CD or Living ABC software

- ✓ Phonics Readers 2b
- ✓ Fluency List G (TGCD)
- ✓ Make a 'Tricky' Word Card: **look**

Optional

- ✓ Individual activities (p.228-238)
- ✓ Letters for Picture Coding (TGCD)

Review previously learned letters and sounds

'Quick Dash' PCCs: ă, c, d, ĕ, f, g, h, ĭ, o, s, t, ŭ, ck, ff, ll, th

'Live Spelling'

When the child holding the **ff** or **ll** PCC is needed in a word he or she chooses another child to be the 'Best Friend on the End' and help hold the PCC. Then that child passes the PCC on to another child who chooses their own best friend in the next word, etc.

Words: **tell, fill, huff, sell, cuff, ill, gull, off**

Sound

Picture Code Cards

Show the plain letter side of the PCC to see what Bouncy Ben looks like in words. Then the children can use the Sound Trick (page 181) to remind themselves of the sound he makes in words: **Bouncy Ben**, /b/.

Action

Teach the Action Trick (page 182). Ask the children to do the action and make the sound in response to the plain letter side of the PCC.

Song

Sing Bouncy Ben's *Alphabet Song*. Show the picture side of his PCC when you sing his name. Turn to the plain letter every time you sing his sound.

Action Trick (see p.182)

Phonemic awareness and language development

Alliteration

Read about Bouncy Ben in the *ABC* book or use the *Living ABC* software. Emphasise his sound and explore the picture together.

Ask questions and discuss

Does **B**ouncy **B**en live in a house halfway up a high hill or in a **b**urrow under a **b**ridge? What does **B**en like **b**est: walking, hopping, or **b**ouncing along in the Reading Direction? What might **B**en like **b**est for **b**reakfast: fresh fruit or **b**rown **b**read, **b**utter and **b**lueberries? Which of these might Ben like to **b**uild? (**b**ridge, house, **b**oat, **b**ookcase) Do you think he **b**oasts about his **b**eautiful **b**ig **b**rown ears? Praise word: **B**rilliant!

Bouncy Ben in
ABC book

Beginning sound games

Pages 232-238 and the *Living ABC* software.

Shape: b and B

Song

Sing or say the verse from the *Handwriting Songs* as you trace both sides of

Ben's *PCC* (lyrics on *TGCD*).

Write

Write a huge **b** on the board or project the Bouncy Ben scene of the *Living ABC* software for children to air-trace as they sing. Follow up with a handwriting activity.

Uppercase

Show the *PCC* **b** and then the *BPCC* **B** and introduce the Uppercase Trick. Whenever Bouncy Ben starts a name or sentence he **b**alances his **b**est **b**lue **b**all **b**etween his **b**ig, **b**rown ears.

Blending

Blending with Picture Code Cards

Make these words for children to do the Roller Coaster Trick.

PCCs from 'Guess Who?' plus **b**

Words: **bed, bell, big, bug, but, cub, back, bath**

Reading and fluency

'Tricky' word

'Tricky' word

Show the word card **look**.* Use it in a sentence or two. Ask the children to stretch and segment to discover which letters need a wavy line.

Ask the children to make up oral sentences about things that **Bouncy Ben** might like to **look** at that begin with his sound (e.g. "He **look**s at **b**ugs.").

* The word **look** is taught as a useful 'tricky' word now, but it will be decodable after Lesson 81, Section 5.

Phonics Readers 2b

Phonics Readers 2b: *Ben and the cub*

Guide children in reading the story. (See suggestions, page 217.)

Fluency List G *(TGCD)*

Practise this new list with the children (page 214).

Lesson 36: Jumping Jim
J j

You'll need

- ✓ *PCCs* for 'Guess Who?' plus **j**
- ✓ *ABC* book
- ✓ *BPCC - Uppercase* **J**
- ✓ *Alphabet Songs CD* and *Handwriting Songs CD* or *Living ABC* software
- ✓ *Phonics Readers 2c*
- ✓ 'Tricky' Word Cards for review

Optional

- ✓ Individual activities (p.228-238)
- ✓ Letters for Picture Coding (*TGCD*)

Review previously learned letters and sounds

'Guess Who?' *PCCs*: ă, b, ě, g, ĭ, m, n, o, s, t, ŭ, ff, ll

Sound

Show the plain letter side of the *PCC* to see what Jumping Jim looks like in words. Then the children can use the Sound Trick (page 181) to remind themselves of the sound he makes in words: **Jumping Jim**, /j/.

Action

Teach the Action Trick (page 182). Ask the children to do the action and make the sound in response to the plain letter side of the *PCC*.

Song

Sing Jumping Jim's *Alphabet Song*. Show the picture side of his *PCC* when you sing his name. Turn to the plain letter every time you sing his sound (lyrics on *TGCD*).

Picture Code Cards

Action Trick (see p.182)

Phonemic awareness and language development

Alliteration

Read about Jumping Jim in the *ABC* book or use the *Living ABC* software. Emphasise his sound and explore the picture together.

Ask questions and discuss

What kind of shoes does Jumping Jim wear, boots or jogging shoes? Remember – he always jumps in the Reading Direction. So always make sure his jogging shoes are behind him! A healthy drink that begins with his sound? (juice) He's a very jolly fellow, so which emotion do you think he feels most? (anger, sadness, or joy)

Beginning sound games

Pages 232-238 and the *Living ABC* software.

Jumping Jim in *ABC* book

Shape: j and J

Song

Sing or say the verse from the *Handwriting Songs* as you trace both sides of Jim's *PCC* (lyrics on *TGCD*).

Write

Write a huge **j** on the board or project the Jumping Jim scene of the *Living ABC* software for children to air-trace as they sing. Follow up with a handwriting activity.

Uppercase

Show the *PCC* **j** and then the *BPCC* **J** and introduce the Uppercase Trick. Whenever Jumping Jim can start an important word, he is so pleased that

he does a big jump and his head disappears in the clouds. We can no longer see even one of his juggling balls.

Blending and segmenting

'Live Reading'
Line children up to make the words.

PCCs from 'Quick Dash' plus **j**

Words: **job, jog, jet, jam, Jim, Jill, bat, beg, bun, bus**

Reading and fluency

Review 'tricky' words
Use the word cards you have made to review recently introduced 'tricky' words and any others which children need to practise.

Suggested words: **look, for, of, her, they, you, like**

Phonics Readers 2c: *Look at them go!*
Guide children in reading. (See suggestions, page 217.)

You can build oral vocabulary by using the words **movement** and **transportation** when discussing the illustrations in this story.

Fluency List G *(TGCD)*
Re-read this list chorally with children. Ask them to do it in different types of voices (e.g. whispering, high mousy voices, low giant voices). Another idea for variety is to read the first line fairly loud and then get just a bit quieter with each line (or vice versa).

Phonics Readers 2c

Lesson 37: Giant All
all as in ball

Focus on **all**

You'll need
✓ *PCCs for 'Quick Dash' plus* **b, f, j, p, s, and t**
✓ *Phonics Readers 2c*
✓ *'Tricky' Word Cards made for previous lessons*

Optional
✓ *Individual activities (p.228-238)*
✓ *Blends & Digraphs Songs CD (2014 edition)*

Review previously learned letters and sounds
'Quick Dash' *PCCs:* **ă, ĕ, ĭ, o, p, s, t, s/z/, ŭ, ch, ck, ff, ll, ng, sh, th**

'Live Reading': Vowels-go-round
Try this variation of 'Live Reading' (see page 202).

PCCs from 'Quick Dash' plus **b, f, j, l**

The **p** and **ck** children stand at the front of the class, leaving a space for a third child to stand in between them.

The vowel children stand to the left of the class and take turns to appear in the middle of the word.

The class blends each word and decides if it is a real word or not (e.g **pack, pick, peck, pock, puck**).

Repeat with **s_ng** and **b_t**.

'Live Spelling': Sound Pops

Take up the *PCCs* from the previous activity and redistribute them to other children (see page 229).

PCCs from previous activity

Words: **job, bat, fell, puff, lock, ship, chips, things**

Giant All

Show the *PCC* picture side of Giant All. This is Giant All and he is so **t**all that you can't even see the top of him. **All** we see of him are his **l**ong legs. He seems to be grabbing an apple. Giant All loves apples. In fact he loves them so much that he just strides into words and takes them without asking! So if you spot a word with an **a**pple in it, but to the right of that apple there are the two **l**ong legs of Giant All, don't expect to hear that apple saying /ă/. Instead you will hear Giant All, calling his own name "All".

Turn to the plain letter. Ask the children to repeat the sound and apple stealing action (reaching down to your right as if grabbing an apple) three times as you push the plain letters forward, "**all**...**all**...**all**."

Picture Code Cards

Phonemic awareness and language development

Explore the Giant All scene in the *Story Phonics* software. Watch the animated story of Giant All striding into words, taking apples. Ask the children to hunt for items in the scene that include Giant All's sound.

Role-play

Ask the children to pretend to be Giant All grabbing an apple and saying "**all**" in big, deep giant voices.

Giant All in *Story Phonics* software

Blending with the Picture Code Cards

Make the words below (on screen with the *Story Phonics* software or with *PCCs*.) Then use the Roller Coaster Trick (e.g. "/b/ /aw//l/, ball")

PCCs: **b, c, f, h, t, all**

Words: **all, ball, fall, hall, tall, call**

Giant All wall

You might like to create a Giant All wall display with a picture of a huge giant surrounded by words that contain his sound.

Copymasters

Introduce the Giant All page from the *Blends & Digraph Copymasters* for children to work on independently or in small groups.

Reading and fluency

Phonics Readers 2c: *Let's look*

In this story, children can help the characters find their lost items. Read the story a few times using some of the whole class suggestions on page 217. Then ask the children to re-read this and several previous stories with a partner.

Fluency List G *(TGCD)*

One way to have pairs of children practise this list is to have the first partner read the first line, the other partner read line 2, the first reading line 3, etc. Then they can switch lines and read again.

Phonics Readers 2c

Lesson 38: Red Robot

R r

You'll need

✓ *PCCs* for 'Guess Who?' plus **r**
✓ *ABC* book
✓ *BPCC* - Uppercase **R**
✓ *Alphabet Songs CD* and *Handwriting Songs CD* or *Living ABC* software

✓ *Phonics Readers 2c*
✓ *Reading Racer Charts (TGCD)*

Optional

✓ Individual activities (p.228-238)
✓ Letters for Picture Coding *(TGCD)*

Review previously learned letters and sounds

'Guess Who?' *PCCs*: ă, b, ě, g, ĭ, m, n, o, s, t, ŭ, ff, ll

Sound

Show the plain letter side of the *PCC* to see what Red Robot looks like in words. Then the children can use the **Sound Trick** (page 181) to remind themselves of the sound he makes in words: **Red Robot**, /rrr/.

Picture Code Cards

Action

Teach the **Action Trick** (page 182). Ask the children to do the action and make the sound in response to the plain letter side of the *PCC*.

Song

Sing Red Robot's *Alphabet Song*. Show the picture side of his *PCC* when you sing his name. Turn to the plain letter every time you sing his sound (lyrics on *TGCD*).

Action Trick (see p.182)

Phonemic awareness and language development

Alliteration

Read about Red Robot in the *ABC* book or use the *Living ABC* software. Emphasise his sound and explore the picture together.

Ask questions and discuss

Red **R**obot is always **r**ushing around. Which way does he always **r**un? (to the **r**ight, in the **R**eading Direction) What sorts of things might he **r**un off with? Answer Yes or No: **r**ed **r**oses, **r**ings, watches, **r**eading books, money, cakes, **r**ice, **r**aisins, puzzles, **r**ecipes, **r**are **r**eptiles, **r**ocks.
Red **R**obot's **r**iddle: What **r**uns all over our school but never moves? (the **r**oof) Praise with: **R**ight! or **R**eally good!

Beginning sound games

Pages 232-238 and *Living ABC* software.

Red Robot in ABC book

Shape: r and R

Song

Sing or say the verse from the *Handwriting Songs* as you trace both sides of Red Robot's *PCC* (lyrics on *TGCD*).

Write

Write a huge **r** on the board or project the *Living ABC* software Red Robot scene for children to air-trace as they sing. Follow with a handwriting activity.

Uppercase

Show the *PCC* **r** and then the *BPCC* **R** and introduce the **Uppercase Trick**. Whenever **R**ed **R**obot starts somebody's name or a sentence, he takes a big breath, changes shape and gets bigger. Can you still **rrr**ecognise him?

Blending and segmenting

'Live Reading' and 'Live Spelling'

Distribute *PCCs*. Line children up for each of the first four words for the class to do the Roller Coaster Trick. Ask the children to stretch and segment the last three and 'Live Spell' them.

PCCs for 'Quick Dash' plus **r**

Words for 'Live Reading': **run, rob, rings, red**

Words for 'Live Spelling': **rocks, rib, rag**

Reading and fluency

Phonics Readers 2c: *Red Robot runs*

Guide children in reading the story. See pages 217-224 for suggestions on introducing stories and re-reading them.

Fluency List G *(TGCD)*

Time children on this list before getting a new one in the next lesson. Let them colour in their *Reading Racer Charts*. Compare their rates with the goal rates for the assessment at the end of Section 2.

Phonics Readers 2c

Q q

Focus on

You'll need

- ✓ *PCCs* for 'Quick Dash' plus **qu**
- ✓ *ABC* book
- ✓ *BPCC - Uppercase* **Q**
- ✓ *Alphabet Songs CD* and *Handwriting Songs CD* or *Living ABC* software

- ✓ *Phonics Readers 2c*
- ✓ *Fluency List H (TGCD)*
- ✓ Make a 'Tricky' Word Card: **was**

Optional

- ✓ Individual activities (p.228-238)
- ✓ Letters for Picture Coding *(TGCD)*

Review previously learned letters and sounds

'Quick Dash' *PCCs*: ă, b, ě, f, ĭ, j, l, o, r, s, t, ŭ, ck, ff, ll

Sound

Show the plain letter side of the *PCC* to see what Quarrelsome Queen looks like in words. Then the children can use the Sound Trick (page 181) to remind themselves of the sound she makes in words: **Quarrelsome Queen**, /kw/.

Action

Teach the Action Trick (page 182). Ask the children to do the action and make the sound in response to the plain letter side of the *PCC*.

Picture Code Cards

The Royal Umbrella

She is called Quarrelsome Queen because she is always arguing with other people. That's not a good way to behave, is it? She is so quarrelsome that she won't even face in the Reading Direction like most of the other Letterlanders. And she is very proud of her long beautiful hair that curls out behind her. In fact, (show the **qu** *PCC*) she is so afraid that the weather will mess up her hair

Action Trick (see p.182)

that she never goes into a word without her royal umbrella to protect it. Show the plain **qu** side. When we see these two letters together we know they will almost always say the sound we hear at the beginning of Quarrelsome Queen's name, /**qu**/. Push the *PCC* forward several times as children say, "/**qu**/, **qu**/, /**qu**/..."

Picture Code Cards

Song

Sing Quarrelsome Queen's *Alphabet Song*. Show the picture side of her *PCC* when you sing her name. Turn to the plain letter every time you sing her sound (lyrics on T*GCD*).

Phonemic awareness and language development

Alliteration

Read about Quarrelsome Queen in the *ABC* book or use the *Living ABC* software. Emphasise her sound and explore the picture together.

Ask questions and discuss

Quarrelsome **Q**ueen is very **q**uick to **q**uarrel. She hardly every **q**uits **q**uarrelling unless she is working on a **q**uilt or writing with her **q**uill pen. Praise words: **Q**uite right!

Quarrelsome Queen in *ABC* book

Beginning sound games

See pages 232-238 and *Living ABC* software.

Shape: q and Q

Song

Sing or say the verse from the *Handwriting Songs* as you trace both sides of Quarrelsome Queen's *PCC* (lyrics on T*GCD*).

Write

Write a huge **q** on the board or project the Quarrelsome Queen scene of the *Living ABC* software for children to air-trace as they sing. Follow up with a handwriting activity.

Uppercase

Show the *PCC* **q** and then the *BPCC* **Q** and introduce the Uppercase Trick. When Quarrelsome Queen starts a name or a sentence, she goes into her Quiet Room to recover from all her quarrelling.

Blending and segmenting

Blending with Picture Code Cards

Make the words below for blending using the Roller Coaster Trick.

PCCs: ă, g, ĭ, s, t, ck, ll, ng, qu

> Words: **quit, quits, quick, quacking, quill**

Segmenting with Picture Code Cards

Call out some of the words above. Ask the class to stretch and segment them and then ask one child to make the word with the *PCCs* as **qu**ickly as possible.

Reading and fluency

'Tricky' word

Show your word card **was**. Children stretch and segment it to discover that the **w** and **s** are decodable but the **a** is irregular. Make a wavy line below it.

'Tricky' word

Phonics Readers 2c: *Look, quick!*
First ask the children to identify the four Letterlanders who hurry past behind Jumping Jim and Goldern Girl in the story. Guide the reading (page 217).

Fluency List H *(TGCD)*
Guide children in reading this new list (page 214).

Phonics Readers 2c

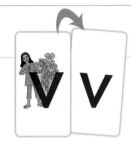

You'll need
- ✓ *PCCs* for 'Guess Who?' plus **f, m, n, t** and **v**
- ✓ *ABC* book
- ✓ *BPCC - Uppercase* **V**
- ✓ *Alphabet Songs CD* and *Handwriting Songs CD* or *Living ABC* software

- ✓ *Phonics Readers 2d*
- ✓ *Magnetic Word Builder* or other letter set

Optional
- ✓ Individual activities (p.228-238)
- ✓ Letters for Picture Coding (*TGCD*)

Review previously learned letters and sounds

'Guess Who?' *PCCs*: ă, b, ĕ, g, ĭ, j, o, s, ŭ, s/z/, ck, ll, qu, sh

Sound

Show the plain letter side of the *PCC* to see what Vicky Violet looks like in words. Then the children can use the Sound Trick (page 181) to remind themselves of the sound she makes in words: **Vicky Violet**, /vvv/.

Picture Code Cards

Action

Teach the Action Trick (page 182). Ask the children to do the action and make the sound in response to the plain letter side of the *PCC*.

Song

Sing Vicky Violet's *Alphabet Song*. Show the picture side of her *PCC* when you sing her name. Turn to the plain letter every time you sing her sound (lyrics on *TGCD*).

Action Trick (see p.182)

Phonemic awareness and language development

Alliteration

Read about Vicky Violet in the *ABC* book or use the *Living ABC* software. Emphasise her sound and explore the picture together.

Ask questions and discuss

Where in Letterland would you go to find **v**ery lovely **v**iolets like the ones in **V**icky's **v**ase, the Letterland Library or **V**olcano **V**alley? What is a healthy group of foods that begin with /**vvv**/? (**v**egetables) Why are **v**egetables so healthy for us? (**v**itamins) What are Mr A, E, I, O and U called? (the five **V**owel Men) What is **V**icky **V**iolet's favourite ice cream flavour, chocolate, strawberry or **v**anilla? Praise word: **V**ery good.

Vicky Violet in ABC book

Beginning sound games

For children needing more practice see pages 232-238, and the *Living ABC* software.

Shape: v and V

Song

Sing or say the verse from the *Handwriting Songs* as you trace both sides of Vicky's *PCC* (lyrics on *TGCD)*.

Write

Write a huge **v** on the board or project the Vicky Violet scene of the *Living ABC* software for children to air-trace as they sing. Follow up with a handwriting activity.

Uppercase

Show the *PCC* **v** and then the *BPCC* **V** and introduce the Uppercase Trick. Whenever Vicky Violet starts a name or a sentence she takes a deep breath and her vase becomes a very big and very valuable vase to show that the word is important.

Blending and segmenting

Blending with Picture Code Cards

Make the following words for the Roller Coaster Trick. Make the word **vanish** as two syllables with a space between to blend each part separately (**van ish**), and then say them together.

PCCs: ă, b, ě, f, g, ĭ, j, m, n, o, s, s/z/, t, ŭ, v, ck, ll, qu, sh

Words: **quit, quack, jam, bill, fog, bug, van, vans, vet, vets, vanish**

Magnetic Word Builder

Spelling with Magnetic Word Builders

Provide children with a *Magnetic Word Builder* or other materials to stretch, segment and spell the words below.

Letters: **a, c, d, e, g, i, k, n, q, s, t, u, v**

Words: **vet, vans, quick, Jim, doll, rug**

Reading and fluency

'Tricky' word

Show your word card **here**. Discover the irregular **ere**. Make a wavy line below it.

'Tricky' word

Phonics Readers 2d: *At the vet's*

Ask the children to look at the first two or three pages and try to decide what is going on before they read the story. Then after they read each page let them change or confirm their predictions. Provide time for the children to re-read this and previous stories for building accuracy and fluency. (Suggestions, page 217.)

Phonics Readers 2d

Fluency List H *(TGCD)*

Revise this list by reading it with the children, then ask them to re-read it with a partner in one of the ways suggested on page 214.

-ve as in have

You'll need

- ✓ PCCs for 'Quick Dash' plus **ve**
- ✓ *Phonics Readers 2d*
- ✓ 'Tricky' Word Card: **too** and for review

- ✓ *Story Phonics* software

Optional

- ✓ Individual activities (p.228-238)
- ✓ Letters for Picture Coding (*TGCD*)

Review previously learned letters and sounds

'Quick Dash' *PCCs*: ă, ĕ, g, h, ĭ, j, l, n, o, r, s/z/, ŭ, v, qu

Vase Prop e

Introduce -ve

There are hardly any English words that end in **v**. Show the picture side of the Vicky Violet *PCC*. All of Vicky Violet's vases have a pointy base, so the slightest breeze can blow them over! Because the winds in Letterland always blow in the Reading Direction, the risk is always that a vase will tip over this way. Tip the *PCC* and ask the children, What would happen if this vase tipped over? **"Her violets and the water would run out."** Very true.

Picture Code Cards

Phonemic awareness and language development

Explore the Vase Prop e scene in the *Story Phonics* software. Watch the animated story and ask the children to hunt for items in the scene that include Vase Prop e.

Vase Prop e in
Story Phonics software

Blending and segmenting

Blending with the Picture Code Cards

Make the word **van** with *PCCs*. Children blend the word. In this word if the wind blows in the Reading Direction, the vase won't tip because the other letters prop it up.

PCCs: ă, g, ĭ, n, v, ve

Words: **van, give**

Let's try another word, **give**. Ask the children to stretch and segment the word and tell you which Letterlanders they hear. Build the word without the final **e**. The wind could blow the vase right over. Replace the **v** *PCC* with **ve**.

This is a special **e** to prop up the vase on the end of a word, called **Vase Prop e,** and the **e** doesn't make any sound. It is completely silent.

So when we use the **Roller Coaster Trick** for this word we don't make a sound for the **e**, we only say the sounds for the first three letters. Demonstrate the **Roller Coaster Trick** for the word **give**: /g/ /ĭ/ /v/, give.

'Live Spelling'

Distribute the *PCCs* below.

Use a Stretching Leader (page 191) for each word and ask different children to hold the **v** and **ve** for each word.

PCCs: ă, g, h, ĭ, l, s/z/, v, ve

Words: **live, have, give, gives**

Children stretch and segment and 'Live Spell' each word with only a **v** on the end at first. Then ask the children in the audience to blow their breath in the Reading Direction. Ask Vicky Violet to pretend to be almost tipped over by the wind. Then the child with the **ve** card steps in beside her and the two hold the **ve** card together with Vicky standing up straight. The class can blend the word.

'Tricky' words

Reading and fluency

'Tricky' words

Introduce the new tricky word **too**. Display the word cards you have made so far or write the words on the board. Point to each one for children to read. Go through them a few times with increasing speed. Suggested words: **was**, **look**, **for**, **of**, **you**, **they**, **see**, **like**

Phonics Readers 2d: *Hugs*

Guide children in reading the story about a busy Mum and her baby. After they have read it once or twice, ask half the class to chorally read the Mum's lines and the other half read the baby's lines.

Phonics Readers 2d

Fluency List H *(TGCD)*

Ask the children to practise reading for fluency (page 214).

Lesson 42: Oscar's Bothersome Little Brother

o as in son

Focus on

You'll need

- ✓ *PCCs for 'Guess Who?' plus* **f**, **g**, **o/ŭ/**, **p** and another **n**
- ✓ *Phonics Readers 2d*
- ✓ *Story Phonics software*
- ✓ *Reading Racer Charts (TGCD)*
- ✓ 'Tricky' Word Cards: **come**, **some**

Optional

- ✓ Individual activities (p.228-238)
- ✓ Letters for Picture Coding *(TGCD)*

Review previously learned letters and sounds

'Guess Who?' *PCCs*: **c**, **d**, **ě**, **ĭ**, **j**, **l**, **m**, **n**, **o**, **r**, **s**, **ck**, **th**, **ve**

Make the word **live**. Point to each letter and ask the children to say the sound (they should remain silent when you point to **e**). Ask a child to explain why the **e** is there and then turn the **ve** *PCC* to the picture side to confirm the child's story logic about Vase Prop **e**.

Over 130 relatively common words in the English language contain an irregular **o** that sounds a bit more like 'uh'. The Letterland story logic to explain this sound follows.

Oscar's Bothersome Little Brother

PCCs: **c**, **d**, **ě**, **ĭ**, **l**, **m**, **n**, **o/ŭ/**, **s**, **th**, **ve**

> Words: **live**, **love**, **son**, **some**, **come**, **month**, **done**

Show the Little Brother *PCC* picture. Can you guess whose little brother this is? Yes, it is Oscar's Bother**s**ome Little Br**o**ther. Say his name with me, "Oscar's Bother**s**ome Little Br**o**ther". Since he is just a baby, he hasn't yet learned to say

Picture Code Cards

/ŏ/ like Oscar. The little brother just says 'uh' /ŭ/ in words. Push the plain letter forward for children to repeat his sound, "/ŭ/ /ŭ/ /ŭ/..."

Change the word **live** to **love** showing the Brother's picture side. Ask the children to blend the word (/l/ /uh/ /v/).

The little brother is bothersome because his letter looks just like Oscar's, but he says /ŭ/ in some words like **love**. It is also bothersome that this little brother *sounds* like another Letterlander. Do you know who that is? ("**Uppy Umbrella**") Let's make some more words with this Bothersome Brother.

Build each word above for children to blend using the Roller Coaster Trick. Use each word in a sentence, e.g. The Bothersome Brother's mother calls him 'son'.

Explain the **e** in words like **some** this way: Another tricky thing about some of the words with the Bothersome Brother's /ŭ/ sound is that they have a silent **e** on the end – even when a Vase Prop **e** is not needed (e.g. **come**, **some**). Use a plain letter **e** and explain, The **e** on the end of a word is almost always silent.

Phonemic awareness and language development

Explore the scene in the *Story Phonics* software. Watch the animated story and ask the children to hunt for items in the scene that include Oscar's Bothersome Little Brtoher.

Oscar's Bothersome Little Brother in *Story Phonics* software

Segmenting

'Live Spelling'

Distribute the *PCCs* below. Use a Stretching Leader (page 191) for each word. Let other children play the roles of Oscar and Baby Brother after each one has been in a word.

PCCs: **c, f, ě, g, j, l, m, n, n, o, o/ŭ/, p, r, s, ck, ve**

> Words: **son, fog, come, rock, love, none, jog, some**

All of our 'Live Spelling' words today will have either Oscar Orange's /o/ sound or his Baby Brother's /ŭ/ sound. Oscar and his brother can stand to the left of the word so we can decide which one we need.

Children stretch and segment and then 'Live Spell' the words. Tell them where a silent **e** is needed on the end. Ask the class to to use the Roller Coaster Trick for each word to check their spelling.

Individual activities

Complete the relevant page in the *Blends & Digraphs Copymasters* independently or in small groups.

Reading and fluency

Phonics Readers 2d: *Fun in the mud*

Guide children in reading this story about Munching Mike and his Mum. After they have read it once or twice, ask everyone to re-read the first two sentences. Then ask half the class to read Mum's lines and the other half to read Mike's lines. Partners can practise reading it this way, too. Ask the children to re-read several previous stories to a partner.

Phonics Readers 2d

Fluency List H *(TGCD)*

Time children reading this list twice (page 214).

W w and wh as in when

Focus on **Ww**

You'll need

- ✓ *PCCs* for 'Quick Dash' plus **w**
- ✓ *ABC book*
- ✓ *Beyond ABC*
- ✓ *BPCC - Uppercase* **W**
- ✓ *Alphabet Songs CD* and *Handwriting Songs CD* or *Living ABC* software
- ✓ *Phonics Readers 2d*
- ✓ Make a 'Tricky' Word Card: **said**
- ✓ *Fluency List I (TGCD)*

Optional

- ✓ Individual activities (p.228-238)
- ✓ Letters for Picture Coding *(TGCD)*
- ✓ *Blends & Digraphs Songs CD*

Review previously learned letters and sounds

'Quick Dash' *PCCs*: ă, b, ĕ, g, ĭ, o, o/ŭ/, s/z/, t, ŭ, v, ve, ll, th

Sound

Show the plain letter side of the *PCC* to see what Walter Walrus looks like in words. Then the children can use the Sound Trick (page 181) to remind themselves of the sound he makes in words: **Walter Walrus**, /www/.

Picture Code Cards

Action

Teach the Action Trick (page 182). Ask the children to do the action and make the sound in response to the plain letter side of the *PCC*.

Song

Sing Walter Walrus's *Alphabet Song*. Show the picture side of his *PCC* when you sing his name. Turn to the plain letter every time you sing his sound (lyrics on TGCD).

Phonemic awareness and language development

Alliteration

Read about Walter Walrus in the *ABC* book or use the *Living ABC* software. Emphasise his sound and explore the picture together.

Action Trick (see p.182)

Ask questions and discuss

Walter **W**alrus is one of the two main trouble makers in Letterland. He often causes trouble for letters next to him in a **w**ord. **W**hat do you think he does? He teases and splashes them and gets them **w**et with **w**ater from his **w**ells. Do you think he runs or **w**addles in the Reading Direction? **W**ould you all **w**ave like **W**alter? Praise with: **W**ow! **W**onderful! **W**hat a **w**inner! or **W**ell done!

Beginning sound games

Pages 232-238 and *Living ABC* software.

Walter Walrus in ABC book

Shape: w and W

Song

Sing or say the verse from the *Handwriting Songs* as you trace both sides of Walter's *PCC* (lyrics on *TGCD*).

Write

Write a huge **w** on the board or project the Walter Walrus scene of the *Living ABC* software for children to air-trace as they sing. Follow up with a handwriting activity.

Uppercase

Show the *PCC* **w** and then the *BPCC* **W** and introduce the Uppercase Trick. Whenever Walter Walrus starts a name or a sentence, he takes a big breath and gets bigger.

Segmenting

*PCC*s: ă, b, ĕ, g, ĭ, n, s/z/, t, w, v, ch, ll, th, wh

Words to segment: **wet, wag, with, wells, web, wig, vet**

Segmenting with Picture Code Cards

Call out the words above for the class to stretch and segment. Ask one child to build the word for all to see (either on a smartboard with the *Story Phonics* software or with the *PCCs* on a shelf. Ask the rest of the class to applaud the child by clapping like Walter might with his flippers.

wh as in when

Sound

Show children the **wh** *PCC* with Walter Walrus splashing Harry Hat Man's hat off. Push the card forward as they say the sound, "/**w**/.../**w**/..."

Picture Code Cards

Phonemic awareness

Share the **wh** scene and story logic in the *Beyond ABC* book or *Story Phonics* software. The children can listen for the sound and look for pictured words that start with the sound. The second sound of **wh** can be saved until later. There are just a few words **wh**o, **wh**ose, **wh**om and **wh**ole, where **w** becomes the silent letter.

Song

Listen to the *Blends & Digraphs Song* about these two characters (lyrics on *TGCD*.) Show the picture side of the **wh** *PCC*.

Walter Walrus and
Harry Hat Man
Beyond ABC book

Blending with Picture Code Cards

Make the words below for children to blend and use in sentences.

Words to blend: **when, which**

Reading and fluency

'Tricky' word

While teaching the word **said**, you can also introduce children to the use of quotation marks. Tell me something fun you did yesterday. Call on a volunteer to briefly answer. Then write your question and the child's answer on the board using **said** and the speaker's name and quotation marks. Read the sentences to the children and discuss where the quotation marks go and also point out the 'tricky' word **said**.

'Tricky' word

Show your **said** word card. Children help decide which letters to mark below with a wavy line to show they are not making their usual sounds (**ai**).

Phonics Readers 2d: *Wet*

Read the story to the children and then with them.

Fluency List I *(TGCD)*

Introduce this new Fluency List (page 214).

Phonics Readers 2d

X x

Focus on **Xx**

You'll need

- ✓ *PCCs for 'Guess Who' plus* **x**
- ✓ *ABC book*
- ✓ *BPCC - Uppercase* **X**
- ✓ *Alphabet Songs CD* and *Handwriting Songs CD* or *Living ABC software*

- ✓ *Phonics Readers 2e*
- ✓ Make a 'Tricky' Word Card: **what**
- ✓ *Fluency List I (TGCD)*

Optional

- ✓ Individual activities (p.228-238)
- ✓ Letters for Picture Coding *(TGCD)*

Review previously learned letters and sounds

'Guess Who?' *PCCs*: ă, b, ĕ, f, ĭ, j, m, o, qu, s, ŭ, v, w, ve

Sound

Show the plain letter side of the *PCC* to see what Fix-it Max looks like in words. Fix-it Max is the only Letterlander who says the sound at the *end* of his name. Discover his sound by separating off the LAST sound in his name: **Fix-it Max**, /**ks**/.

Picture Code Cards

Action

Teach the Action Trick (page 182). Ask the children to do the action and make the sound in response to the plain letter side of the *PCC*.

Song

Sing Fix-it Max's *Alphabet Song*. Show the picture side of his *PCC* when you sing his name. Turn to the plain letter every time you sing his sound.

Phonemic awareness and language development

Alliteration

Read about Fix-it Max in the *ABC* book or use the *Living ABC* software. Emphasise his sound and explore the picture together.

Action Trick (see p.182)

Ask questions and discuss

How old do you think Fix-it Max is, five or si**x**? Would Fix-it Max carry his lunch in a plastic bag or a plastic bo**x**? Would his favourite animal be a fo**x** or a cow? What does Max pretend to drive – a lorry or a taxi? Max makes his /**ks**/ sound in only a few words, because two other Letterlanders, or sometimes three, often do the job for him (e.g. **ks** in **books**, **cks** in **socks**). Praise with: E**x**cellent.

Fix-it Max in ABC book

Beginning sound games pages 232-238, and *Living ABC* software.

Shape: x and X

Song

Sing or say the verse from the *Handwriting Songs* as you trace both sides of Max's *PCC* (lyrics on *TGCD*).

Write

Write a huge **x** on the board or project the scene from the *Living ABC* software for children to air-trace as they sing. Follow with a handwriting activity.

Uppercase

Show the *PCC* **x** and then the *BPCC* **X** and introduce the Uppercase Trick. When Fix-it Max starts a name or a sentence, he takes a deep breath and gets bigger.

Blending

Blending with Picture Code Cards

Build the words below for the children to blend. Separate the two syllables in **exit** (**ex it**). Ask the children to do the Roller Coaster Trick to blend the sounds sin each syllable and then put the whole word together.

PCCs: **ă, b, f, ĭ, m, o, s, x**

Words: **Max, fix, fixes, mix, six, boxes, fox, exit**

Reading and fluency

'Tricky' word

Show the word card **what**. Ask a few volunteer children to use it in sentences. Ask the children to help decide where the wavy line needs to go.

'Tricky' word

Phonics Readers 2e: *Can you fix it, Max?*

Read this story about Fix-it Max and Jumping Jim with the children. Then divide children into three groups for re-reading. One reads Jim's quotes, one reads Max's and the other group reads 'said Jim', etc. Then let children re-read the story in groups of three with each taking a different role each time.

Fluency List I *(TGCD)*

Revise this list with the children. Ask the children to try reading the sentences emphasing various words or phrasing differently. Then ask partners to practise the list together as you walk about checking on accuracy and fluency.

Phonics Readers 2e

> **Note:** Does Max ever whisper his /ks/ sound at the start of a word? (No, never. When he starts the words 'xmas' and 'X-ray' he first makes an /eh/ sound before /ks/ and at the start of 'xylophone' he has a quick snooze so he makes a /zzz/ sound instead!

Lesson 45: Yellow Yo-yo Man
Y y

Focus on

You'll need

- ✓ *PCCs for 'Quick Dash' plus* **m, n, t** *and* **y**
- ✓ *ABC book*
- ✓ *BPCC - Uppercase* **Y**
- ✓ *Alphabet Songs CD* and *Handwriting Songs CD* or *Living ABC* software

- ✓ *Phonics Readers 2e*
- ✓ *Reading Racer Charts (TGCD)*
- ✓ *Fluency List I (TGCD)*

Optional

- ✓ Individual activities (p.228-238)
- ✓ Letters for Picture Coding *(TGCD)*

Review previously learned letters and sounds

'Quick Dash' *PCCs:* ă, ě, g, ĭ, o, o/ŭ/, r, s, s/z/, ŭ, v, w, x, ck, ll, ve

Sound

Show the plain letter side of the *PCC* to see what Yellow Yo-yo Man looks like in words. Then the children can use the Sound Trick (page 181) to remind themselves of the sound he makes in words: **Yellow Yo-yo Man** /yyy/.

Picture Code Cards

Action

Teach the Action Trick (page 182). Ask the children to do the action and make the sound in response to the plain letter side of the *PCC*.

Song

Sing Yellow Yo-yo Man's *Alphabet Song*. Show the picture side of his *PCC* when you sing his name. Turn to the plain letter every time you sing his sound.

Action Trick (see p.182)

Phonemic awareness and language development

Alliteration

Read about Yellow Yo-yo Man in the *ABC* book or use the *Living ABC* software. Emphasise his sound and explore the picture together.

Ask questions and discuss

Yellow Yo-yo Man only has a few chances to make his /yyy/ sound in words. Can you guess some of them. What do you think his favourite colour is? (yellow) When he is sleepy, he opens his mouth and...? (yawns). He has a birthday once a...? (year). You will hear him in a few more words like **y**ou, **y**esterday, **y**oung and **yyyy**es! The rest of time he takes the yo-yos out of his sack and works for Mr E or Mr I. If he is at the end of your name, he is probably working for Mr E. (Harr**y**, Rub**y**, Lil**y**, etc.) Sometimes he works for Mr I (m**y**, tr**y**, b**y**), but we will learn more about that later. Praise with: **Yes!**

Yellow Yo-yo Man in
ABC book

Beginning sound games

Pages 232-238 and *Living ABC* software.

Shape: y and Y

Song

Sing or say the verse from the *Handwriting Songs* as you trace both sides of Yo-yo Man's *PCC* (lyrics on *TGCD*).

Write

Write a huge **y** on the board or project the Yellow Yo-yo Man scene of the *Living ABC* software for children to air-trace as they sing. Follow up with a handwriting activity.

Uppercase

Show the *PCC* **y** and then the *BPCC* **Y** and introduce the Uppercase Trick. Whenever Yo-yo Man starts a name or a sentence, he quickly empties out some of his yo-yos (which are heavy) so that he can step lightly up onto the line to show how important that word is.

Blending and segmenting

Blending with Picture Code Cards

Build the words below for children to blend.

PCCs from 'Quick Dash' plus: **m, n, t, y**

Words: **yes, wag, yell, yet, tax, yams, six, win, yuck, give**

Spelling with Magnetic Word Builders

Say the words below and a sentence, then repeat the word. Children stretch and segment, and then build the words using the *Magnetic Word Builder* or *PCCs*.

Letters: **a, c, e, f, g, i, k, l, l, m, o, s, t, u, v, w, x, y**

Words: **yell, wet, fix, vets, yuck, wig, yams, love**

Magnetic Word Builder

Reading and fluency

'Tricky' word review

Review the 'tricky' words below with the cards you have made for previous lessons. All three are used in the story for this lesson.

'Tricky' Word Cards: **see, what, you**

Phonics Readers 2e: *Let's go and see Yo-yo Man*

Quarrelsome Queen and Kicking King are going to visit another Letterlander. Who do you think it might be?

Guide the children in reading and discussing the story (see page 217). Re-read it with groups of children taking the roles of the three characters (and another group acting as narrator reading the words 'yells Yo-yo Man'. Small groups of four could then take the roles and read together. Then each child in the group could take a different role and read again.

Fluency List I *(TGCD)*

Children read with partners as you time them all (page 214).

Phonics Readers 2e

Lesson 46: Zig Zag Zebra
Z z

You'll need
✓ *PCCs* for 'Guess Who?' plus **z**
✓ *ABC* book
✓ *BPCC - Uppercase* **Z**
✓ *Alphabet Songs CD* and *Handwriting Songs CD* or *Living ABC* software
✓ *Phonics Readers 2e*

✓ *Fluency List J (TGCD)*
✓ Make a 'Tricky' Word Card: **they**
✓ Make an extra **z** letter on a card the size of the *PCCs*

Optional
✓ Individual activities (p.228-238)
✓ Letters for Picture Coding *(TGCD)*

Review previously learned letters and sounds

'Guess Who?'*PCCs*: ă, b, ĕ, f, g, ĭ, o, p, t, ŭ, v, x, y, ll

Sound

Show the plain letter side of the *PCC* to see what Zig Zag Zebra looks like in words. Then the children can use the **Sound Trick** (page 181) to remind themselves of the sound she makes in words: **Zig Zag Zebra**, /zzz/.

Picture Code Cards

Action

Teach the **Action Trick** (page 182). Ask the children to do the action and make the sound in response to the plain letter side of the *PCC*.

Song

Sing Zig Zag Zebra's *Alphabet Song*. Show the picture side of her *PCC* when you sing her name. Turn to the plain letter every time you sing her sound (lyrics on T*GCD*).

Action Trick (see p.182)

Phonemic awareness and language development

Alliteration

Read about Zig Zag Zebra in the *ABC* book or use the *Living ABC* software. Emphasise her sound and explore the picture together.

Ask questions and discuss

Zig **Z**ag **Z**ebra is very quiet and shy, so you won't see her letter in a lot of words. In fact she's so shy she doesn't even face in the Reading Direction. (Can children remember why Golden Girl and Quarrelsome Queen don't either?) Do you remember who else makes her /**zzz**/ sound at the end of lots more words? (Sleepy Sammy Snake) Do you think Zig **Z**ag **Z**ebra would rather live on a farm

Zig Zag Zebra in ABC book

or a **zoo**? (**zoo**) What do you think her favourite number is? (**zero**). When she runs very fast, do you think the sound you would hear would be **zzz**oooom or whoosh?

Beginning sound games
Pages 232-238 and the *Living ABC* software.

Shape: z and Z

Song
Sing or say the verse from the *Handwriting Songs* as you trace both sides of Zig Zag's *PCC* (lyrics on *TGCD*).

Write
Write a huge **z** on the board or project the Zig Zag Zebra scene of the *Living ABC* software for children to air-trace as they sing. Follow up with a handwriting activity.

Uppercase
Show the *PCC* **z** and then the *BPCC* **Z** and introduce the Uppercase Trick. When Zig Zag Zebra starts a name or a sentence she takes a deep breath and gets bigger.

Blending

'Live Reading'
Distribute the *PCCs* below and the extra **z** card you have made. Guide children in forming the words for everyone else to blend.

Double consonants zz
Explain that Zig Zag Zebra has a best friend named Zoe Zebra to stand with her at the end of just a few words. Maybe Zoe is so shy she doesn't even want us to see her picture but only her letter.

PCCs for 'Quick Dash' plus: **z**, **z**, **ll**

Words: **zip, zig, zag, buzz, fuzz, fox, vet, yet, yell**

Reading and fluency

'Tricky' word

'Tricky' word
Teach the word **they*** with the card you have made (page 210).

Phonics Readers 2e: *Zig and zag*
Guide children in reading and re-reading this story (for more ideas see page 217). Ask partners to re-read several previous stories together.

Call out one or two of the sentences from the story for children to write.

Fluency List J *(TGCD)*
Practise this new list as preparation for the assessment that follows this lesson.

Phonics Readers 2e

---

* **they** is probably the most frequently misspelled word in the English language because the **e** sounds exactly like an **a**.
In Letterland this **e** is depicted as 'Mr Mean-E', a crotchety old man who says:
"Hee, hee, hee, I'm an **e**, but I say '**a**' in the little word **they**.
I'll be glad so long as you spell **they** wrong!"
You could introduce this old meany as a challenge to your class. "Don't let him catch you out spelling **they** with an **a**!"

Let's review and celebrate

At this point you have not only completed Section 2 of this Teacher's Guide, but more importantly you have thoroughly taught the entire alphabet. Why not celebrate this event with a special day or a special lesson, or some review activities? Here are a few suggestions. Children could make suggestions, too.

- **Review Story** There is one more story to read in *Phonics Readers 2e*. It is kind of guessing game with the title *Who said that?*

Phonics Readers 2e

- **Letterland Fruit Feast** Ask the children to bring in a fruity snack for one of the letters of the alphabet, e.g. apple, blueberry, cranberry, date, fig, guava, kiwi, mango, pineapple, quince, raspberry, strawberry, watermelon, etc.

- **Dress Up Day** Each child could dress up as a different Letterlander and have a parade. Be sure to take lots of photos.

- **Favourite Letterlander** Ask everyone to pick their favourite Letterlander and collect words with the initial sound to write and/or illustrate along with the character. Children can write a sentence about it and share their work.

- **Alphabet Book** Ask the children to make pages for a class ABC book with drawings or magazine cuttings.

- **Sing-a-long** Let the children request their favourite songs. Use actions and *Picture Code Cards* for the *Alphabet Songs* and air-tracing for the *Handwriting Songs*.

- **Dramatic Reading/Performing** Divide the class into groups of three to six children. Let each group pick a story from the *Phonics Readers*. Ask them to practise reading it and acting it out and then each group can present it to the class, to parents or other classes.

- **Eyes Shut Riddle Game** (page 237) Pass out the *PCC*s for **a-z**. Call out a riddle and ask the child with the corresponding *PCC* to stand up and call out the Letterlander's name and sound, e.g. **"I am Dippy Duck and I say /d/."**

- **Blends and Digraphs Songs Video** Make a video of groups children dramatising the songs for the digraphs (**ng**, **ch**, **sh**, **th**) while everyone sings. Other children could hold up large signs of words that include the digraph.

Home link

Now that the children have finished Section 2, they are able to start reading little booklets. Take this opportunity to make copies of the three *Take-Home Booklets* for Section 2 on your *TGCD* for children to read in class and then take home to read to their parents.

Cutting, folding and stapling instructions are on the *TGCD*.

Take-Home Booklet

Assessment - Refer to your TGCD

Use the Section 2, Part 2 assessments a few days to two weeks after completing the final lesson in Section 2 (Lesson 46).

All assessment instructions/forms are on the *TGCD*.

Section 3 :
Blending with Adjacent Consonants

Lesson Chart

Lesson	Lesson focus	Example word	Concept	Story from *Phonics Readers*	'Tricky' word	Set/Book
47	sc, sk, sm, sn, sp, st, sw	scab, skip, smash, snap, spot, stuck, swim	s + consonant	It is so hot!	says, do	3a
48	sc, sk, sm, sn, sp, st, sw	scab, skip, smash, snap, spot, stuck, swim	s + consonant	Spin and smash		3a
49	bl, cl, fl, gl, pl, sl	block, clock, flag, glad, plug, slug	Consonant + l	Lucy likes to help	wants	3a
50	bl, cl, fl, gl, pl, sl	block, clock, flag, glad, plug, slug	Consonant + l	A bird hops in		3a
51	br, cr, dr, fr, gr, pr, tr	brick, crab, drip, frog, grin, press, track	Consonant + r	What do you see?	into	3a
52	br, cr, dr, fr, gr, pr, tr	brick, crab, drip, frog, grin, press, track	Consonant + r	Can a crab grab?	can't, ask	3b
53	Review	–		Snow on the hill	don't	3b
54	-nd, -nk, -nt	hand, tank, tent	Final blends	Sink or float?	asked, gave	3b

Further resources

 Blends & Digraphs CD

Picture Code Cards

 *Magnetic Word Builder*

Story Phonics software

 *Blends & Digraphs Copymasters*

 *Word Bank Copymasters*

Teacher's Guide CD

Section 3 Assessment

Take-Home Booklets

Fluency Lists J-K

Blending with Adjacent Consonants

In these eight lessons, children blend and segment adjacent consonants. This enables them to read hundreds more short vowel words and consolidate their decoding and spelling skills. Since these sounds are not new there is no need to memorise them. Instead they learn to seamlessly blend the sounds as they read words. To spell, they slow-speak words to hear each consonant as a separate sound.

Contents

Consonant + s	**sc sk sm sn sp st sw**
Consonant + l	**bl cl fl gl pl sl**
Consonant + r	**br cr dr fr gr pr tr**
Final blends	**-nd -nk -nt**

Objectives

By the end of this section, children should be able to:

- Blend CCVC (glad, spill), CVCC words (hand, best) and CCVCC words (stand, plant)
- Segment CCVC and CVCC words
- Read nine additional 'tricky' words (total: 30)
- Read decodable text with adjacent consonant words and new 'tricky' words with accuracy, fluency, and comprehension.

Practise and apply

Children continue to learn with activities such as 'Quick Dash', 'Guess Who?' and 'Live Reading' and Spelling. In addition they try the new strategies below that keep your lessons fresh and interesting.

Turn 'lip' into 'slip' In 'Live Reading', you and the children imagine Sammy Snake **ssss-s**liding along **sss-s**neaking up on a word to change **lip** to **slip** or **pin** to **spin**. Similar word changing fun works with consonants adjacent to **l** and **r**.

Act out the word After children build a word, they 'act out' the meaning. For **glad** they smile, or for **block** they pretend to stack blocks. They will think up creative actions for almost any word.

Word Detectives Children act as detectives looking for adjacent consonants to Picture Code in sentences on the board.

Blends & Digraph Songs CD 20 songs feature adjacent consonants with **l**, **r**, and **s**. Children listen for words with these as they sing.

Reading Children get lots of practice reading their new words in the eight stories in the *Phonics Readers*, in *Fluency Lists* and *Take-Home Booklets*.

'Tricky' words introduced in Section 3

says	do	wants	into	
can't	ask	don't	asked	gave

S plus consonant

You'll need

✓ *PCCs for 'Quick Dash' plus* **b, g, p, t** *and* **ck**
✓ *Phonics Readers 3a*
✓ *Fluency List J (TGCD)*
✓ *Make a 'Tricky' Word Card:* **do**

Optional

✓ A toy snake or headband
✓ Individual activities (Activity Bank)
✓ Large words for Picture Coding

Review previously learned letters and sounds

'Quick Dash' *PCCs:* ă, c, d, ě, ĭ, k, l, m, n, o, s, ŭ, w, ll

Adjacent consonants with s

PCCs from 'Quick Dash' plus **g, p, b, t**

Words: **s_ep, step, scab, skip, sled, smell, spot, swim, snug**

Missing letter

Make the word **s_ep** with *PCCs* with a space for the missing letter. Sammy Snake hisses so much at the beginning of words, it can be hard to hear the consonant that comes next in the word.

Tell children their job is to discover the missing letter and put it in place.

This word has *four* sounds that we need to segment out. Use the word **step** in a sentence and toss it to them. Use the **Rubber Band Trick** to stretch out the word and segment the sounds to discover what letter is missing, "ssssteeep, /s/ /t/ /e/ /p/". It's Talking Tess! She makes such a quick, quiet /t/ sound. No wonder it is hard to hear her.

Ask a child to place the **t** *PCC* to complete the word. Then ask everyone to do the **Roller Coaster Trick** to blend the word, "/s/ /t/ /e/ /p/, sssssteeeeep, **step**." Children will need to tap the sounds at four points along their arm and then slide their hand down the roller coaster to blend.

Make the additional words with the second letter left out and do the same.

Ask a child to write the words on the board as each is completed. Read the list on the board with the children and ask what letter all these words begin with.

Yes, they all begin with Sammy Snake's letter and have a consonant as the second letter – not a vowel. When we have two consonants together with each making their own sound, it can be tricky to read and spell the words. You've listened well for that second consonant.

'Live Reading'

Sammy Snake at your service

Sammy Snake likes to slide up to his other consonant friends to make new words. He does his best to help us blend the sounds together by holding out his /sss/ sound until we can say the next consonant sound.

Distribute the *PCCs*: ă, b, c, ě, ĭ, k, l, m, n, o, p, s, t, ŭ, w, ll, ck

Words: **nap - snap, tuck - stuck, mock - smock, pill - spill, cab - scab, kin - skin, well - swell, lap - slap**

Ask one child to stand off to the side holding the Sammy Snake *PCC*. Line up the children with the letters in the word (**nap**).

Sammy slides into place

Ask Sammy Snake to come slithering in with everyone hissing /sss/ until he stops by the **n**. Next the other letters say their sounds in turn /n/ /ă/ /p/. Then the class does the Roller Coaster Trick for the word, first touching their arm for each of the four sounds and then blending as shown in the margin.

Let a different child be Sammy Snake after each word or two. Do as many words as time and children's attention allow.

"s...n...a...p"

Reading and fluency

'Tricky' words

Show the card **says**. Read the word and say it in a sentence or two. With the Rubber Band Trick, guide children to discover that **a** and **y** do not say their usual sounds and Sammy Snake is making his sleepy /zzz/ sound on the end. Make a wavy line below **ay** and a small **z** above the final **s**. Then children say the word each time you push the word card forward, "says, says..."

Go on to teach the 'tricky' word **do**.

'Tricky' word

Phonics Readers 3a: *It is so hot!*

For a change in routine, let pairs of children read to each other first. Then all read together (page 217).

Fluency List J *(TGCD)*

Children continue practising this list (page 214).

Phonics Readers 3a

Individual activity

Picture Coding

Ask the children to Picture Code some words with Sammy Snake plus a consonant.

Lesson 48: Spelling words

S plus adjacent consonants

You'll need

✓ PCCs for 'Guess Who?' plus **b, k, l, n** and **p**
✓ Magnetic Word Builder or other letter set
✓ Phonics Readers 3a
✓ Blends & Digraphs Songs CD or Story Phonics software

✓ Write the Word Detectives sentence (p.113) on the board at child level

Optional

✓ A toy snake or headband
✓ Individual activities (Activity Bank)
✓ Large words for Picture Coding

Review previously learned letters and sounds

'Guess Who?' PCCs: ă, d, ĕ, ĭ, s, s/z/, t, ŭ, w, ck, ll, ng

'Live Spelling'

We need to listen closely as we use the Rubber Band Trick on our words today. We want to be sure we hear all four sounds especially Sammy Snake's /sss/ sound and the consonant that comes after it.

Distribute *PCCs* from 'Guess Who?' plus **b, k, l, n, p**

Words: **skin, slid, spell, swings, snuck, stacks, best, ask**

Lead children in stretching and segmenting and forming the first word or two.

Then ask one of the children who doesn't have a *PCC* to act as Stretching Leader to demonstrate the stretch and segment strategy before the rest of the class does it. Change leaders after every word or two.

When you make the words **best** and **ask**, tell children that sometimes Sammy Snake likes to be next to a consonant friend on the end of words, too.

Write the words on the board as each is completed (or ask a child to do it).

Children then read the list on the board in order as you point to the words. Repeat once or twice, a bit faster each time. Then point to the words in a random order for children to read.

Group activities

Spelling with Magnetic Word Builders
Letters: **a, c, e, i, k, l, m, n, o, p, s, t, u**

Words: **step, stop, stuck, stick, stack, snack, snap, snip, rest, mask**

Call out each word above, say it in a sentence and repeat the word. Children repeat, stretch and segment it and spell it with their own letter sets.

Make sure that everyone has the correct spelling by observing or by providing the spelling on the board. Remove the model and ask them to cover the word with their hands and spell it aloud by saying the letter sounds in sequence.

Ask them to leave their letters in place as you call out the next word to stretch and spell. Then they will only need to change one or two letters.

Magnetic Word Builder

Word Detectives
Ask the children to come to the board and Picture Code or underline the **s** and the consonant after it in the sentences below. If underlining, put a separate line under each of the letters. Then read the sentences a few times with the children.

Scott skips on the steps. Then he slips and smashes into the bin.

Songs
Enjoy listening to and singing some of the seven songs on the *Blends & Digraphs CD* or the *Story Phonics* software featuring Sammy Snake and an adjacent consonant. After singing a song, ask the children to recall some of those consonant blend words (lyrics on *TGCD*).

The *Story Phonics* software also includes some simple chants to link the blended sound and vocabulary together.

Reading and fluency

Phonics Readers 3a: *Spin and smash*
Tell children that they will read about two Letterlanders who decide to go ice skating on an outdoor rink. After all have read the story once or twice, you may want to let one group of children read the speech bubbles for Vicky, another read for Max and a third group read the text below the illustrations. (More suggestions on pages 217-224).

Phonics Readers 3a

Consonants plus l

You'll need

- ✓ *PCCs for 'Quick Dash' plus* **k**, **m** *and* **s**
- ✓ *Phonics Readers 3a*
- ✓ *Fluency List J (TGCD)*
- ✓ *Blends & Digraphs Songs CD*
- ✓ Make a 'Tricky' Word Card: **wants**
- ✓ A torch

Optional

- ✓ Individual activities (Activity Bank)

Review previously learned letters and sounds

'Quick Dash' *PCCs:* ă, b, c, d, ĕ, f, g, h, ĭ, l, o, p, s, ŭ, ck, ss

Adjacent consonants with l

PCCs from 'Quick Dash' plus **k**, **m**

> Words: **cap, clap, block, flip, glad, plug, help, milk**

Blending with Picture Code Cards

Make the word **cap** with *PCCs* for children to blend using the Roller Coaster Trick.

Lucy Lamp Light likes to line up with her consonant friends at the beginning of a word. When she does, she becomes the second letter in the word. Let's put Lucy's /lll/ sound into this word as the second letter.

Change **cap** to **clap** and lead children in the Roller Coaster Trick for the four sounds in this word. Then give them a clap for reading this new word.

Let's see what other consonants Lucy likes to line up with in words.

After children blend each word, ask them to do an action or quick mime that demonstrates the meaning of the word (e.g. smile for **glad**, stacking pretend **blocks**). For the words **help** and **milk** point out that sometimes Lucy likes to line up at the end of a word with a consonant friend as well.

'Live Reading' - Lucy lights up words

Dim the lights in the classroom and have your torch ready for this variation on 'Live Reading'.

Distribute the *PCCs*: ă, b, c, f, g, l, o, p, s, ŭ, ck, ss

> Words: **glass, clock, plus, black, flag**

After lining up the children to make the first word, shine the light on each child's *PCC* to signal for the class to make each sound in the word as they begin the Roller Coaster Trick. Then sweep the light across the whole word as the children slide their hands doing the Roller Coaster Trick to blend it. Do the same with each word.

Songs

Enjoy listening to and singing some of the six songs on the *Blends & Digraphs CD* featuring Lucy Lamp Light and an adjacent consonant. Ask the children to recall words with a consonant plus **l**.

Reading and fluency

'Tricky' word

Teach the word **wants** with the children helping to decide on the letter that needs a wavy line. (More on page 210.)

'Tricky' word

Phonics Readers 3a: *Lucy likes to help*

Guide children in reading today's story. Then display *PCCs* for Lucy Lamp Light, Clever Cat, Firefighter Fred, Golden Girl and Peter Puppy. Ask the children to tell how Lucy helped each Letterlander. Then ask the children to re-read this story and previous ones with a partner.

Fluency List J *(TGCD)*

Ask the children to practise their list with a partner. You may want to use one of the sentences for dictation.

Phonics Readers 2c

Lesson 50: Spelling words

Consonant plus l

You'll need

- ✓ *PCCs for 'Guess Who?' plus* **b, c, d**
- ✓ *Phonics Readers 3a*
- ✓ *Fluency List J (TGCD)*
- ✓ *Magnetic Word Builder or other letter sets*

✓ Write the Word Detective sentences (p.116) on the board

Optional

- ✓ Individual activities (Activity Bank)
- ✓ Large words for Picture Coding

Review previously learned letters and sounds

'Guess Who?' *PCCs:* **ă, f, g, ĭ, l, m, o, p, ŭ, ck, ff, sh**

'Live Spelling'

Distribute *PCCs* from 'Guess Who?' plus **b, c, d**

Words: **club, flop, blush, flock, cliff, glad, plum**

Lead children in stretching and segmenting and forming the first word or two. Write each word on the board after 'Live Spelling' it (page 202.)

Then ask the children without *PCCs* to take turns as Stretching Leader.

Words on the board

After 'Live Spelling' all the words, children read the list on the board in order, as you point. Repeat once or twice, a bit faster each round. Then point to the words in a quick random order for children to re-read.

Segmenting

Spelling with Magnetic Word Builders

Letters: **a, c, c, f, g, i, k, l, n, o, p, s, s, t, u**

Words: **flat, glass, class, cluck, click, plan, plod**

Call out the words above, say them in a sentence and repeat the word. Children repeat, stretch and segment it and spell it with their own letter sets. Ask them to check their spelling with the Roller Coaster Trick. (Full details, page 188.)

Magnetic Word Builder

Word Detectives

Ask the children to come to the board and Picture Code or underline the **l** and the consonant before it in the sentence below. If underlining, put a separate line under each of the letters. Then read the sentence a few times with the children.

We plan to build a club house with the big blocks in the back of the class.

Reading and fluency

Phonics Readers 3a: *A bird hops in*
Guide children in reading and re-reading the story. You may want to use the Story Stone activity for re-telling this story. (See more comprehension and fluency strategies, page 217-224.)

Fluency List J *(TGCD)*
Time children and ask them to graph their scores (page 214).

Dictation
Call out one or two sentences from the above story or the *Fluency List* for children to write. To help children remember the sentence as they write, say the whole sentence with rhythm and expression and ask the children to repeat it twice in the same way.

Phonics Readers 3a

Individual activity

Writing topic
The above story may bring out children's own experiences with animals in unexpected places. Encourage them to draw and write about them.

Picture coding
Children may enjoy Picture Coding some of the consonant–plus–l words. Use their colourful contributions to decorate your walls.

Lesson 51
Consonant plus r

You'll need
✓ *PCCs for 'Quick Dash' plus* **f, g, s**
✓ *Phonics Readers 3b*
✓ *Fluency List K (TGCD)*
✓ *Blends & Digraphs Songs CD*

✓ Make a 'Tricky' Word Card: **into**
Optional
✓ Individual activities (Activity Bank)
✓ A helmet for Red Robot

Review previously learned letters and sounds

'Quick Dash' *PCCs*: ă, b, c, d, ě, ĭ, o, p, r, t, ŭ, ck, ng, sh, ss

Blending
Set out the word **fog** with *PCCs* for children to blend.

Red Robot likes to see if he can catch you out by running into words. He often runs right up and squeezes in just after the first letter and changes the word and its meaning. Watch how he changes the word **fog**.

PCCs from 'Quick Dash' plus **f, g**

Words: **fog, frog, brush, crib, dress, grab, press, trap, bring**

Move the picture side of the Red Robot *PCC* as if he is running toward the word and then insert it to change the word to **frog**.

Lead children in the Roller Coaster Trick for this four-sound word. Then ask them to hop like frogs, make frog noises, or pretend their hands are hopping frogs.

Make the rest of the words above for the children to blend. Give children turns as the Blending Leader for some of the words.

After children read the word, ask them to do an action or mime to demonstrate the meaning of the word (e.g. paint with a **brush**, lift a baby into a **crib**).

'Live Reading'
Distribute the *PCCs*: **ă, b, d, g, ĭ, o, p, r, t, ck**

Words: **bag-brag, tip-trip, gab-grab, dip-drip, tick-trick**

The Red Robot child stands to the left of the class ready to rush into the word to change it. After every word or two, let a different child be Red Robot.

Line up the children to make the first three-sound word for the Roller Coaster Trick. Use the word in a sentence.

Red Robot rushes in. Ask Red Robot to rush into the word after the first letter. Now the class does the Roller Coaster Trick for the new four-sound word.

Songs
Enjoy listening to and singing some of the seven songs on the *Blends & Digraphs Songs CD* featuring a consonant-plus-**r**. After singing a song, ask the children to recall some of the consonant-plus-**r** words.

Reading and fluency

'Tricky' word
Show the 'Tricky' Word Card: **into**. Cover half the card and ask the children to read **in** and then read the other half, **to**. Mark the **o** with a wavy line below, as it is not making its usual sound. Then show the whole word and ask the children to read it when you push it forward several times, "**into, into...**"

'Tricky' word

Phonics Readers 3b: *What can you see?*
Today's story is about Golden Girl watching things up close in her garden. Guide children in reading the story. Then re-read this one and a few previous stories with a partner.

Fluency List K *(TGCD)*
Introduce this new list with echo reading and then choral reading (page 214).

Phonics Readers 3a

Lesson 52: Spelling words
Consonant plus r

You'll need
✓ *PCCs for 'Guess Who?' plus* **c, f** *and* **g**
✓ *Phonics Readers 3b*
✓ *Fluency List K (TGCD)*
✓ *Whitebard or other writing materials*

✓ Make the 'Tricky' Word Cards: **can't, ask**
Optional
✓ *Individual activities (Activity Bank)*
✓ *Letters/words to Picture Code*

Review previously learned letters and sounds

'Guess Who?' *PCCs*: **ă, b, ĕ, d, ĭ, m, n, o, p, r, ŭ, ck, sh, ss**

'Live Spelling'

Spelling with Picture Code Cards

Distribute *PCCs* from 'Guess Who?' plus **c**, **f**, **g**

Words: **brick, crab, drum, grin, drop, fresh, press**

Lead children to stretch and segment and then form the first word. They can then do the Roller Coaster Trick to check their spelling.

Ask one child who doesn't have a *PCC* to act as Stretching Leader to demonstrate the stretch and segment strategy before the rest of the class does it. Change leaders after every word or two.

Write the words on the board as each one is completed (or ask a child to do it).

After 'Live Spelling' all the words, children then read the list on the board in order as you point to the words. Repeat once or twice, a bit faster each time.

Segmenting

Written spelling (page 209)

Call out the words below, say them in a sentence and repeat the word. Children repeat, stretch and segment it, then write it on erasable whiteboards or on paper. Ask them to check their spelling with the Roller Coaster Trick.

Words: **crush, bring, frog, dress, grass**

Make sure that everyone has the correct spelling by observing, or by providing the spelling on the board after they have written it. Then remove the word. Children cover their word with their hands and spell it aloud.

Word Detectives

Read the sentences on the board with the children a few times. Then ask the children to Picture Code or underline the **r** and the consonant before it (separate underlines).

Can you grab that frog that is hopping on the grass?

Who is that going trip-trap, trip-trap on my bridge?

Reading and fluency

'Tricky' word

Show the word card **can't**. Say the word and use it in a sentence or two. Explain that this an important little word to know because it is one of the 65 most used words in the English language. It is a contraction, or a quick way of saying '**cannot**'. (See more on contractions, page 213.) The other 'tricky' word introduced in this story is **ask**. Depending on regional accents, let children tell you if there needs to be a wavy line below it.

'Tricky' word

Phonics Readers 3b: *Can a crab grab?*

Guide children in reading these silly rhymes. Ask them to re-read it with a partner and also a few previous stories.

Fluency List K *(TGCD)*

Revise the list with children and ask them to re-read it with a partner at some time during the day.

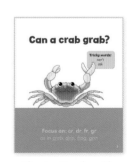

Phonics Readers 3b

Individual activity

Picture Coding

Provide large letter words with consonant-plus-**r** pairs (e.g, **crib**, **trap**) for children to Picture Code.

Lesson 53
Review

You'll need
- ✓ PCCs for 'Quick Dash'
- ✓ Blends & Digraphs Songs CD
- ✓ Phonics Readers 3b
- ✓ Fluency List K (TGCD)
- ✓ Reading Racer Charts
- ✓ Make a 'Tricky' Word Card: **don't**

Optional
- ✓ Individual activities (Activity Bank)
- ✓ Workbooks 1-6

'**Quick Dash**' *PCCs*: ă, b, c, ĕ, g, ĭ, l, n, o, p, r, s, t, ŭ, ck, ll, ss

'Live Reading' and 'Live Spelling'

'Live Reading'

Line children up to make the first word for the class to do the Roller Coaster Trick. For each subsequent word you will only need to change a few letters so you can build all the words at a quick pace for review.

Distribute the 17 *PCCs* from 'Quick Dash' above for 'Live Reading' and 'Live Spelling'.

Words for 'Live Reading': **spill, snap, trap, press, plan, clap**

Pop up 'Live Spelling'

Use the same *PCCs* as in 'Quick Dash' above. Say the first word and ask the children to stretch and segment it. Children with the *PCCs* needed in the word pop up and line up to form the word. The rest of the class blends the word to check the spelling and suggests changes if needed. (See page 229.)

Children in the first word stay in place as everyone segments the next word.

Children who are not in the word sit down. Those children needed in the new word pop up and help form it. The class checks the spelling of each word with the Roller Coaster Trick.

Songs

Review or listen for the first time to some of the songs on the *Blends & Digraphs CD* featuring adjacent consonants with **s**, **l** and **r**. After singing a song, ask the children to recall some of the words beginning with the featured pair of consonants.

Reading and fluency

'Tricky' word

Show the word card **don't**. Say the word and use it in a sentence or two. Explain that this is an important little word to know how to read because it is one of the 65 most used words in our English language. It is a contraction, or a quick way of saying '**do not**', with an apostrophe taking the place of the missing letter. Use the Rubber Band Trick to guide children to discover that Mr O is saying his name in this word. Picture code the **o** with a stick figure Mr O. Then children say the word each time you push the word card forward, "**don't**, **don't**..." (For more on contractions, see page 213.)

'Tricky' word

Phonics Readers 3b: *Snow on the hill*

Guide children in reading *the story*. Then ask them to re-read this story and the previous one with partners (page 217).

Phonics Readers 3b

Fluency List K *(TGCD)*

Ask children to practise their list with a partner (page 214).

Call out one or two sentences from the story or the *Fluency List* for children to write. Help them make corrections as needed for spelling, punctuation, and capitalisation. (For more suggestions, see page 214.)

Individual activity

Writing topic

Children may enjoy sharing their own experiences with snow or other outdoor events. This could lead to writing and illustrating.
Workbooks 1-6 Complete the pages in Workbook 3.

Lesson 54
Final -nd, -nt, -nk

You'll need

✓ *PCCs for 'Guess Who?'* plus **c, d, h**
✓ *Phonics Readers 3b*
✓ *Fluency List K (TGCD)*
✓ *Reading Racer Charts*

✓ Make an apostrophe card to match *PCCs* in size
✓ Make the 'Tricky' Word Cards: **asked, gave**

Optional

✓ Individual activities (Activity Bank)

Review previously learned letters and sounds

'Guess Who?' *PCCs*: ă, b, ĕ, ĭ, k, l, n, p, s, t, ŭ, w, ck, th, ng

Introducing -nd

We will often find Noisy Nick near the end of a word with Dippy Duck but we will still hear him making his /**nnn**/ sound and Dippy Duck saying /**d**/ as usual, as well. Let's try a few words.

Blending

Blending with Picture Code Cards

Make the –**nd** words below and guide children in the Roller Coaster Trick.
PCCs from 'Guess Who?' plus **c, d, h**

Words with –**nd**: **and, hand, sand, stand, end, send**

After children read the word, use it in a sentence or ask them to do an action that demonstrates the meaning of the word (e.g. wave with their **hand**, point to two other children as if saying 'you **and** you',).

Introducing -nt

We may also hear Noisy Nick at the end of words with Talking Tess. Make the -**nt** words for the Roller Coaster Trick.

Words with –**nt**: **went, ant, pant, plant**

Introducing -nk

Display the *PCCs* **n** and **k**.

Now when Noisy Nick gets behind Kicking King's back he doesn't make his usual /**nnn**/ sound. Instead he makes his singing sound /**ng**/ even though Golden Girl isn't there to make it with him. And something else unusual happens, too.

Blending with Picture Code Cards

Make the word **pick** as shown and ask the children to blend it. Then ask the children to explain why Clever Cat likes to be at the end of a word with Kicking King. (**"She likes to watch him kick when he has plenty of room to do it at the end of a word."**)

PCCs from 'Guess Who? plus **d**

> Words **pick/pink, in/ink, thin/think, tan/tank, sun/sunk, drink**

Replace **ck** in **pick** with the **n** and **k** to make **pink**.

When Noisy Nick makes his singing sound, Clever Cat is startled by this change of tune and runs away instead of staying to watch Kicking King kick.

Lead children in the Roller Coaster Trick for **pink** with Nick's singing sound /**ng**/.

To help children hear Nick 'change his tune', make the word **in** for children to read. Then add **k** to make **ink** for them to read. Do the same with the other pairs of words listed above. Finally make the five-sound word, **drink**.

'Tricky' words

Reading and fluency

'Tricky' words

Teach the words **asked** and **gave**.

After Lesson 56 **gave** will be decodable.

Phonics Readers 3b

Phonics Readers 3b: *Sink or float?*

Guide children in reading the story (for suggestions, see page 217). Children may want to plan and carry out their own sink-or-float activity.

Fluency List K *(TGCD)*

Time children reading this list (page 214).

Home link

Make copies of the Section 3 *Take-Home Booklets* from the *TGCD* for children to read in class and then take home to read to their parents. For further instructions, see *TGCD*.

Take-Home Booklet

Assessment - Refer to your TGCD

> Use the Section 3 assessments a few days to two weeks after completing the final lesson in Section 3.
>
> All assessment material including full instructions and Assessment forms are on the *TGCD*.

Section 4 :
Long Vowels

Lesson Chart

Lesson	Lesson focus	Example word	Letterland Concept	Story from *Phonics Readers*	'Tricky' word	Set/Book	
55	**y**	my	Yo-yo Man works for Mr I	Can Zig Zag fly?		3b	
56	**a_e**	make	Silent Magic e	You and me	your, does	3c	
57	**i_e, wr**	like, write	Silent Magic e	Ben rides his bike	put	3c	
58	**e_e, o_e, u_e** (ph)	these, home, cube (phone)	Silent Magic e	Rose bakes a cake	play	3c	
59	Revision	-	-	Pete and Nate's fun and games	now, later	3c	
60	**ed, ed, ed**	skated, smiled, hoped	Magic ending	What they liked to do		3c	
61	**ed, ed, ed**	landed, slammed, clapped	Magic ending	Look what happened!	story, reading	3d	
62	**y**	baby	Yo-yo Man works for Mr E	Happy times		3d	
63	**ai, ay**	rain, say	Vowels out walking	My puppy	down	3d	
64	**ee**	bee	Vowels out walking	Mr E's trees	out, our, eat	3d	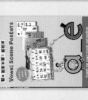
65	**ea**	sea	Vowels out walking	Molly and me by the sea	water, two	3e	
66	**oa**	boat	Vowels out walking	The bad goat		3e	
67	**ie, ue**	tie, blue	Vowels out walking	What a mess	one	3e	
68	Revision	-	-	Stop the train!	there	3e	
69	**ild, ind, old**	mild, kind, cold	Vowel Men's habits	Gifts	about	4a	

Further resources

Blends & Digraphs CD

Picture Code Cards

Beyond ABC

Far Beyond ABC

Vowel Scene Posters

Magnetic Word Builder

Story Phonics Software

Teacher's Guide CD

Section 4 Assessment

Fluency Lists L–O

Take-Home Booklets

Long Vowels

Long vowel patterns require children to look beyond a single vowel letter to pronounce the sound of the vowel. By learning the story logic of the split digraph, children learn not one long vowel pattern but five patterns that signal long vowel sounds. Also in this section, the Vowel Men out walking story is applied to six long vowel digraphs. Together these and other phonic concepts help children read and spell thousands of new words.

Contents

y as a vowel	**y** /ī/ **y** /ē/
Split digraph	**a_e e_e i_e o_e u_e**
-ed suffix	**ed**/ed/ **ed**/d/ **ed**/t/
Vowel digraphs	**ai ay ea ee ie oa ue**
Single long vowels	**-ind -ild -old**

Objectives

By the end of this section, children should be able to:

- Say the sound of split digraphs and long vowel digraphs when shown the plain letters
- Say three sounds for **y** and three for **–ed** when shown the plain letters
- Blend and segment words with long vowels
- Decode words with suffix **-ed**
- Read seventeen additional 'tricky' words (total: 47)
- Read decodable text containing long vowel words with accuracy, fluency, and comprehension.

Practise and apply

Children continue to use learning activities and practise content from previous sections along with the new strategies and variations below:

Role-playing the story logic Children enjoying enacting the Letterland stories.

Animation Children enjoying watching the Letterland stories come to life in the *Story Phonics* software.

Word Detectives This activity is especially important with vowel digraphs and split digraphs because children practise looking beyond single letters to decode new words.

Vowel Scene Posters The posters remind children to look for patterns in their reading and writing.

Blends & Digraph Songs The songs help make the story logic even more engaging and memorable for children.

Phonics Readers There are 15 *Phonics Reader* stories to accompany this section. The stories are more in-depth and interesting.

'Tricky' words introduced in Section 4

your	does	put	play
now	later	story	reading
down	out	our	eat
water	two	one	there
about			

y as in my

You'll need

- ✓ *PCCs* for 'Quick Dash' plus **y**/ī/
- ✓ *Phonics Readers 3b*
- ✓ *Fluency List L (TGCD)*
- ✓ Make a 'Tricky' Word Card: **ask**

- ✓ Write sentences for Word Detectives (p.126) on the board

Optional

- ✓ Individual activities (Activity Bank)
- ✓ Large words for Picture Coding

Review previously learned letters and sounds

'Quick Dash' *PCCs*: ǎ, b, c, d, f, k, l, m, p, r, s, t, y, sh

Yellow Yo-yo Man works for Mr I

Display the picture side of the Yellow Yo-yo Man *PCC* with his yo-yo's.

Yellow Yo-yo Man likes to appear in words, but there are not many words that start with his /**yyy**/ sound. So he doesn't get many chances to sell his yo-yos. Luckily, he sometimes gets to work for Mr I in words.

Let's see how that happens in the word **my**. Say a sentence using the word **my**. Ask the children to repeat the word and then stretch and segment it.

PCCs from Quick Dash plus **y**/ī/.

> Words: **my, by, try, fly, sky**

Picture Code Cards

Show the plain letter **m** *PCC*. First we hear /**mmm**/. Then we hear / ī /. Place the Mr I *PCC* (picture side) to make **mi**.

Mr I comes rushing up to Yellow Yo-yo Man and says, "Oh, my. Almost every time I have to be at the end of a word, I start to feel dizzy... as if I were about to fall off a cliff! (Rock Mr I's *PCC* back and forth a bit.) Do you think you could take my place right at the end of a few little words and say my name for me? I'll even give you one of my fine ice creams, if you will." Yellow Yo-yo Man cries, "Yes, yes please!"

Replace Mr I with the Yo-yo Man with an ice cream *PCC* to make **my**. Yellow Yo-yo Man is happy to help – in fact he loves to appear at the end of words, because Mr I gives him a yummy, big ice cream as a reward every time! We will even find him saying / ī / for Mr I inside a few words, as well. Make each word above for children to blend.

Group activities

'Live Spelling'

Distribute these *PCCs*: c, d, ī, m, p, r, s, y/ī/, sh

> Words: **mi/my, dri/dry, spi/spy, shi/shy, cri/cry***

After children stretch and segment the first word, ask them to form it with Mr I on the end (**mi**). Ask Mr I to act as if he is dizzy and ask the Yo-yo Man to take his place. Children can then use the Roller Coaster Trick to blend the now correctly spelled word, **my**.

Let different children play the roles of Yellow Yo-yo Man and Mr I for each word. Follow similar steps as with **my** to 'Live Spell' the rest of the words above.

* There are only about 25 further English words that end in **y** saying **i** that children might need early on. They include **identify**, **multiply** and **magnify**.

Word Detectives

Children Picture Code the **y**'s with ice cream cones.

Why did the Zebra jump to the sky?

Oh, my, she thinks she can fly!

Reading and fluency

Phonics Readers 3b: *Can Zig Zag fly?*

Read the story and ask the children to practise this brief rhyming story until they can read it with some zing! (page 217)

Fluency List L *(TGCD)*

Introduce this new list (more on page 214).

Phonics Readers 3b

Note: For **y** sounding like **e** (as in baby), see Lesson 62, page 136.

Lesson 56: Silent Magic e

a_e as in make

Focus on **a_e**

You'll need

✓ *PCCs for 'Guess Who?' plus* **l**, **m**, **n**, *Silent Magic* **e**
✓ *Far Beyond ABC and/or Story Phonics Software*
✓ *Blends & Digraphs Songs CD*

✓ *Phonics Readers 3c*
✓ *Fluency List L (TGCD)*
✓ Make 'Tricky' Word Cards: **your, does**
✓ Write Word Detective sentence on the board
✓ A magic wand

Review previously learned letters and sounds

'Guess Who?' *PCCs*: ă, ā, c, d, ĕ, f, h, ĭ, k, p, s, t, ŭ, ch

---

New concept - Silent Magic e

Teacher reference

Show the Silent Magic **e** *PCC*. Do you know this special kind of **e**? This is a Silent Magic **e**, invented by Mr E. When he made this **e**, he announced:

'Introducing the **e** you cannot hear
with the power to make Vowel Men appear.'

The magic sparks always jump back over one letter to land on a vowel.

You can see this story animated on the *Story Phonics* software or read more about Mr E's invention in the *Far Beyond ABC* book.

All the Vowel Men were delighted with what Silent Magic **e** could do! They decided to call it their Naming Game.

* Note: Silent letters in Letterland products are usually coloured grey, but the final **e** here, although a silent letter, is a 'Stop-Look-and-Listen' colour, red. This is to emphasise its power and to signal the presence of a long vowel earlier in the word.

Silent Magic e poster

Group activities

Blending a_e words

Make the word **tap** with the Mr A *PCC* hidden behind Annie Apple. Ask the children to blend it using the **Roller Coaster Trick**. Use it in a brief sentence.

PCCs for 'Guess Who?' plus **m**, **n**, *Silent Magic* **e**.

Words: **tap/tape, can/cane, Sam/same**

Now let's put Mr E's Silent Magic **e** on the end. Place the Silent Magic **e** *PCC* to make **tape**. Wave the magic wand that you have made above Annie Apple as shown. Swap Mr A to the front. The Silent Magic **e** shoots its sparks back over one letter. They land on Annie Apple and make her disappear! In her place Mr A appears and calls out his name! Remember the **e** is silent. It doesn't make a sound at all, but it is powerful. Making that Vowel Man appear has even made a completely new word! Lead children in blending to discover the new word **tape**. Let volunteers wave the wand and move the *PCCs* as you do the same with **can/cane**, **Sam/same**.

Picture Code Cards

Song

Enjoy the Silent Magic **e** song on the *Blends & Digraphs Songs CD* and/or *Story Phonics* software (lyrics on *TGCD*).

'Live Reading'

Distribute *PCCs* for 'Guess Who?' plus Silent Magic **e**, **l**, **n** .

Words: **cap/cape, hat/hate, plan/plane, chase, chat, safe, lake**

Children with vowels show the picture side, the rest show the plain letter.

Ask the children to make the word **cap** with the Mr A child hiding behind Annie Apple. All blend **cap** using the **Roller Coaster Trick**. Now let's play the Naming Game. The Silent Magic **e** child joins the word, waves the magic wand above Annie Apple who 'disappears' as Mr A takes her place and the class blend **cape**. Do the same with **hat/hate** and **plan/plane**. (You could also remove the **e** child and see Annie Apple 'reappear'.)

Children predict

Beginning with the word **chase**, children all show plain letters. Then let the class decide if the Letterlander behind the letter **a** will be Annie Apple or Mr A. The child holding the vowel *PCC* flips it over to confirm their decision. Then all the children do the **Roller Coaster Trick** to blend the word.

Word Detectives

Ask the children to Picture Code Mr A, Silent Magic **e** and the magic sparks in this sentence on the board:

It's fun to gaze at the crane as it wades in the lake.

Mr A and Silent Magic e
Far Beyond ABC

Phonemic awareness and language development

Share the **a_e** scene in the *Story Phonics* software and/or *Far Beyond ABC* book for children to listen for words and look for pictures of words with **a_e**.

Reading and fluency

'Tricky' words

Teach the 'tricky' words **your** and **does**.

'Tricky' words

Phonics Readers 3c: *Tales of two*

Ask the children to hunt for and decode the Silent Magic **e** words in this story before they read it (for more suggestions, see page 217).

Fluency List L *(TGCD)*

Revise this list with the children and provide time for them to practise it with partners. (Full details on page 214.)

Phonics Readers 3c

Lesson 57: Silent Magic e
i_e as in like

You'll need
- ✓ PCCs for 'Quick Dash' plus **d, f, ĭ, ī, l, r, z**
- ✓ *Far Beyond ABC* and/or *Story Phonics* software
- ✓ Magic wand from previous lesson

- ✓ *Phonics Readers 3c*
- ✓ *Fluency List L (TGCD)*
- ✓ Make a 'Tricky' Word Card: **put**
- ✓ Write the Word Detectives sentence on the board

Review previously learned letters and sounds
'Quick Dash' *PCCs:* ă, ā, b, c, Silent Magic e, ĭ, ī, k, m, n, s, t, sh

Review Silent Magic e concept - 'Live Reading'
Distribute the *PCCs* from 'Quick Dash' except for ĭ, ī

> Words: **back/bake, snack/snake, make, take, cake, shake**

Line children up to form the word **back** using the separate **c** and **k** *PCCs* instead of **ck**. Ask Mr A to hide behind Annie Apple. Children use the **Roller Coaster Trick** to blend **back**. Then ask why Clever Cat likes to be on the end of the word with Kicking King ("to watch him kick"). Now let's add Silent Magic **e** on the end. The Silent Magic **e** child stands after Kicking King and reaches over waving the magic wand above Clever Cat. Clever Cat doesn't want magic sparks on her fur so she runs away. (Clever Cat sits down.) Now Silent Magic **e**'s sparks make Annie Apple disappear as the Mr A, appears. (They change places.) Children use the **Roller Coaster Trick** to blend the word **bake**.

Do the same with different children for **snack/snake** and other words above.

Picture Code Cards

Silent Magic e makes Mr I appear
PCCs: **b, d,** Silent Magic **e, f, ĭ, ī, k, l, n, r, s, z**

> Words: **fin, fine, like, skin, size, bike, bid, ride**

Set out the word **fin** for children to blend, with the Mr I *PCC* hidden behind Impy Ink. Ask the children to predict what will happen when Silent Magic **e** is added to the end of the word. Then place Silent Magic **e** at the end. Wave the magic wand above Impy Ink and move Mr I in front of Impy Ink to make the word **fine**. Make the additional words above with plain letters. Ask the children to predict who is hiding behind the vowel and flip it to the picture side before they do the **Roller Coaster Trick**.

Mr I and Silent Magic e
Far Beyond ABC

Phonemic awareness and language development
Share the **i_e** scene in the *Story Phonics* software and/or *Far Beyond ABC* book for children to listen for words and look for pictures of words with **i_e**.

Word Detectives
Ask the children to Picture Code Mr I, Silent Magic **e** and the magic sparks in this sentence on the board:

> **Ben rides his bike for nine miles.**

'Tricky' word

Reading and fluency

'Tricky' word Teach the word **put** as shown. (Fully decodable after Lesson 81).

Phonics Readers 3c: *Ben rides his bike*
Guide the children in reading the story (page 217).

Fluency List L *(TGCD)* Ask partners to practise this list as you observe.

Phonics Readers 3c

wr as in write

Sound

A word children are guranteed to come across early on in their learning is 'write', so it is worth looking briefly at the explanation for the sound they hear at the start of this word. Show children the **wr** PCC with Walter Walrus being captured by Red Robot. Push the card forward as they say the sound, "/r/..."

Phonemic awareness and language development

Share the **wr** scene in the *Story Phonics* software and/or *Beyond ABC* Book about these two trouble-makers. Ask the children to listen for the sound and look for pictured words that start with the sound.

Song

Listen to the *Blends & Digraphs* song (lyrics on *TGCD*). Show the picture side of the **wr** PCC. When we see these two together, we just hear /r/.

Blending wr words

Make the words below for children to blend and use them in sentences.

Walter Walrus and
Red Robot in
Beyond ABC

> Words to blend: **write, wrist, wreck, wrong**

Lesson 58: Silent Magic e

e_e, o_e, u_e as in these, home, cube

You'll need

- ✓ PCCs for 'Guess Who?' plus **b, h, j, l, m, n, ss**
- ✓ *Far Beyond ABC* and/or *Story Phonics* software
- ✓ Magic wand from previous lesson
- ✓ *Phonics Readers 3c*
- ✓ *Fluency List L (TGCD)*
- ✓ 'Tricky' Word Card: **play**

Review previously learned letters and sounds

'Guess Who?' *PCCs:* **c, ĕ, ē,** Silent Magic e, **l, o, ō, p, r, s/z/, t, ŭ, ū, th**

As you know, there are three more Vowel Men in Letterland: Mr E, Mr O and Mr U. Do you remember the Naming Game?

'Introducing the **e** you cannot hear
with the power to make Vowel Men appear.'

Let's play that game with these other Vowel Men

Mr E, Mr O, Mr U and Silent Magic e

Set out the word **pet** for children to blend, with the Mr E PCC hidden behind Eddy Elephant.

Children predict what will happen when Silent Magic **e** is added to the end of the word. Wave the magic wand above Eddy Elephant and move Mr E in front to make the name **Pete**. Children use the Roller Coaster Trick to blend the sounds to discover or confirm the new word. Follow the same procedure as described for **e_e** with Silent Magic e making Mr O and Mr U appear creating the words **hop/hope** and **cut/cute.**

Phonemic awareness and language development
Share these three scenes in the *Story Phonics* software and/or *Far Beyond ABC* Book for children to listen for words and look for pictures of words with each of the split digraphs.

Silent Magic e in *Far Beyond ABC*

Group activities

Blending split digraph words
PCCs from 'Guess Who' plus **h, m, n**

> Words: **hop/hope, cut/cute, pet/Pete, home, rope, plus, use, tune, hunt, these**

'Live Spelling'
Distribute *PCCs* from 'Guess Who?' plus **b, j, l, n, ss**

> Words: **hope, cone, crop, tube, June, less, close, these**

Keep the Silent Magic **e** child in front of the class.

Call out the words above. After children stretch and segment each word, ask them to decide which vowel is needed and whether or not Silent Magic **e** is needed.

Reading and fluency

'Tricky' word
Teach the 'tricky' word **play**.

'Tricky' word

Phonics Readers 3c: *Rose bakes a cake*
Ask the children to read the title and look at the first few illustrations and then make predictions about the story.

Partner reading
Ask partners to re-read this story and a few previous ones, either at this point or later in the day.

Fluency List L *(TGCD)*
Continue with this list using some of the suggestions on page 214.

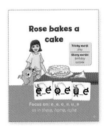

Phonics Readers 3c

ph as in phone

Sound
Another word children will inevitably come across early on in their learning is 'phone', so it is worth looking briefly at the explanation for the sound they hear at the start of this word.

Phonemic awareness and language development
Share the **ph** scene in the *Story Phonics* software and/or *Far Beyond ABC* book that explain the story logic. Ask the children to listen for the sound and look for pictured words that start with the sound.

Show children the **ph** PCC with Harry Hat Man taking a photo of Peter Puppy. Push the card forward as they say the sound, "/**fff**/.../**fff**/..."

Peter Puppy and Harry Hat Man in *Beyond ABC*

Blend
Make the words **phone** and **graph** with *PCCs* for blending.

Song
Listen to the *Blends & Digraphs Song* about these two characters.

Review

You'll need

✓ PCCs for 'Quick Dash' plus ā, ē, Silent Magic e, g, ī, l, m, n, ō, o/ŭ/, s/z/, ū, th
✓ Magic wand from previous lesson

✓ Phonics Readers 3c
✓ Fluency List L (TGCD)
✓ Reading Racer Charts (TGCD)
✓ Magnetic Word Builder or other letter sets
✓ 'Tricky' Word Cards: **now**, **later**

Review previously learned letters and sounds

'**Quick Dash**' PCCs: ā, ē, Silent Magic e, g, ī, l, m, n, ō, o/ŭ/, s/z/, ū, th

Blending and segmenting

'Live Reading'

Distribute the 15 PCCs from 'Quick Dash' plus **c, d, f, ĭ, p, s, t**

Words: **game, mine, mile, pole, those, these, use, tune, inside, confuse**

Line children up to make each word for the rest of the class to blend. For the words **inside** (**in side**) and **confuse** (**con fuse**), leave a space between the children in the first syllable and the last. Ask the class to do the Roller Coaster Trick to blend the sounds in each syllable. Then ask them to close the gap between the syllables and read the whole word.

Spelling with Magnetic Word Builders

Letters: **a, b, c, d, e, e, h, i, k, l, m, m, o, p, r, s, t, u, v**

Words: **lick, like, mile, drive, drop, rose, use, cube, cut, cute, homemade**

Children use the Magnetic Word Builder (or other sets of letters).

As you use the Rubber Band Trick on the words to spell, listen closely for the vowel sound. If it is a Vowel Man's name, what will you need on the end? "**Silent Magic e**"

Say the word, say it in a sentence and repeat the word. Children repeat the word and stretch and segment it. Then they build the word with their own set of letters (see page 214.) For the compound word **homemade** (**home made**) ask the children to stretch and segment and spell one syllable at a time.

Magnetic Word Builder

Reading and fluency

'Tricky' words

Show the cards you have made **now** and **later**. Read them out, say the words in a sentence and guide children to stretch and segment them. Ask them which letters are not making their usual sounds and mark them with a wavy line as shown in the margin. Practise the word by pushing it forward a few times for children to read it: "**now, later**..." Both of these words will become fully decodable in lessons to follow.

'Tricky' words

Phonics Readers 3c: *Pete and Nate's fun and games*

After reading this story, encourage the children to talk about all the things that the two boys did and why Pete thanked Nate at the end.

Partner reading

Ask partners to re-read this one and a few previous stories again.

Phonics Readers 3c

Fluency List L *(TGCD)*

Time the children reading this list with partners (twice each) to check their fluency (page 214). Ask them to graph the results on their charts.

Individual activities

Writing topic

- This story may spur children to talk about their own visits to the sea or other places. They may want to draw and write about their experiences.
- Introduce the relevant pages to revise these sounds in the *Blends & Digraphs Copymasters*.
- Introduce the relevant pages *Workbook 4*.
- Ask the children to fill some words in their *Word Bank Copymasters*.

a-e words		**e-e words**		**i-e words**		**o-e words**		**u-e words**	
came	race	these	theme	like	slide	bone	stone	June	huge
made	same	Pete	gene	time	prize	pole	woke	flute	cube
make	snake	Eve	scene	pine	nice	home	note	prune	tube
take	amaze	Steve	complete	ripe	invite	alone	explode	rude	use
game	escape	even	extreme	shine	inside	those	envelope	rule	

Lesson 60: Magic ending

ed as in skated, smiled, hoped

You'll need

✓ PCCs for 'Guess Who?' plus **b, c, d, l, m, ed**/ed/, **ed**/d/, **ed**/t/

✓ Phonics Readers 3c
✓ Fluency List M (TGCD)
✓ Write the Word Detective sentences on the board

Review previously learned letters and sounds

'Guess Who?' *PCCs:* ā, Silent Magic **e, h, ī, k, l, m, ō, r, s, s/z/, v, w, ch**

New concept - The three sounds of -ed

Teacher reference

1. Sometimes at the end of a word you will hear Eddy Elephant and Dippy Duck making their usual sounds, as expect**ed**.

as expect**ed**

2. At other times Eddy Elephant has completely disappear**ed**!

disappear**ed**

3. More amazing still, sometimes both Eddy Elephant and Dippy Duck have vanish**ed**. The only person who notic**ed** them do this trick is Talking Tess who, quite astonish**ed** says '**t**!'.

vanish**ed**ᵗ

These are all Magic Endings, and the magic never disappears.

We are now going to look at the endings of some words. Many words end in **ed**, but **ed** makes three different sounds.

First ed /ed/

Make the word **skate** with *PCCs* with picture sides for Mr A and Silent Magic **e** only. Use it in a sentence, e.g. "We like to skate in winter."

Now let's turn **skate** into skat**ed**. (Remove the Magic **e** card and add **ed**, plain letter side.) We can say, "We skat**ed** yesterday." It means we did it in the past.

Base words and suffixes

So we have added a suffix **ed** to our base word **skate**. This **ed** is a suffix just like –**s** added onto words. We add the suffix –**ed** to the base word to tell us that something happened in the past.

Sound of ed/ed/

Now, let's listen to see what this suffix sounds like in **skated**. Let's say **skated** in two parts like this **skate-ed**, "**skat-ed**." I can hear both Eddy Elephant and Dippy Duck's sounds at the end. Can you?

Magic Ending

But Mr A is still there saying his name even though we took away Silent Magic **e**! So this must be a Magic Ending!

Turn to the picture side. Point out the top hat, the magic wand and the sparks on the **ed**/ed/ *PCC*.

Eddy Elephant enjoyed Mr E's magic tricks so much that Mr E kindly gave Eddy his own top hat and wand, asked him to take a friend (Dippy Duck who was delight**ed**) and put him in charge of every **ed** ending.

Just like Silent Magic **e**, Magic **ed** has the power to make a Vowel Man appear.

Write '**ed**' on the board, with **skated** under it.

Make the words below. The children can read them and use them in sentences.

Words with **ed**/ed/: **skate/skated, trade/traded, wade/waded**

Picture Code Cards

ed words

hated	quoted
sided	voted
invited	skated

Second ed/d/

Make the word **wave** for children to blend. Now let's add the past tense suffix to our base word **wave** and read this word, "**waved**." Here's Magic **ed** again, but I can't hear Eddy. Can you? ... Sometimes Eddy Elephant has disappeared, hiding behind his letter – just for fun. When he's hiding, we just hear /**d**/ at the end, but he still uses his magic wand to make a Vowel Man appear.

Show picture side of the *PCC*. Make these pairs of words:

Words with **ed**/d/: **smile/smiled, close/closed**

Picture Code Cards

ed words

blamed	saved
lined	surprised
phoned	used

Third ed/t/

PCC as shown on the right, plain side first.

Make the word **bake** for the Roller Coaster Trick. Now if we want to say, "We **baked** a cake yesterday," we will need our Magic **ed** again. Ask the children to stretch and segment **baked**. Now what can you hear at the end? "/**t**/". Yes, you have just discovered the third sound of –**ed**!

Sometimes Eddy Elephant and Dippy Duck *both* play a disappearing game. Talking Tess is the only one that sees them do it. She is too astonished^t to say anything except her usual quiet /**t**/ sound. Show *PCC* picture side to confirm.

Make the additional words for the Roller Coaster Trick:

Words with **ed**/t/: **bake/baked, hope/hoped, chase/chased**

Picture Code Cards

ed words

choked	produced
coped	scraped
priced	stroked

Word Detectives

Ask the children to write little letters above each **ed** to indicate the sound: **ed**,

d, or **t**, in this sentence on the board.

> The big walrus waded into the water, dived and chased after a fish.

Reading and fluency

Phonics Readers 3c: *What they liked to do*
Read the story with children using some of the usual strategies (page 217).
Later children can make three columns of words from the story, for the three
sounds of **ed**.

Fluency List M *(TGCD)*
Distribute this new list to children which revises words from *Phonics Readers 3c*
and the latest five lessons. Echo read one line at a time with the children. Then
read chorally. Make time later for children to re-read the list with a partner.

Phonics Readers 3c

Lesson 61: Best friends to the rescue
ed as in landed, slammed, clapped

You'll need
✓ *PCCs for 'Quick Dash' plus* **ă, b, g, h, ĭ, k, ng, sh** *and
   a second PCC for* **b, g, p, t**

✓ *Phonics Readers 3d*
✓ *Fluency List M (TGCD)*
✓ Magic wand from previous lessons
✓ 'Tricky' Word Cards: **story, reading**

Review previously learned letters and sounds
'Quick Dash' *PCCs:* **ā**, Silent Magic **e, h, ī, k, l, m, ō, r, s, s/z/, ū, v, w, ch**

'Live Spelling': Review of Magic -ed
Distribute the *PCCs* from 'Quick Dash' plus **sh**

> Words: **trade/traded, shape/shaped, use/used, dive/dived,
> hate/hated, like/liked**

Ask the three children with the picture sides of the three **–ed** *PCCs* to go to the
right of your 'Live Spelling' area where everyone can see them.

Give other children the remaining *PCCs*. Children stretch and segment **trade**.
After they 'Live Spell' it, ask them to say and listen to the past tense **traded**
and decide which **–ed** is need. Ask the **ed**/ed/ child to replace Silent Magic **e**
on the end to make the word **traded**.

Now let's look at that magic ending more carefully.

Build the word **land** for children to blend using the Roller Coaster Trick. Add
the **ed**/ed/ *PCC*, plain side. Ask the children to fill in the last word of a sentence
ending with **landed** (e.g. *"It was two o'clock when the plane _____."*).
Children decide what the **–ed** sounds like and predict who they think it will be.
(**"Eddy Elephant and Dippy Duck"**). Confirm or correct them with the picture
side. Remember that magic sparks can only go over one letter so you can still
hear Annie Apple's sound in the word: **landed**

New concept - Best Friends to the Rescue

Teacher reference

Your aim here is to show that the most frequent function of double consonants is to protect short vowel sounds.

tăp   tāped   tăpped

hŏp   hōped   hŏpped

You might want to share this bit of additional lore as you teach this lesson. Now Mr E's Magic Endings were working so well in Letterland that the Vowel Men were getting a bit tired having to appear in so many words. Mr e can't undo his magic so what could they do? The clever idea they had was to bring in a **Best Friend to the Rescue!**

PCCs from 'Quick Dash' plus ă, **b** (Bouncy Ben), **b** (Bouncy Barbara), **g**, (Golden Granny) ĭ, **n, o, p** (Patsy Puppy), **t** (Talking Tom)

spotted /ed/, **hugged** /d/, **grabbed** /d/, **slipped** /t/

Make the word **spot**, with only Oscar's picture side and the Mr O card hidden behind it. Now listen to this sentence and finish it by adding **ed** to the word **spot**: *A zebra is striped but a leopard is _____. Yes, spott-ed!* We hear **ed** so we need Eddy and Dippy Duck.

Place the **ed**/ed/ *PCC* to temporarily spell **spoted**. Now we have a problem. Look, Eddy is shooting the magic sparks over one letter, so what is going to happen when they land on the vowel? Yes, Mr O is going to appear.

Move Mr O to the front, covering Oscar Orange.
That would turn our word into **spōted** (rhymes with voted). That's not even a word! Luckily the Letterlanders have worked out a way to fix this problem. They call it 'Best Friends to the Rescue.' They know that the magic sparks can only reach back over ONE letter to land on a vowel. So the last letter calls their best friend to help block the magic, Best Friends Together make only ONE sound.

Talking Tess's best friend Talking Tom joins her. Show both **t**s' picture sides in the word. Replace Mr O with Oscar. Now when the magic sparks fly over one letter, they can't reach Oscar Orange. Talking Tess and Talking Tom have blocked them, rescuing Oscar from disappearing. And we have the word we wanted to spell, **spotted**. Say it with me, "**spotted.**"

Make more words with some of the best friends coming to the rescue. Ask the children to add the best friends and retell why they are needed.

Note: At this point children are not expected to always spell words correctly with consonants that double before a vowel suffix. Teaching this concept now is mainly to clear up any confusion in reading such words.

Bouncy Barbara

Diana Duck

Firefighter Frank

Golden Granny

Linda Lamp Light

Munching Maria

Noisy Nicola

Patsy Puppy

Sally Snake

Talking Tom
'Best Friend'
Picture Code Cards

Reading and fluency

'Tricky' words Teach the words **story** and **reading**.

Phonics Readers 3d: *Look what happened!*
Read the story with children. Afterwards, ask the children to make lists of words with **ed** that include 'Best Friends to the Rescue.'

'Tricky' words

Fluency List M *(TGCD)*
Re-read this list with the children and ask partners to read it to each other.

Phonics Readers 3d

Lesson 62: Yellow Yo-yo Man works for Mr E

y as in baby

You'll need

- ✓ *PCCs* for 'Guess Who?' plus **y**/ē/ and a second PCC for **b, p, n, t**
- ✓ Make a third plain letter **p** card similar to the others

- ✓ *Phonics Readers 3d*
- ✓ *Fluency List M (TGCD)*
- ✓ *Far Beyond ABC* and/or *Story Phonics* software
- ✓ Write the Word Detective sentences on the board

Review previously learned letters and sounds

'Guess Who?' *PCCs*: ā, ă, b, d, ĭ, ī, l, h, n, p, ŭ, y/ī/, ck, qu

Teacher reference

This lesson will really help those children who, in their earliest efforts to spell words ending in **y**, regularly chose **e** (e.g. cos**e** for cos**y**). There are over 5000 words which end in **y** sounding like an ē, so this is a ver**y** good lesson to learn!

Yellow Yo-yo Man works for Mr E

Tell children that you want to make the word **baby** with the *PCCs*. Guide them to stretch and segment the word. Build the word **babe** with *PCCs* with the Silent Magic **e** on the end. Can you hear /ē/ on the end? Oh no! This is Silent Magic **e**. Mr E has made almost all his final **e**'s into Silent Magic **e**'s. The word we have made is not **baby**, it's **babe**! I'd better tell you this story:

> One day Mr E discovered that he had used up too many of his **e**'s making his Silent Magic **e**'s. He was upset. "Oh no!" he cried. "I totall**y** forgot that in man**y** words people don't want an **e** to be silent at the end!" But there was no way he could change his Silent Magic **e**'s back.
>
> What could he do? He was terribl**y** upset until he saw Yellow Yo-yo Man. "Help, Yellow Yo-yo Man, can you say ē for me?" he called out, desperatel**y**. "I...don't know," said Yellow Yo-yo Man, slowl**y**. He put down his yo-yos and took a deep breath. Then he said, "ē", quite easil**y**! Mr E was so pleased. Immediatel**y** he gave Yellow Yo-yo Man the job of saying ē for him in nearl**y** every word which sounds like it ends in **e**. So now Yellow Yo-yo Man works ver**y** hard for Mr E. Mr E has even given him a tin**y** little ē to carry with him to show everybod**y** how man**y** words he finishes.

Picture Code Cards

Phonemic awareness and language development

You can find a shortened version of the above story and many words and illustrated items with **y**/ē/ for children to identify in the *Story Phonics* software and *Far Beyond ABC* book. They also revise the story of Yellow Yo-yo Man working for Mr I in short words like **try**.

Show the **y**/ē/ *PCC* and replace Silent Magic **e** with it to make the word **baby** as shown. So now we have...? "**baby**." If time allows, try acting out this story.

y as e in Far Beyond ABC

Group activities

Blending y (as e) words

Follow the steps below setting out the *PCCs*.

PCCs from 'Guess Who?' plus **f, s, t, y**/ē/ and a second card for **b, n,** and **p**

> Words: **funny, happy, tiny, lucky, sadly, quickly**

Let's read some more words with Yellow Yo-yo Man working for Mr E.

Make each word using picture sides only for the vowels and for **y**.

'Live Reading'

Distribute the *PCCs*: **b**, **ĭ**, **k**, **n**, **n**, **ō**, **p**, **p**, **t**, **t**, **ŭ**, **y/ē/**, and your prepared third **p**

Words: **puppy, pony, bunny, kitty**

Let's make some animal words with Yellow Yo-yo Man working for Mr E. The children make each word using plain sides, but picture sides for the vowels and Yellow Yo-yo Man. Use the extra **p** card you have made for **puppy**.

Word Detectives

Ask the children to Picture Code Yellow Yo-yo Man with a little **e** in his yo-yo sack.

> **Dippy Duck and Sammy Snake are happy it is sunny for their picnic.**

While some children are Picture Coding at the board, ask the rest to try to think of all the Letterlanders whose names end with an /ē/ sound. You could write the names on the board (They will discover that Annie Apple is the only one with an /ē/ at the end that isn't spelled with **y**).

Reading and fluency

Phonics Readers 3d: *Happy times*

Read the story with the children. After they re-read it once or twice, you may want them to make a list of **y**/ē/words in the story and read the list to a partner.

Fluency List M *(TGCD)*

Ask the children to continue practising this list (page 214).

Individual activities

- Introduce the relevant pages to revise these sounds in the *Blends & Digraphs Copymasters*, or use *Workbook 4*.

y as e words	
body	mummy
empty	quickly
funny	slowly
	very

Phonics Readers 3d

New concept - Vowels Out Walking

The next few lessons concentrate on a particular long vowel spelling pattern of pairs of vowels together in words. The generalisation of the rule is:

first long vowel - second vowel silent

To ensure children both understand and apply this rule Letterland presents it as a memorable rhyme.

When two vowels go out walking,

the FIRST one does the talking.

This rule makes a vast number of new words decodable.
Display the *Vowels Out Walking Poster* and listen to the *Vowels Out Walking Song* on the *Blends & Digraphs Songs CD*, to begin familiarising children with the concept.

Note: there are exceptions to this rule.

A less frequent spelling is **oe** (as in **toe**). This not included in the Vowels Out Walking lessons because it is often irregular (e.g. d**oe**s, sh**oe**).

Teacher reference

Vowels Out Walking Poster

Blends & Digraphs Songs CD

Lesson 63: Mr A and Mr I out walking

ai, ay as in rain and say

You'll need

- ✓ *PCCs for 'Quick Dash' plus* **ai, ay**
- ✓ *Beyond ABC and/or Story Phonics software*
- ✓ *Phonics Readers*
- ✓ *Fluency List M (TGCD)*
- ✓ *Reading Racer Charts (TGCD)*
- ✓ Make a 'Tricky' Word Card: **down**

Review previously learned letters and sounds

'Quick Dash' *PCCs:* l, m, n, p, r, s, t, w, y/ī/, y/ē/, ed/ed/, ed/d/, ed/t/

Mr A and Mr I out walking

Display the picture side of the **ai** PCC. The Vowel Men like to go out walking in Letterland together, but... it can be dangerous! When Mr A and Mr I go out walking, Mr A waves to everyone and says his name /ā/. Let's pretend we are Mr A waving and saying /ā/.

But look at Mr I. Is he waving and saying his name? "**No.**" Can you do what he is doing? Children imitate Mr I, as if looking for something. Mr I is the Lookout Man. He is silent because he is busy looking out for robots who sneak up on Vowel Men and try to capture them while they are out walking!

So when we see Mr A and Mr I out walking, who will we hear saying his name? "**Mr A.**" And what is Mr I doing? "**Looking out for robots!**"

Picture Code Cards

Phonemic awareness and language development

Explore the **ai** scene in the *Story Phonics* software and/or *Beyond ABC* book. Listen to or watch the animated story of Mr A and Mr I out walking and ask the children to hunt for items in the scene that include Mr A's name.

ai in Beyond ABC

Group activities

Role-play

Pair children up to play the roles of Mr A and Mr I. They can walk about with Mr A saying his name and Mr I on the lookout. Swap roles and repeat.

'Live Reading'

Distribute the *PCCs:* l, m, n, p, r, s, t, w, ai

Words with **ai: rain, train, trail, tail, wait, paint**

Ask two children to hold the **ai** PCC. Mr A waves and Mr I mimes being the Lookout Man each time they say /ā/ in a word. Make the seven **ai** words.

Mr A and Yellow Yo-yo Man out walking

Distribute the *PCC:* **ay**

Keep the children in the word **wait** in place as you share the story logic for **ay**. If we ask Talking Tess to sit down, do we have another word? (**wai**) Let's do the Roller Coaster Trick and see. "/w/ /ā/, **way**." Yes we do! But remember what happens to Mr I when he is on the end of a word? Yes, he gets dizzy! He actually feels like he's on the edge of a cliff and about to fall off. A dizzy Lookout Man wouldn't be much use, would he? That's why Mr I has made a deal with Yellow Yo-yo Man to take his place, so he won't ever have to be on the end of a word when he goes out walking with Mr A.

The Mr I child walks as if dizzy to his seat. Yellow Yo-yo Man comes forward to take Mr I's place, sharing the **ay** PCC with Mr A. Now Yellow Yo-yo Man is the

Lookout Man. Mr A waves and says his name while Yellow Yo-yo Man silently looks out for robots. Blend **way**.

Repeat the steps above going from **pai** to **pay** with different children.

Phonemic awareness and language development

Explore the **ay** scene in the *Story Phonics* software and/or *Beyond ABC* book. Children listen for Mr A's name in words as you read and as they talk about the illustration.

Word Detectives

Ask the children to underline the Vowel Men out walking in these sentences.

Tess waited in the rain all day for the train.

May we play with clay today?

ay in Beyond ABC

ay words	
day	clay
play	spray
may	tray
say	delay
stray	

Reading and fluency

'Tricky' word

Teach the word **down** as shown. This will be decodable after Lesson 85.

Phonics Readers 3d: *My Puppy*

After you read the story with the children you may want to try the Plan and Play strategy (page 222).

Fluency List M *(TGCD)*

Time children on this list today (page 214).

'Tricky' word

Phonics Readers 3d

Individual activities

- Introduce the relevant pages to revise these sounds in the *Blends & Digraphs Copymasters*, or use *Workbook 4*.

Lesson 64: Mr E and Mr E out walking

ee as in bee

Focus on **ee**

You'll need

- ✓ PCCs for 'Guess Who?' plus **g, k, l, ee**
- ✓ Vowels out walking poster
- ✓ Beyond ABC and/or Story Phonics software
- ✓ Phonics Readers 3d
- ✓ Fluency List N (TGCD)
- ✓ Blends & Digraphs Songs CD
- ✓ Make the 'Tricky' Word Cards: **out, our, eat**

Review previously learned letters and sounds

'Guess Who?' PCCs: d, l, m, n, p, r, s, t, w, ai, ay, ch, qu

Show the **ai** and **ay** PCCs picture sides. Ask the children to share the story logic and explain why Yellow Yo-yo Man takes Mr I's place in **ay**.

'Live Spelling'

Ask two children to hold the **ai** card and two more hold the **ay**. Distribute the PCCs from 'Guess Who?' except **qu**

Words: **main, chain, say, tray, mail, day, play, wait, rain**

After children spell a word, ask one child to explain the choice of **ai** or **ay**.

Mr E and Mr E out walking

Look at the *Vowels Out Walking* poster again. Mr A and Mr I aren't the only Vowel Men who like going out walking. Ask the children to name some of the pairs they see and find the tiny lurking robots. Point to the twin E's. Did you know that Mr E has a twin brother whose name is also Mr E? The two Mr E's like to go out walking together. The first Mr E says his name and his twin...what does he say? "**Nothing.**" What is he doing? "**Looking out for robots!**"

Vowels Out Walking Poster

Group activities

Song

Listen to the first verse of the *Vowels Out Walking Song*. Play again and sing along (lyrics on *TGCD*).

Show the picture side of the **ee** PCC. So when we see two e's together, we just hear one /ē/. Push the *PCC* forward for children to say: "/ē/, /ē/, /ē/..."

Picture Code Cards

Role-play

Partners take turns in the roles of Mr E and his brother. As they walk, the first Mr E says his name and his twin acts as the Lookout Man.

Phonemic awareness and language development

Share the **ee** scene in the *Story Phonics* software and/or *Beyond ABC* book. Children listen and look for Mr E's name in words in the picture. If you are using the software on a whiteboard the children could come up to the front and press on the things they see in the scene.

ee in Beyond ABC

Blending ee words

PCCs: d, ĕ, g, k, l, n, p, r, s, w, ee, qu

Words: **see, seed, sleep, feel, keep, week, weekend, green, queen**

ee words	
seem	jeep
feel	meet
weep	week
feet	deep

Word Detectives

Ask the children to Picture Code the twin Mr E's.

The queen sees some bees by the green trees.

Individual activities

Complete the **ea** page in the *Blends & Digraph Copymasters*. See Letterland Resources (page 12).

Reading and fluency

'Tricky' words

'Tricky' words

Show the word cards **out** and **our** and **eat**. Guide children to discover the irregular letters, mark as shown and practise the word cards. All of these words will become fully decodable in later lessons.

Phonics Readers 3d: *Mr E's trees*

Read this rhyming story to the children the first time. Then ask them to join in on a second reading. You might assign a different small group to each verse to rehearse and present.

Phonics Readers 3d

Fluency List N *(TGCD)*

Introduce this new list to children and ask them to practise it chorally with you and then with partners (page 214).

ea as in sea

You'll need

- ✓ *PCCs for 'Quick Dash' plus* **ea**
- ✓ *Beyond ABC and/or Story Phonics software*
- ✓ *Phonics Readers 3e*
- ✓ *Fluency List N (TGCD)*
- ✓ Write the Word Detective sentences on the board
- ✓ Make a 'Tricky' Word Card: **water**

Review previously learned letters and sounds

'Quick Dash' *PCCs*: **b, c, d**, Silent Magic **e, l, m, n, p, r, s**/z/, **t, ai, ay, ch, ee**

Mr E and Mr A out walking

Display the **ea** PCC. Ask the children to look at the two Vowel Men and explain what they are doing and saying based on what they know about other Vowel Men out walking. In this instance, the rhyme to remember is:

The first man **usually*** says his name, but his friend won't do the same.

Ask the children to pair up and mime the actions and sound of Mr E and Mr A.

Push the plain letter side forward a few times as children repeat, "/ē/, /ē/, /ē/".

* The word 'usually' is needed because of the other sound of **ea** (as in h**ea**d) where Eddy Elephant gets a turn to talk.

Picture Code Cards

Phonemic awareness and language development

Share the **ea** scene in the *Story Phonics* software and/or *Beyond ABC* book. Children listen and look for Mr E's name in words in the picture. If you are using the software on a whiteboard the children could come up to the front and find the things they see in the scene.

ea in Beyond ABC

Group activities

Blending ea words

Make the word **eat** for children to blend using the Roller Coaster Trick.

PCCs for 'Guess Who?' plus **ea**

> Words: **eat, meat, beans, peas, peach, tea**

We can make some more words that are something you can eat or drink. After children do the Roller Coaster Trick for each word, ask them to tell with a show of hands if they like that food.

'Live Reading'

Distribute the *PCCs*: **b, c, d**, Silent Magic **e, l, n, p, r, s**/z/, **ai, ay, ch, ea, ee**

> Words: **beach, reach, read, lead, clean, please, play, plain, need**

Help children form the word for the class to blend. Then quickly make the changes needed for the next word for blending. For the word **please**, explain: sometimes Mr E puts a Silent Magic **e** on the end after an **s** even if there is no magic needed. Then we know it's not a plural **s**, so the **s** does not mean there are two or more of something.

Word Detectives

Ask the children to Picture Code Mr E and Mr A in the sentence:

> **Mr E and Mr A have a seat on the beach and read about the beasts that live in the sea.**

ea words	
sea	treat
seat	heap
bead	least
read	steamy
meat	repeat

Individual activities

Complete the **ea** page in the *Blends & Digraph Copymasters* or in *Workbook 4*. See Letterland Resources (page 12).

Reading and fluency

Tricky word

Show the word card **water**. Lead the children to discover the letters with irregular sounds, mark as shown and practise it.

'Tricky' word

Phonics Readers 3e: *Molly and me by the sea*

Before reading this story, you might ask the children to guess what it might be about based on the 'tricky' word. Read this story with the children a few times. Then ask partners to re-read this one and a few previous stories.

Fluency List N *(TGCD)*

Revise this list with the children. Ask them to read it to a partner later in the day (page 214).

Phonics Readers 3e

Lesson 66: Mr O and Mr A out walking

oa as in boat

Focus on

You'll need

✓ PCCs for 'Quick Dash' plus **c, f, k, m, oa**
✓ *Phonics Readers 3e*
✓ *Fluency List N (TGCD)*
✓ *Beyond ABC* and/or *Story Phonics* software

Review previously learned letters and sounds

'Quick Dash' *PCCs*: **b, c, d, f, Silent Magic e, g, ī, l, r, s, t, ai, ay, ea, e**

Mr O and Mr A out walking

Display the **oa** *PCC* plain letter side. Tell the children that Mr O and Mr A are on the other side. Ask them to predict what the two will be doing and saying. Confirm or correct them with the picture side. Then remind them of the rhyme,

When two vowels go out walking, the FIRST man does the talking.

The first man says his name, but his friend won't do the same.

Let's ask everyone on this side of the class to be Mr O, wave and say your name together. Everyone on the other side of the class be Mr A and put your hand to your forehead and look all around without saying anything. Then ask the sides to swap roles. Push the plain letter side forward a few times as children repeat, "/ō/, /ō/, /ō/".

Picture Code Cards

Group activities

Blending oa words

Make the following words for children to blend using the Roller Coaster Trick.

PCCs for 'Quick Dash' plus **oa**

oa words	
coat	soap
load	oak
goat	toad
loaf	foal
road	boat

Words: **coat**, **goat**, **goal**, **soap**, **road**, **lifeboat**

Phonemic awareness and language development

Share the **oa** scene in the *Story Phonics* software and/or *Beyond ABC* book. Children listen and look for /ō/ sound of **oa** in words in the picture.

'Live Spelling'

Distribute the *PCCs*: **b, d, f, k, l, m, r, s, t, ea, oa**

oa in Beyond ABC

Words: **boat**, **team**, **float**, **load**, **dream**, **soak**, **oatmeal**

Ask two children to hold the **oa** card and two more hold **ea**. These Vowel Men pairs stand to the left of your 'Live Spelling' area so they can 'go walking' into the word when they are needed. Follow the usual steps for 'Live Spelling'. Children stretch and segment to help decide on the required letters.

Word Detectives

Ask the children to Picture Code Mr O and Mr A in the words of this sentence:

The foal with the spotted coat ran down the road to get her oats.

Reading and fluency

Review 'tricky' words

Ask the children to practise these recent 'tricky' words or others using either the cards you have made previously or your classroom board: **now**, **down**, **out** and **water**.

Phonics Readers 3e: *The bad goat*

Read the story with the children a few times. Then ask partners to re-read this one and a few previous stories.

Phonics Readers 3e

Fluency List N *(TGCD)*

Children continue to build fluency by practising this list with partners (page 214).

Lesson 67: Vowel Men out walking

ie, ue as in tie and blue

Focus on

You'll need

- ✓ *PCCs* for 'Quick Dash' plus **c, f, m, oa**
- ✓ *Vowels out walking* poster
- ✓ *Beyond ABC* and/or *Story Phonics* software
- ✓ *Phonics Readers 3e*
- ✓ *Fluency List N (TGCD)*
- ✓ Make 'Tricky' Word Card: **one**
- ✓ *Reading Racer Charts (TGCD)*

Review previously learned letters and sounds

'Quick Dash' *PCCs*: **b, d, g, l, r, s, t, ai, ay, ea, ee**

'Live Spelling'

Distribute the *PCCs*: **k, l, p, s, t, w, ay, ee**

Words: **week**, **peek**, **pay**, **play**, **peel**, **steel**, **stay**

Ask two children to hold the **ay** card and two more hold **ee**. These Vowel Men stand to the left of your 'Live Spelling' area so they can 'go walking' into the word when needed. Follow the usual steps for 'Live Spelling' including asking the children to stretch and segment to help decide on the letters required.

Mr I and Mr E out walking

Review the five pairs of Vowel Men already studied by pointing to them *Vowels out walking* poster while the children say the sounds (**ay, ai, ee, ea, oa**).

Then point to Mr I and Mr E and ask the children, What is Mr I doing and saying? What is Mr E doing?

Show children the **ie** *PCC* picture side. Point to Mr I and ask the children to tell a partner what Mr I is doing and saying. Let the other partner talk about Mr E.

Push the plain letters forward a few times for the children to repeat "/ī/, /ī/, /ī/." Note with this pair of vowels out walking you must say,

When Mr I and Mr E go out walking,

Mr I **usually** does the talking.

Emphasise **usually**. There are times when **ie** makes another sound (as in **field**).

Phonemic awareness and language development

Share the **ie** scene in the *Story Phonics* software and/or *Beyond ABC* book. Children listen and look for the /ī/ sound of **ie** in words in the picture.

ie in Beyond ABC

ie words		ue words	
pie	cried	cue	value
lie	tried	due	queue
tie	spied	hue	statue
die	fried	venue	rescue

Mr U and Mr E out walking

Follow similar steps with Mr U and Mr E out walking. Explain that Mr U is walking so fast that we often don't hear his full name. In most words it comes out as /oo/ (as in **blue**). Can you say both ways we might hear these sounds as I push these two letters forward? /ū/ or /oo/

Picture Code Cards

Phonemic awareness and language development

Share the **ue** scene in the *Story Phonics* software and/or *Beyond ABC* book. Children listen and look for the /ū/ or /oo/ sound of **ue** in words in the picture.

ue in Beyond ABC

Group activities

Let's blend some words with these Vowel Men out walking. For the word **rescue**, separate it into two syllables for blending (**res cue**). Then put them together for reading the whole word.

PCCs for 'Quick Dash' plus **ie, ue**

Words: **tie, tried, cried, pie, blue, clue, true, rescue**

Reading and fluency

'Tricky' words
Teach the word **one**.

'Tricky' word

Phonics Readers 3e: *What a mess*
Read the story with the children a few times. Then ask partners to re-read this one and a few previous stories.

Fluency List N *(TGCD)*
Time children on this list to check their accuracy and fluency. Ask them to graph the results on their *Reading Racer Charts* (TGCD).

Phonics Readers 3e

Lesson 68: Review Vowel Men out walking

ai, ay, ea, ee, ie, oa, ue

You'll need

✓ PCCs for 'Quick Dash'
✓ Phonics Readers 3e

✓ Fluency List O (TGCD)
✓ Make 'Tricky' Word Card: **there**
✓ Reading Racer Charts (TGCD)

Review previously learned letters and sounds

'Quick Dash' *PCCs:* b, d, l, p, r, t, ai, ay, ee, ea, ie, oa, ue

Vowel Men-go-round

Walking into words

PCCs: **ai, ay, b, d, ee, ea, l, oa, p, r, t, ue**

> Word groups:
>
> **laid, lead, load, lied**   **bait, boat, beat, beet**
> **tree, tray, true**   **pay, pea, pie**

Give these *PCCs* to pairs of children: **ai, ay, ee, ea, ie, oa, ue**. Ask them to line up on the left side of your classroom ready to walk in the Reading Direction to be a part of words.

Ask two more children with the **l** and **d** *PCCs* to stand at the front of the room with enough space between them for two Vowel Men.

Then ask the **ai** pair to walk into position between **l** and **d**. As they walk, ask the first one to wave and say his name, the second to look for robots with his hand to his forehead.

Use the Roller Coaster Trick to blend the resulting word **laid**. Use it in a quick sentence as the Vowel Men quietly return to their place at the left and **l** and **d** remain at the front. Ask other Vowel Men pairs to do the same to form the other words above with **l** and **d**. Do likewise with the other consonants and Vowel Men listed.

Written spelling

Part 1 - Words

Display these *PCCs:* **ie, ee, ue**

You are going to write some words and each one will have one of these pairs of Vowel Men out walking as part of the spelling.

> Words to read out: **cried, teeth, blue, green, tie**

Say each word, a sentence containing that word, then repeat the word. Children repeat the word, stretch and segment it, then write the word on paper or a whiteboard. When they have finished, write the word on the board for them to check their spelling.

Finally, ask the children to read all the words on the board.

Part 2 - Sentence

Display these *PCCs:* **ai, ay, ea**

> Say this sentence: **Did the team play in the rain?**

Ask the children to attempt to write the sentence using each of the displayed pairs of Vowel Men at least once. After they have written it, write the sentence on the board for all to check and correct their own. Read the sentence together.

Reading and fluency

Introduce prefix un-

The prefix **un-** is included in several words of the *Phonics Reader*s story for this lesson. Write these words on the board: **tie, pack, lock, helpful**. Ask the children to read the first word and define it or give a sentence with it (e.g. "I **need to tie my shoes**"). Let's see what happens when we add the prefix **un-** to the beginning of the base word **tie**. Write **untie** and discuss the change in meaning. Do the same with the other words and encourage children to use the terms 'prefix' and 'base word' as you discuss them.

'Tricky' word

Phonics Readers 3e

Phonics Readers 3e: *Stop the train!*

Teach the 'tricky' word **there**. Then read this story with the children.

Fluency List O *(TGCD)*

Introduce this new list to children.

---

ild, ind, old as in mild, kind, cold

You'll need

✓ PCCs for 'Guess Who?' plus **c, h, k, n, r, s, t, w**

✓ Phonics Readers 4a
✓ Fluency List O (TGCD)

Review previously learned letters and sounds

'Guess Who?' *PCCs*: b, d, ī, l, m, ō, ai, ay, ch, ee, ea, ie, ll, oa, ue, th

---

By now your class will be accustomed to looking out for split digraph patterns and vowel pair patterns to help them predict when the previous vowel will be long. By contrast, this lesson focuses on the few words where there is no such signal. They just learn that the Vowel Men have a habit of appearing in these words and saying their names.

Mr I's mild and kind words

Making the word **mild,** explain, Mr I is a **mild** man which means he doesn't usually get angry. Here is the word **mild** and some words that rhyme with it.

Make the word **mild** and the two other **ild** words for children to blend.

You could follow on by asking, Are you a mild child or a wild child, or somewhere in between?

Make the word **kind** with only Mr I on the picture side for blending.

Mr I is also very kind. You will always find him in the word **kind** saying his name /ī/. You will also see and hear him in some words that rhyme with **kind**, like **find**, **behind**, **mind** and **wind**.

i words	
find	mild
kind	child
remind	wild
behind	

Blending Mr I's words

Make each of the **ind** words below by changing the initial letter. Let the children use the **Roller Coaster Trick** to blend them and make up a sentence for each.

PCCs: **b, d, f, ī, k, l, m, n, w, ch**

Words: **mild, child, wild, kind, find, mind, blind**

Mr O's old words

Display your Mr O *PCC*. Mr O, the Old Man, is the oldest person in Letterland. Nobody knows exactly how old he is, but one thing is certain. Mr O is so old that he knows almost everything there is to know in Letterland! If you want to be sure to find him, look for him right at the start of the word **old**, and in most other words that rhyme with **old**. That means you will find him saying his name /ō/ in **old, bold, cold, fold, unfold, gold, hold, sold, scold** and **told** because they all rhyme with **old**.

o words	
old	sold
hold	fold
cold	gold
	told

Blending Mr O's words

Make the words below with only Mr O on the picture side. Children use the Roller Coaster Trick to blend, and make up a sentence for each word.

PCCs needed: **b, c, d, h, l, m, ō, r, s, t, ll, th**

Words: **old, cold, told, hold, most, roll, both**

Before making **most, roll** and **both** explain, Mr O has a habit of saying his name in three more useful words.

Word Detectives

Ask the children to Picture Code Mr I and Mr O in these words:

> **You will find that Mr I is kind and mild to every child.**
>
> **I am told that Mr O has an old golden hat for the cold.**

Reading and fluency

Phonics Readers 4a: *Gifts*

In the story Mr I has a gift for Mr O but before he can have the gift he has to guess what it is. And Mr O reciprocates. The choice of gifts are obvious but the children will enjoy explaining the riddles (e.g. as a clue for the gift of an ice cream, Mr I says, "If you hold it too long, it goes away.") .

Fluency List O *(TGCD)*

Revise this list with the children and ask them to practise it with partners.

Phonics Readers 4a

Take-Home Booklet

Home link

Make copies of the Section 4 *Take-Home Booklets* from the *TGCD* for children to read in class and then take home to read to their parents.

Assessment - Refer to your TGCD

Use the Section 4 assessments a few days to two weeks after completing the final lesson in Section 4.

All assessment material including full instructions and Assessment forms are on the *TGCD*.

Section 5 :
Further Vowel Sounds and Spellings

Section 5: Long Vowels
Lesson Chart

Lesson	Lesson focus	Example word	Letterland Concept	Story from *Phonics Readers*	'Tricky' word	Set/Book
70	ar	farm	Arthur Ar, the Apple Stealer	In the dark	were, who	4a
71	or	for	Orvil Or, the Orange Stealer	The day of the big match		4a
72	Review			Carly and the sharks		4a
73	ir	girl	Irving Ir, the Ink Stealer	The bird girls	Mrs	4b
74	ur	fur	Urgent Ur, the Umbrella Stealer	My very bad morning		4b
75	er	her	Ernest Er, the Elephant Stealer	Snapshots	doesn't	4b
76	Review	-		Ben's birthday surprise	saw	4b
77	ow	show	Oscar Orange, Mr O and Walter Walrus	When the cold wind blows	know	4c
78	igh	night	Mr I, Golden Girl and Harry Hat Man	Cats' eyes and humans eyes	talk, how	4c
79	Review	-		Lost in the Queen's maze		4c
80	oo	moon	The Boot Twin	Penguins on the loose	walk	4c
81	oo, u	book, put	The Foot Twin	The biggest carrot ever	would, little, always	4d
82	aw, au	saw, cause	Annie Apple and Walter Walrus	In art class	could, colour	4d
83	ew, ew	few, grew	Eddy Elephant and Walter Walrus	The Hat Man's new roof	should, friend	4d
84	Review	-		Who will help?	laugh	4d
85	ow, ou	out, how	Oscar Orange and Walter Walrus	What big flippers you have	their	4e
86	oi, oy	coin, boy	A boy called Roy	Nick's noisy new toy		4e
87	Review	-		Squeaks, the house mouse	people	4e
88	air, ear	fair, year		Lily and the fairies	through	4e

Teacher's Guide CD

Section 5 Assessment

Fluency Lists P-T

Take-Home Booklets

Further resources

*Blends &
Digraphs CD*

Picture Code Cards

Beyond ABC

Far Beyond ABC

*Vowel Scene
Posters*

*Magnetic Word
Builder*

Further Vowel Sounds and Spellings

In this section children learn the story logic for **r**-controlled and **w**-controlled vowels. Enter the Vowel Stealers! These rascally robots motivate young readers to become detectives and catch them in words. They learn to look out for Walter Walrus as well, who has his own ways of changing vowel sounds. They also learn memorable story logic that explains all the other common vowel sounds to further expand their reading and writing horizons.

Contents

r-contolled vowels	**ar er ir or ur air ear**
Long vowel patterns	**igh ow**
Other spellings/sounds	**oi oy ou ow oo oo u aw au ew**

Objectives

By the end of this section, children should be able to:

- Say the new sound when shown the letters
- Blend and segment words with the various vowel patterns and sounds
- Read an additional twenty-one 'tricky' words (total: 68)
- Apply the new sounds in reading with increasing accuracy, fluency and comprehension.

Practise and apply

Children continue to use learning activities and practise content from previous sections along with the new strategies and variations below:

Role-playing the story logic Children will remember to look out for new spelling patterns and recall the pronunciations after hearing the story logic, seeing it illustrated, singing about it and role-playing the letter characters' interactions.

Word Detectives Children catch the vowel stealing robots and the mischievous Walter Walrus at their tricks to get those sounds right.

Vowel Scene Posters Children use the Vowel Stealers Poster to help them catch those rascally robots whenever they are reading or writing.

Blends & Digraph Songs Lively songs help make learning fun and memorable.

Reading Practice With a growing stock of decodable and 'tricky' words children can read longer, more complex stories to help build fluency, vocabulary and comprehension. There are more *Phonics Readers* to accompany this section.

'Tricky' words introduced in Section 5

were	who	Mrs	doesn't
saw	know	talk	how
walk	would	little	always
could	colour	should	knew
friend	laugh	their	people
through			

New concept - The Vowel Stealers

In the pages that follow, a remarkable fact about the English language is introduced. Almost every time a single vowel is followed by an **r**, that **r** will alter the vowel's sound. Consider **tap** but **tar**, **hen** but **her**, **fist** but **first**, **pot** but **port**, **fun** but **fur**. The vowels become **r**-controlled and the new phonemes **ar**, **er**, **ir**, **or** and **ur** are created.

Letterland explains this phonic fact at a child's level by depicting all **r's** as running robots who capture vowels in their sacks.

Display the *Vowel Stealers Poster* and explain:

There is a gang of vowel stealing robots in Letterland. Red Robot is the ringleader. These robots all have a bad habit of running off with vowel sounds! We must become sharp-eyed detectives to spot these robots. Let's find out what they get up to so they won't stop us from reading words!

Vowel Stealers Poster

Lesson 70: Arthur Ar, the apple stealer
ar as in farm

Focus on

You'll need

- ✓ PCCs for 'Quick Dash' plus **g, r, s, t, ar**
- ✓ *The Vowel Stealers* poster
- ✓ *Far Beyond ABC* and/or *Story Phonics* software
- ✓ *Blends & Digraphs Songs CD*
- ✓ *Phonics Readers 4a*
- ✓ *Fluency List P (TGCD)*
- ✓ Make 'Tricky' Word Cards: **who** and **were**
- ✓ Write sentences for Word Detectives on the board

Review previously learned letters and sounds

'Quick Dash' *PCCs:* ā, c, d, ĕ, k, m, n, p, ee, ea, ie, oa, ss, ue

Introducing Arthur Ar, the apple stealer

Show the picture side of the **ar** *Picture Code Card*.

Arthur Ar is a robber who steals apples. When he captures an Annie Apple, don't expect her to be making her usual 'a' sound. Instead you will hear Arthur Ar reporting back to his ringleader, Red Robot, with a tiny radio device in his outstretched **ar**m. He calls in with just one word: his surname "**Ar!**"

Can you say it with me? "**Ar!....Ar!**"

Phonemic awareness and language development

Explore the **ar** scene in the *Story Phonics* software and/or *Far Beyond ABC* book. Listen to or watch the animated story of Arthur Ar and ask the children to hunt for items in the scene that include Arthur Ar's /**ar**/ sound.

Picture Code Cards

Arthur Ar in Far Beyond ABC

Group activities

Blending ar words

Words: **car, park, star, smart, dark, darkness, radar, garden***

Make these words one at a time with plain letter side of the PCC's or on screen. For each word, let a child be the Chief Detective. The detective comes forward, points out Arthur Ar and turns the card to the picture side, showing

that Arthur has not fooled anybody!

Then the chief leads the class in the Roller Coaster Trick for the word.

* Leave a space between the syllables of **garden** (gar den) and ask the children to do the Roller Coaster Trick for each syllable. Then close the space for reading the whole word. The sound of the **e** is a schwa, the almost inaudible ŭ or ĭ sound we say quickly in unaccented syllables.

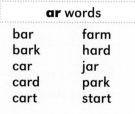

ar words	
bar	farm
bark	hard
car	jar
card	park
cart	start

Word Detectives

Write these sentences on the board and help children to Picture Code or underline the **ar**'s in the words. Then read the sentences together.

He parks his radar car in the dark yard.

On the farm, we set the alarm to start the day on time.

'Live Spelling'

Now let's 'Live Spell' some words. We'll need to listen like good detectives to hear the sounds and spell them.

PCCs: ă, ā, **d**, Silent Magic **e**, **g**, ĭ, **k**, **l**, **m**, **n**, **p**, **s**, **r**, **t**, **t**, **ar**, **sh**

Words: **park, lake, start, sharp, glad, shark, snap, smart, artist***

* After saying the whole word **artist**, say each syllable (**art ist**) for the children to repeat, stretch and segment, and 'Live Spell' separately and then join them.

Song

Arthur Ar's song is on the *Blends & Digraphs Songs CD* and *Story Phonics* software. Your children have reached a stage in their decoding where they will be able to decode some of the song lyrics (*TGCD*) but the primary function of the songs is to increase phonemic awareness and to have fun singing along, rather than using them as decodable texts.

Individual activities

Introduce the relevant page from the *Blends & Digraph Copymasters* for children to work on independently or in small groups.

Ask the children to fill some **ar** words in their *Word Bank Copymasters* from the board. Add a few distractors to make this more of a challenge.

Reading and fluency

'Tricky' words: **were** and **who**. Irregular letters as shown.

'Tricky' words

Phonics Readers 4a: *In the dark*

The first few pages provide some suspense about what these two shadowy characters are up to. Ask the children to make predictions and revise their predictions as they gather more information.

Phonics Readers 3e

Fluency List P *(TGCD)*

Ask the children to practise the list with partners. You may want to use some words or sentences from the list for dictation.

Focus on

Lesson 71: Orvil Or, the orange stealer
or as in for

You'll need

- ✓ *PCCs for 'Guess Who?' plus* **ā, d, f, ĭ, r, t, t, or**
- ✓ *The Vowel Stealers* poster
- ✓ *Far Beyond ABC* or *Story Phonics* software
- ✓ *Phonics Readers 4a*
- ✓ *Fluency List P (TGCD)*
- ✓ *Reading Racer Chart (TGCD)*
- ✓ *Blends & Digraphs Songs CD*

Review previously learned letters and sounds

'Guess Who?' PCCs: **ă**, Silent Magic **e, g, h, k, l, m, n, p, s, ar, ie, a_e, th, sh**

Introducing Orvil Or, the orange stealer

Show the plain letter side of the **or** PCC.

Now, we have another robber for you to go after, Reading Detectives. Do you want to see what he looks like?

Turn to the picture side. This is Orvil Or and he steals oranges. Whenever he does, don't expect to hear the orange saying 'o' anymore, instead you will just hear the sound of Orvil Or reporting back to his ringleader, Red Robot, with a tiny radio device as he runs off to his get-away boat by the shore. He reports in with just one word: his surname "**Or!**"

Can you say it with me? "**Or!....Or!**"

Show the plain letter side again. So whenever you see an orange just behind a robot's back, the chances are that you have caught Orvil Or! /**or**/. Push the card forward a few times to cue children to say, "**or... or...**".

Picture Code Cards

The Vowel Stealers poster

Ask the children to find Orvil Or on the poster and note objects in the illustration that have his sound (**oar, shore**). See variant spellings of /**or**/ below.

Vowel Stealers Poster

Phonemic awareness and language development

Explore the **or** scene in the *Story Phonics* software and/or *Far Beyond ABC* book. Listen to or watch the animated story of Orvil Or and ask the children to hunt for items in the scene that include his /**or**/ sound.

Orvil Or in
Far Beyond ABC

Group activities

Blending or words

PCCs: **c**, Silent Magic **e, f, h, k, m, n, s, t, or, th**

Words: **or, for, fork, horn, north, storm, more, store, score**

Let children take turns being the Chief Detective who turns over the **or** card to show Orvil Or that he can't fool them. Then the class does the Roller Coaster Trick for that word.

When you make the word **more** and the other words with **-ore** begin with plain letter sides of all the letters including Silent Magic **e**. Let the children 'catch' Orvil Or as before and explain, In **-ore** words, Silent Magic **e**'s sparks don't work because Orvil Or absorbs them into his robot arm.

Word Detectives

Ask the children to come to the board and underline the **or** in the words of the sentences below. Then read the sentence a few times with the children:

Orvil Or wore his torn shorts to play sport.

Song

Orvil Or's song is on the *Blends & Digraphs Songs CD* and the *Story Phonics* software. Teach the words **stealer**, **corner**, **called** and **orange** if you intend to show the song lyrics (*TGCD*). The lyrics are not decodable texts, they are simply to increase phonemic awareness and aid language development.

or words	
for	born
fork	worn
cord	fort
cork	torn
sort	glory

Individual activities

Complete the **or** page in the *Blends & Digraph Copymasters* and the *Workbooks*. See Letterland Resources (page 12).

Reading and fluency

Fluency List P (*TGCD*)

Time children on this list and ask them to record their scores on their *Reading Racer Charts*.

Phonics Readers 4a: *The day of the big match*

Before reading the story you may want the children to be detectives and find Orvil Or words in the text. They could call them out as they find them for you to list on the board. Review the list before the children read the story.

Read the story with the class a few times. Then ask partners to re-read this one and other stories for fluency practice when time allows.

Phonics Readers 4a

Variant spellings: our, oor, oar

Blending with Picture Code Cards

Display the Orvil Or *PCC* for all to see. Sometimes Orvil Or is running so fast when he steals a vowel, he actually picks up two vowels behind his back. In many of these words, whether Orvil Or takes one vowel or two, it is all the same to him! He just goes on rep**or**ting back with his last name, "Or!".

Make the words below with **plain letters** for children to blend using the **Roller Coaster Trick**.

PCCs: **d, f, l, o, r, u, y, or**

Words: **door, poor, floor, oar, roar, soar, your, four, pour, fourteen, court** (but *not* **our, hour, sour**)

Blending and segmenting ar, or

You'll need

- ✓ PCCs for 'Quick Dash'
- ✓ The Vowel Stealers poster
- ✓ Magnetic Word Builder or other letter sets
- ✓ Phonics Readers 4a
- ✓ Fluency List P (TGCD)

Review previously learned letters and sounds

'Quick Dash' *PCCs*: **d, ē**, Silent Magic **e, f, l, m, o, ŭ, p, r, s, t, y, ar, or, sh**

Blending

'Live Reading'

Ask two children to hold the **ar** PCC. The Arthur Ar child holds a sack and the other child holds on to the sack to show she or he has been captured. Ask another pair to do the same with **or**. These pairs could stand just to the left of your 'Live Spelling' area, ready to rush into a word when you call for them.

Distribute the *PCCs*: **d**, Silent Magic **e, f, m, p, r, s, t, y, ar, or, sh**

Words: **for, far, farm, sore, shore, sharp, yard, fort**

Spelling with Magnetic Word Builders

Provide children with a *Magnetic Word Builder* or other letter sets. Call out the words as usual for children to stretch and segment and build with their letters.

Letters: **a, c, d, e, h, n, o, p, r, s, t**

Words: **star, scar, store, short, part, corn, card, core, chore**

Magnetic Word Builder

Reading and fluency

Phonics Readers 4a: *Carly and the sharks*

Read the story with the class a few times. You may want to share some images or information from the internet on sharks, public aquariums or Eugenie Clark, 'The Shark Lady', in conjunction with this story.

Fluency List P *(TGCD)*

Introduce this new list to children by echo reading each line or by choral reading. Later ask partners to re-read to each other.

Phonics Readers 4a

New concept - the Robot Brothers

Point to the poster as you talk with the children (alternatively use *PCCs*). Here we have all the robots in Letterland. Let's name the ones we have already met: **"Red Robot, Arthur Ar, Orvil Or."**

Now there are three more robots. They look alike. That's because they are brothers. They all say their last name the same way /**er**/, but look! They spell it three different ways because each one captures a different vowel.

Write the names **Irving Ir, Ernest Er** and **Urgent Ur** for the children to compare. Ask the children to practise these names as you point to them.

You also might want to listen to the Er/Ir/Ur Brother's Song on the *Blends & Digraphs Songs CD* that clusters **ir, er**, and **ur** words.

Vowel Stealers Poster

Blends & Digraphs Songs CD

ir as in girl

You'll need

- ✓ *PCCs for 'Guess Who?' plus* **ir**
- ✓ *Far Beyond ABC or Story Phonics software*
- ✓ *Blends & Digraphs Songs CD*
- ✓ *Phonics Readers 4b*
- ✓ *Fluency List P (TGCD)*
- ✓ Make a 'Tricky' Word Card: **Mrs**

Review previously learned letters and sounds

'Guess Who?' *PCCs*: b, d, g, l, n, t, w, ay, ee, sh, th, ar, or

Irving Ir, the ink stealer

Show the picture side of the **ir** PCC.

Here is the first of the brothers, Irving Ir. Just like with the other Vowel Stealers, we need to be good detectives to catch him.

In Letterland everyone writes with ink pens. But Irving Ir likes to run off with ink bottles. The ink splashes as he runs and virtually every shirt he has is dirty. As he runs he calls out his last name, "Ir". . Push the plain letters forward several times cueing the children to say, "**Ir**...".

Phonemic awareness and language development

Explore the **ir** scene in the *Story Phonics* software and/or *Far Beyond ABC* book. Ask the children to hunt for items in the scene that include his sound.

Picture Code Cards

Irving Ir in
Far Beyond ABC

Group activities

Blending ir words

PCCs for 'Guess Who?' plus **ir**

Words: **girl, shirt, bird, birthday, third, thirteen, twirl**

Let's make some words with Irving Ir's /**ir**/sound from the story.

Let the children take turns being the Chief Detective who turns over the **ir** card to show Irving that he can't fool them. Then the class blends the word. Ask the children to blend the words one syllable at a time, and then read the whole word (**birth day, thir teen**). Ask someone to say a sentence with each word perhaps relating to the content of the **ir** pages in *Far Beyond ABC*.

Song

Play *Irving Ir in Person* from the CD or software and sing along with the children (lyrics on *TGCD*).

Word Detectives

Ask the children to come to the board and underline the **ir**'s in the words of the sentence below. Then read the sentence a few times together.

> **Irving Ir has more than thirty dirty shirts!**

ir words	
girl	birth
sir	third
bird	first
shirt	thirteen
skirt	thirsty

Mrs

Reading and fluency

'Tricky' word: Mrs Irregular letters as shown.

Phonics Readers 4b: *The bird girls*

This story has lots of dialogue. Try using Plan and Play (see page 222).

Fluency List P *(TGCD)*

Review the list with the children and ask partners to re-read to each other. You may want to use some of the words or sentences for dictation.

Phonics Readers 4b

Lesson 74: Urgent Ur, the umbrella stealer
ur as in fur

You'll need

- ✓ PCCs for 'Quick Dash' plus Silent Magic **e**
- ✓ The Vowel Stealers poster
- ✓ Far Beyond ABC or Story Phonics software
- ✓ Blends & Digraphs Songs CD
- ✓ Phonics Readers 4b
- ✓ Fluency List P (TGCD)
- ✓ Reading Racer Charts (TGCD)

Review previously learned letters and sounds

'Quick Dash' PCCs: ă, b, d, h, n, s, s/z/, t, ar, ay, er, ir, or, th, ur

Urgent Ur, the umbrella stealer

Display *The Vowel Stealers* poster (alternatively use *PCCs* for **er** and **ir**) and show the **ur** PCC. Here's another of these purple brothers, Urgent Ur. Write his name on the board. As we have learned, all three brothers' last names sound the same and that is what we hear in words, /ur/. Urgent Ur steals umbrellas and reports back with his last name, "**Ur!**"

What makes Urgent Ur different from his brothers? Yes, he wears boots that are covered in curly purple fur. Write 'curly purple fur' on the board so children can see these **ur** spellings.

Those boots slow Urgent Ur down, so you don't see him as often as his other brothers. Show the plain letter **ur** side and ask the children to say "/ur/" several times whenever you push the card forward.

Picture Code Cards

Phonemic awareness and language development

Explore the **ur** scene in the *Story Phonics* software and/or *Far Beyond ABC* book. Ask the children to hunt for items in the scene that include his /**ur**/ sound.

Urgent Ur in
Far Beyond ABC

Group activities

Blending ir words

*PCCs for 'Quick Dash' plus Silent Magic **e***

Words: **burn, turn, nurse, hurt, Thursday, Saturday**

Let's make some words with Urgent Ur's /**ur**/ sound from the story we just shared.

Let the children take turns being the Chief Detective who turns over **ur** card to show Urgent Ur that he can't fool them. Then the class does the **Roller Coaster Trick** to blend the word. Ask the children to blend the longer words, one syllable at a time and then read the whole word (**Thurs day, Sat ur day**). Ask someone to say a sentence with each word, perhaps relating to the content of the **ur** pages in *Far Beyond ABC*.

Word Detectives

Ask the children to come to the board and underline the **ur**'s in the words of the sentence below. Then read it a few times together.

> **On Thursday Urgent Ur hurt his toe on the curb.**

Song

Play *Urgent Ur in Person* and sing along with the children (lyrics on *TGCD*). The lyrics are not decodable texts, they are simply to increase phonemic awareness and aid language development.

ur words	
burn	hurt
burp	surf
burst	turn
curl	turnip
disturb	

Reading and fluency

Phonics Readers: *My very bad morning*
Read the story together a few times. Children can make a list of **ur** words in the story. Then they can tell a partner how each word relates to the story.

Fluency List P *(TGCD)*
Time children on this list and ask them to record their scores on their *Reading Racer Charts*.

Phonics Readers 4b

Lesson 75: Ernest Er, the elephant stealer
er as in her

Focus on

You'll need
- ✓ PCCs for 'Guess Who?' plus ĕ, **n**, **n**, ō, **s**, **s**/z/, ū
- ✓ *The Vowel Stealers* poster
- ✓ *Far Beyond ABC* or *Story Phonics* software

- ✓ *Blends & Digraphs Songs CD*
- ✓ *Phonics Readers 4b*
- ✓ *Fluency List Q (TGCD)*
- ✓ *Reading Racer Charts*
- ✓ Make a 'Tricky' Word Card: **does**

Review previously learned letters and sounds
'Guess Who?' *PCCs:* ă, **b**, **d**, Silent Magic **e**, **f**, o/ŭ/, **m**, **r**, **t**, **er**, **ir**, **or**, **th**, **ur**

Ernest Er, the elephant stealer

Display *The Vowel Stealers* poster (or use *PCCs* for **ur** and **ir**) and show the **er** PCC. Here is Ernest Er, another brother. Write his name on the board. As we have learned, all three brothers' last names sound the same and that is what we hear in words. As Ernest Er likes to run off with Elephants, he says his last name, **Er**.

Can you see how **Er**nest **Er**'s feet look different from his broth**er**s'? Yes, he wears train**er**s that help him run. In fact, let me tell you a secret about **Er**nest **Er**: (whispering) Ernest Er is a fast**er** runn**er** than both of his oth**er** broth**er**s because he has long**er** legs. Ask the children to whisp**er** the secret with you a few times and then whisp**er** it to a neighbour. Write the secret on the board so children can see these **er** spellings.

You can see that Ernest Er is often on the end of words. That's because most of the time, as he is fast**er** he runs ahead of his broth**er**s to the end of words.

But just like with all the Vowel Steal**er**s, we have to be good detectives to catch Ernest Er in words by calling out his last name, **Er**. Show the plain letter **er** side and ask the children to say "/**er**/" as you push the card forward.

Picture Code Cards

Phonemic awareness and language development
Explore the **er** scene in the *Story Phonics* software and/or *Far Beyond ABC* book. Ask the children to hunt for items in the scene that include his /er/ sound.

Group activities

Blending er words
Let's make some words with Ernest's /**er**/ sound from the story and illustration

Ernest Er in
Far Beyond ABC

we just shared.

Make the words, leaving a space between the first syllable and the **er**. Use picture sides for **o**/ŭ/ and **er** only. Ask the children to blend the sounds in the first syllable. Then close the space and ask them to read the whole word.

PCCs from 'Guess Who?'

> Words: **faster, brother, other, mother**

Song

Play *Ernest Er in Person* from the *Blends & Digraphs Songs CD* and ask the children to sing along (lyrics on *TGCD*). The lyrics are not decodable texts, they are simply to increase phonemic awareness and aid language development.

'Live Reading'

Let one child be Ernest Er, the faster runner. He or she stands to the left of your 'Live Reading' area. Distribute the *PCCs* and form each word without the **er** and then ask Ernest Er to run to the end of the word to finish it. Ask the class to do the Roller Coaster Trick for each syllable and then read the whole word. (For the second **s** in **sister**, use the plain letter side of the Sleepy Sammy card.)

PCCs: ě, ĭ, n, n, ō, r, s, s/z/, t, v, er

> Words: **runner** (run ner), **ever** (ev er), **never** (nev er), **over** (o ver), **sister** (sis ter)

Word Detectives

Ask the children to come to the board and Picture Code or underline the **er**'s. Then read this sentence a few times together, emphasising the final **er**'s:

> All winter and summer, Ernest Er is a faster runner than both of his other brothers.

Individual activities

Complete the **er** page in the *Blends & Digraph Copymasters* and the *Workbooks*. See Letterland Resources (page 12).

Reading and fluency

Phonics Readers 4b: *Snapshots*

Teach the new 'tricky' word **doesn't** and enjoy the story with the children.

Fluency List Q *(TGCD)*

Introduce this new list to children by echo reading each line or by choral reading. Later ask partners to re-read to each other.

---

er words

hammer	dinner
letter	better
ladder	summer
supper	banner

Note: In many words **er** can be an unstressed syllable, or schwa sound, making it sound more like /uh/.

'Tricky' word

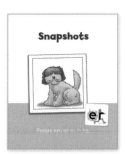

Phonics Readers 4b

er, ir, ur

You'll need

- ✓ PCCs for 'Quick Dash' plus **b, f, l, m, n, s, t, v**
- ✓ The Vowel Stealers poster
- ✓ Phonics Readers 4c
- ✓ Fluency List Q (TGCD)
- ✓ Make a 'Tricky' Word Card: **saw**

Review previously learned letters and sounds

'Quick Dash' PCCs: ĕ, ĭ, ō, o/ŭ/, ar, ch, ea, er, ir, or, th, th, ur

'Live Spelling' - Three Brothers

Let three children be Ernest Er, Irving Ir and Urgent Ur. Give each one a bag or backpack and their *PCC* (picture-side). The three of them stand to the left of your 'Live Reading' area.

Here are the /er/ brothers. Let's say their names.

Vowel Stealers Poster

Our first group of words for 'Live Spelling' will have the /er/ sound on the end of the word. Which one of the Er/Ir/Ur Brothers do you think will be on the end of these words? **"Ernest Er."**

Why does Ernest Er usually get to be the /er/ sound at the end of words? **"He's a faster runner than his other brothers."**

That's right. In a moment our brothers are going to have a pretend race to the end of some words and Ernest Er is going to get there before Irving Ir and Urgent Ur. The other brothers don't need to worry, we will make some words with them in a while.

Distribute the *PCCs* from 'Quick Dash' plus **b, f, l, m, n, s, t, v**

> Ernest Er Words: **never** (nev er), **over** (o ver), **teacher** (teach er),
> **mother** (moth er), **winter** (win ter)

First syllable

To begin, say the whole word and then say it again with a pause between syllables. Ask the children to repeat the syllables. Then ask them to stretch and segment the first syllable. Children with *PCCs* form the syllable.

Er syllable

Then ask the children to say the second syllable. If it has more than one sound (e.g. **o ver**), they segment the syllable (/v/-/er/) and put the letter before **er** in place. Then the three brothers pretend to race with Ernest Er winning and finishing the word. The other two brothers look disappointed.

Irving Ir

Now make some Irving Ir words. Ernest Er could still be on the end.

> Words: **birth, shirt, third, twirler** (twirl er)

Urgent Ur

Now make Urgent Ur words (some may also have Ernest Er on the end).

> Words: **turn, burner** (burn er), **nurse** (nurse), **surfer** (surf er)

Segmenting

Spelling with Magnetic Word Builders

Provide the children with a *Magnetic Word Builder* or other letter sets. Display the *PCC* for **er**, **ir**, or **ur** for each group of words so that the children do not

Magnetic Word Builder

have to guess at which spelling to use.

Letters needed: **a, b, c, d, e, e, h, i, l, n, o, q, r, r, s, s, t, t, u, v, y**

ur words: **curly** (curl y), **Thursday** (Thurs day), **disturb** (dis turb)

ir words: **dirty** (dir ty), **squirt**, **thirteen** (thir teen)

er words: **better** (bet ter), **ever** (ev er), **dresser** (dress er), **brother** (broth er), **colder** (cold er)

'Tricky' word

Reading and fluency

Phonics Readers 4c: *Ben's birthday surprise*
Teach the new 'tricky' word **saw** and enjoy the story.

Fluency List Q *(TGCD)*
Review the list. Then partners re-read to each other.

Phonics Readers 4c

Lesson 77: Oscar Orange, Mr O and Walter Walrus

ow as in show

Focus on **OW**

You'll need

- ✓ *PCCs for 'Guess Who?' plus* **ow**/ō/
- ✓ *Beyond ABC or Story Phonics software*
- ✓ *Phonics Readers 4c*
- ✓ *Fluency List Q (TGCD)*
- ✓ Make 'Tricky' Word Card: **know**
- ✓ Write the Word Detective sentence on the board
- ✓ Picture code **kn** on the board

Review previously learned letters and sounds

'Guess Who?' *PCCs:* b, d, g, ǐ, k, l, n, r, s, w, ar, er, ir, or, sh, ur

Walter Walrus, the troublemaker

We've been learning about some troublemakers, the vowel stealing robots, but did you know that there is another troublemaker in Letterland? He's not a robot and he doesn't capture vowels in a net. Instead he likes to tease them by splashing them with waves of cold, salty water from his two water wells.

Show the plain letter side of the **ow**/ō/ *PCC* or show the *Story Phonics* software. Some Letterlanders that you know are hiding behind these letters. Point to the **o**. Oscar Orange and...Point to the **w**. Who is hiding behind this one? **"Walter Walrus!"** That's right and Walter Walrus is trying to splash cold, salty water on Oscar Orange, but let's see what happens.

Picture Code Cards

Show the picture side and give children a moment to look at it. You know that Mr O takes care of all the talking oranges, don't you. And so here he steps in and stops Walter Walrus from teasing Oscar Orange with his splashing. Mr O steps in between, puts his hand up and says, "Oh, no, you don't!" Repeat the action and the words. Let's all do that like Mr O. Children put up a hand in a 'stop' gesture and say, **"Oh, no you don't!"**

Show the plain letters. That's why when we see these two letters together they often say /ō/. Push the card forward several times and o say /ō/ each time.

Role-play

Ask three children to come forward and role-play the scene with Oscar, Mr O and Walter. Then ask all the children to get in groups of three and do the same. Repeat twice more so that everyone gets a chance to play all three roles.

Phonemic awareness and language development

Explore the **ow**/ō/ scene in the *Story Phonics* software and/or *Beyond ABC* book. Ask the children to hunt for items in the scene that include the **ow**/ō/ sound.

Mr O and Walter Walrus in *Beyond ABC*

ow words	
arrow	follow
blow	grow
borrow	low
crow	show
elbow	snow

Group activities

Blending ow words

PCCs for 'Guess Who?' plus **ow**/ō/

Words: **low, blow, slow, grow, show, window** (win dow), **know**

Make the words with picture sides for **ow**/ō/ only.

Only 36 high frequency words begin with **k**. Nearly half of those begin with silent **kn**. The most important **kn** words to read and spell correctly are **know**, **knows** and **knew**. Before making the word **know,** share with the children the Letterland story logic for **kn** below.

Kicking King likes kicking but he never kicks when he is next to Nick in a word. Noisy Nick has a knack of getting in his way so he can't kick. Kicking King points at Nick and frowns but says nothing.

Word Detectives

Ask the children to come to the board and Picture Code or underline the **ow**'s. Then read the sentence a few times together.

I know the snow will blow by my window all day.

Individual activities

Complete the **ow** page in the *Blends & Digraph Copymasters* and the *Workbooks*. See Letterland Resources (page 12).

Reading and fluency

Phonics Readers 4c: *When the cold wind blows*

Enjoy the story with the children. As this is a poem with some less familiar words and word order, you may want to read it all to them the first time. Then read each verse to the children for them to echo read. You could also assign each verse to a small group to practise and then have all read their part to the class. The new 'tricky' word is **know**.

Phonics Readers 4c

Fluency List Q *(TGCD)*

Ask partners to practise with each other. You may want to use some of the words or sentences for dictation.

Lesson 78: Mr I, Golden Girl and Harry Hat Man

igh as in night

You'll need

✓ *PCCs for 'Quick Dash' plus* **igh**
✓ *Beyond ABC or Story Phonics software*
✓ *Phonics Readers 4c*
✓ *Fluency List R (TGCD)*
✓ *Reading Racer Charts (TGCD)*
✓ Write the Word Detective sentences on the board
✓ Make 'Tricky' Word Cards: **how** and **talk**
✓ An ice cream

Review previously learned letters and sounds

'Quick Dash' *PCCs*: b, d, h, ĭ, k, l, m, n, r, s, t, ar, ai, oa, ow

Introducing igh

Show the children the picture side of the **igh** PCC. Let's name these Letterlanders as I point... "Mr I, Golden Girl, Harry Hat Man."
Mr I is a kind man and he gives Golden Girl an ice cream for being a good girl. She is always careful to be completely silent when she sits next to Harry Hat Man because she knows he hates noise. Harry Hat Man smiles.
All we hear when these three are together is Mr I saying /ī/ as he holds out a fine ice cream for Golden Girl.

Push the plain letters forward several times. Children say /ī/ each time.

Picture Code Cards

Role-play

Ask three children to come forward and role-play the scene with Mr I, Golden Girl and Harry Hat Man. Use the ice cream you have prepared or the children can just pretend. Golden Girl could cover her mouth to show she is making no noise as she sits quietly with Harry Hat Man. You could role-play the scene at least three times so all the children get a chance to be each character.

Phonemic awareness and language development

Explore the **igh** scene in the *Story Phonics* software and/or *Beyond ABC* book. Ask the children to hunt for items in the scene that include the **igh** sound.

Group activities

Blending igh words

PCCs for 'Quick Dash' plus **igh** *or Story Phonics software - word building*

Mr I, Golden Girl and Harry Hat Man in *Beyond ABC*

> Words to blend: **high, night, light, right, knight, starlight**

Make the words with picture side for **igh** only. Children blend the words. For the word **knight** ask the children to tell the story logic that explains the **kn** sound you shared in the previous lesson.

Segmenting igh words

Call out the words for all the children to stretch and segment. Ask the group to help decide on the letters needed. Let individual children come forward and build the words on screen or on a shelf for all to see. For **midnight** ask them to stretch and segment each syllable separately.

> Words to segment: **sight, fight, fright, midnight** (mid night).

Word Detectives

Ask the children to come to the board and Picture Code or underline **igh**. Then read the sentences a few times together.

> **It might not be right for two knights to fight late in the night by the bright starlight. It might be a slightly frightening sight.**

igh words	
bright	night
fight	right
flight	thigh
high	sunlight
knight	tight

Reading and fluency

Phonics Readers 4c: *Cats' eyes and human eyes*
Teach the new 'tricky' words **talk** and **how** and read this story in play form with the children.

Fluency List R *(TGCD)*
Time children on this list and record their scores on their *Reading Racer Charts*.

'Tricky' words

Phonics Readers 4c

Lesson 79: Review
ow, igh

You'll need
✓ *PCCs* for 'Guess Who?'

✓ *Phonics Readers 4c*
✓ *Fluency List R (TGCD)*
✓ *Magnetic Word Builder* or other letter sets

Review previously learned letters and sounds

'Guess Who?' *PCCs*: b, f, g, l, n, r, s, t, t, ai, ar, igh, ow/ō/

'Live Spelling'

Revise the story logic by displaying the **igh**, **ow**/ō/*PCCs*. Ask the children to help retell the story logic. You may want to ask the children to role-play these stories again or watch the animated versions on the *Story Phonics* software. Distribute the *PCCs*. Call out the words for the children to stretch and segment. *PCCs* from 'Guess Who?' above.

Words: **slow**, **grown**, **sigh**, **fight**, rainbow (rain bow), **starlight** (star light)

Picture Code Cards

Spelling

Segmenting

Provide *Magnetic Word Builders* or other letter sets. Call out the words for children to stretch and segment.

Letters needed: **d, e, f, g, h, h, i, l, m, n, o, r, t, w**

Words: **fight**, **mow**, **flow**, **might**, **high**, **throw**, **delight** (de light), **window** (win dow)

Reading and fluency

Phonics Readers 4c: *Lost in the Queen's maze*
Enjoy reading and re-reading the story with the children a few times. Then you could assign three children to play the part of each of the three characters. The rest of the class can chorally read the words not in quotes. Cue each part by saying the character's name whenever it is their turn.

Fluency List R *(TGCD)*
Introduce this new list to the children by echo reading each line or by choral reading. Later ask partners to re-read to each other.

Phonics Readers 4c

oo as in moon

You'll need

✓ PCCs for 'Quick Dash' plus ĭ, r, z, oo (boot), th
✓ Far Beyond ABC or Story Phonics software
✓ Phonics Readers 4d
✓ Fluency List R (TGCD)
✓ Write the Word Detective sentences on the board
✓ Make a 'Tricky' Word Card: **walk**

Review previously learned letters and sounds

'Quick Dash' PCCs: **b, c, d,** Silent Magic **e, f, g, h, l, m, n, p, s, s/z/, t, ch, igh, ow/ō/**

Introducing the Boot and Foot Twins

To explain the sound of two **oo**'s appearing together in a word, you need to meet the Boot and Foot Twins. These twins are Mr O's grandsons. They are rather cheeky little boys who spend a lot of their time fighting over their boots.

You might like to start the lesson listening to the *Boot and Foot Twins song* on the *Blends & Digraphs Songs CD* or *Story Phonics* software to get an initial impression of this cheeky pair and the sounds they make.

*Blends & Digraphs
Songs CD*

The Boot Twin

Show the picture side of the **oo** (boot) *PCC*. Look closely at the picture. What do you notice about their feet? Yes, the one of them has boots on but the other doesn't. Ask the children to examine the picture further and comment on what they see, including the expressions on the face of each twin.

Point to the twin on the left. This one is called the Boot Twin. He teases his twin brother by taking his boots. Then he says (use a mocking tone), "**Oo**, I have your b**oo**ts." Can you hold up an imaginary pair of boots and say that with me?

Show the plain letters. That's why when we see these two letters together they often say /**oo**/. Push the card forward several times to cue children to say /**oo**/.

Picture Code Cards

Phonemic awareness and language development

Explore the **oo** scene in the *Story Phonics* software and/or *Far Beyond ABC* book. Ask the children to hunt for items in the scene that include the **oo** sound.

The Boot and Foot Twins in
Far Beyond ABC

Group activities

PCCs for Quick Dash plus **oo** (boot)

Words: **boot, moon, food, soon, spoon, choose, goose**

'Live Reading'

Distribute the *PCCs*. Use the plain letter sides except for **oo**. Ask two children to hold the **oo** *PCC*. Ask them to explain why their letters say /**oo**/ before you make the first word. After every two words or so let another pair be the twins and explain their sound again.

Special words

Note the different sounds for **s** in the similarly spelled words **choose** /**z**/ and **goose** /**s**/. (One has Sleepy Sammy's sound).

'Live Spelling'

Call out the words for all the children to stretch and segment. Then call on individual children to help build the words at the front of the class.

PCCs for 'Quick Dash' plus ĭ, r, z, oo (boot), th

oo words	
bamboo	proof
cool	room
igloo	shampoo
moon	spoons
	zoo

> Words: **broom, cool, smooth, loose, zoo, igloo** (ig loo).

Word Detectives

Ask the children to come to the board and underline the **oo's**. Then read the sentence a few times together.

This afternoon a moose got loose at the zoo.

Reading and fluency

Phonics Readers 4d

Phonics Readers 4d: *Penguins on the loose*

Teach the 'tricky' word **walk**.

This story would work well with **Plan and Play** as there are lots of roles to play: penguins, children and zookeepers (see page 222).

walk

'Tricky' word

Fluency List R *(TGCD)*

Review the list with children. Partners re-read to each other.

Lesson 81: The Foot Twin and Upside Down Umbrella

oo, u as in book and put

You'll need

- ✓ *PCCs for 'Guess Who?' plus **oo** (foot), **u***
- ✓ *Far Beyond ABC or Story Phonics software*
- ✓ *Fluency List R*
- ✓ *Phonics Readers 4d*
- ✓ Write the Word Detective sentences on the board
- ✓ Make the 'Tricky' Word Cards: **would, little**

Review previously learned letters and sounds

'Guess Who?' *PCCs*: **b, c, d, f, g, k, l, p, t, igh, ll, oo** (boot), **ow**/ō/, **sh**

The Foot Twin

Picture Code Cards

Display the picture sides of both the Boot Twin *PCC* and the Foot Twin *PCC*. Ask the children to examine the two pictures and talk about the differences.

You already know that the Boot Twin has taken his brother's boots. When we see these twin letters in words, we often hear the B**oo**t Twin say /oo/. Show the Boot Twin card. But sometimes we hear the F**oo**t Twin instead. He steps in a cold puddle with his bare f**oo**t and says, "**Oo**, just l**oo**k at my f**oo**t!"

Ask the children to pretend to step in a cold puddle and say, "**Oo, just look at my foot!**" Write the sentence on the board. Talk about the three times you hear the Foot Twin's sound.

Turn to the plain letter side. Ask the children to say the sound several times as you push the plain letters forward: "/**oo**/, /**oo**/..."

The Boot and Foot Twins in *Far Beyond ABC*

Phonemic awareness and language development

Explore the **oo** scene in the *Story Phonics* software and/or *Far Beyond ABC* book. Ask the children to hunt for items that include the Foot Twin's **oo** sound.

Group activities

Blending oo words

Make the words below with only the picture side for **oo** (f**oo**t). Children do the **Roller Coaster Trick** for each word.

*PCCs for 'Guess Who?' plus **oo** (foot)*

> Words: **foot, look, good, cook**

oo words	
look	took
foot	wood
cook	wool
good	hook
book	hood

Upside Down Umbrellas

There is another way we sometimes find this sound spelled in words. Show the picture side of the Upside Down Umbrella *PCC*.

There is another giant in Letterland called Giant Full. He helps Mr U put umbrellas in words but sometimes he can be a bit rough. He pushes and pulls at the umbrellas.

Write this sentence on the board:

Giant Full, you pushed me in, now pull me out!

Point to this sentence on the board. Ask the children to repeat it several times. Point out the words in the sentence that have the /**oo**/ sound spelled with the letter **u**.

Push the plain letter side of the **u** /**oo**/ *PCC* forward a few times as children repeat the sound, "/**oo**/, /**oo**/...".

Phonemic awareness and language development

Explore the **u** scene in the *Story Phonics* software. Ask the children to hunt for items in the scene that include the **u** sound.

Picture Code Cards

Upside down umbrella in
Story Phonics software

Group activities

Blending with u words

Make the words below with the picture side for **u** /**oo**/ only. Ask the children to blend each word.

*PCCs for 'Guess Who?' plus **u**/**oo**/*

Words: **push, pull, full, put, bush**

u words	
bull	pull
bush	push
full	put

Word Detectives

Ask the children to come to the board and underline the target sound. Then read the sentences a few times together.

> **Clever Cat looked in her cookbook for something good to cook.**
>
> **I pushed my foot into my sock and pulled it up.**

Individual activities

Introduce the relevant page from the *Blends & Digraph Copymasters* for children to work on independently or in small groups.
Ask the children to fill some **u** words in their *Word Bank Copymasters* from the board. They could also complete the relevant pages in their *Workbooks*.

Reading and fluency

Phonics Readers 4d: *The biggest carrot ever*
Teach the 'tricky' words **would** and **little** and enjoy the story.

Fluency List R *(TGCD)*
Partners practise reading to each other.

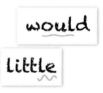

'Tricky' words

Phonics Readers 4d

aw, au as in saw and cause

You'll need

- ✓ *PCCs* for 'Quick Dash' plus **f, k, m, n, p, t, aw, au**
- ✓ *Beyond ABC* or *Story Phonics* software
- ✓ *Phonics Readers 4d*

- ✓ *Fluency List R (TGCD)*
- ✓ *Reading Racer Charts (TGCD)*
- ✓ Write the Word Detective sentence on the board
- ✓ Make 'Tricky' Word Cards: **could, colour**

Review previously learned letters and sounds

'Quick Dash' *PCCs*: **b, c, d, f, g, k, l, p, t, igh, ll, oo**(boot), **ow**/ō/, **sh**

Annie Apple and Walter Walrus

Display the picture side of the **aw** *PCC*. Ask the children to examine the picture and talk about the characters and what they are doing.

We know that Walter Walrus can be a troublemaker. He is splashing his salty, cold water right in Annie Apple's face and even in her eyes. When he does this, Annie Apple cries out, "**Aw**! Don't be so **aw**ful!" Write this sentence on the board, talk about the **aw** spelling and sound and rehearse the sentence together.

Picture Code Cards

Role-play

Ask the children to pair up to be Annie and Walter. 'Walter' pretends to splash 'Annie.' She wipes her face and says, "**Aw**, don't be so **aw**ful." Then ask them to swap roles and repeat.

Turn to the plain letter side of **aw**. Ask the children to say the sound each time you push the plain letters forward: "/**aw**/, /**aw**/...".

Phonemic awareness and language development

Explore the **aw** scene in the *Story Phonics* software and/or *Beyond ABC* book. Ask the children to hunt for items in the scene that include the **aw** sound.

Annie and Walter in Beyond ABC

Walter Walrus in Uppy Umbrella's letter

Display the picture side the **au** *PCC*. Walter is a troublemaker. Sometimes he even sneaks into Uppy Umbrella's letter when she is away. He fills up the letter with his salty water and surprises Annie Apple by splashing her in the face again. So what does she say? The same thing again! "**Aw! Don't be so awful!**"

Push the plain letter side of **au** forward a few times for children to say the sound: "/**aw**/, /**aw**/..."

Picture Code Cards

Phonemic awareness and language development

Explore the **au** scene in the *Story Phonics* software and/or *Beyond ABC Book*. Ask the children to hunt for items in the scene that include the **au** sound. (The full list is at the back of the book.)

Group activities

Make the words below with the picture side for **aw** or **au** only. Children blend each word. Use the plain letter side of an **e** for **pause**, etc. as this is a final silent **e**.

PCCs for 'Quick Dash' plus **p, aw, au**

Annie and Walter in Beyond ABC

Words: **saw, draw, claw, pause, cause**

Spelling with Picture Code Cards

Display the picture sides: **oo** (boot), **oo** (foot), **aw, au**. Ask the children to help tell the story logic and sounds.

Call out each word for the children to repeat. Then ask them to stretch and segment and decide on the letters needed. They will need some guidance on choosing between **aw** and **au** as these have the same sound. Let children come forward to help build the words at the front of the class.

PCCs for 'Quick Dash' plus **f, k, m, n, t, aw, au**

Words: **moon, lawn, book, food, straw, stood, launch**

aw /au words	
paw	August
claw	haul
jaw	haunted
lawn	launch
yawn	laundry

Word Detectives

Ask the children to come to the board and Picture Code or underline each **aw** and **au**. Then read the sentence a few times together.

I saw that Walter Walrus was the cause of an awful splash.

Chant

Enjoy the chant for Annie Apple and Walter Walrus's sound on the *Story Phonics* software.

Reading and fluency

Phonics Readers 4d: *The art class*

Teach the 'tricky' words **could, colour**. This is the second story of four in a row that feature a theme of cooperation. As you read each one, ask the children to compare how the characters work together in each of the stories.

Phonics Readers 4d

'Tricky' words

Fluency List R *(TGCD)*

Time the children on this list and ask them to record their scores on their *Reading Racer Charts*.

Lesson 83: Eddy Elephant and Walter Walrus

ew as in grew and few

Focus on **ew**

You'll need

✓ *PCCs for 'Guess Who?' plus* **f, k, m, n, p, t, aw, au**
✓ *Beyond ABC or Story Phonics software*
✓ *Blends & Digraphs Songs CD*
✓ *Phonics Readers 4d*
✓ *Fluency List S (TGCD)*
✓ *Write the Word Detective sentence on the board*
✓ *Make 'Tricky' Word Cards:* **should, knew**

Review previously learned letters and sounds

'Guess Who?' PCCs: **d, ě, ǐ, k, v, r, s, t, aw, au, ch, sh, th, oo** (boot), **oo** (foot)

Eddy Elephant and Walter Walrus

Display the picture side of the **ew** PCC. Examine the picture together and talk about what the characters are doing.

We know that Walter Walrus likes to splash Letterlanders. Eddy Elephant knows it, too. But he has something that no one else in Letterland has – a long trunk that can suck up water. Before Walter gets a chance to splash, Eddy sucks up water from the wells and blows it right at Walter. Walter is so upset, he cries out, "**Ew, you!**"

Picture Code Cards

Let's all say, "**Ew, you!**" This is our clue for remembering that these two letters sometimes say /**oo**/ and sometimes say /**yoo**/.

Turn to the plain letter side of **ew**. So when I show you these plain letters, you say, "/**oo**/, /**yoo**/." Ask the children to say the sounds each time you push the plain letters forward: "/**oo**/, /**yoo**/.../**oo**/, /**yoo**/...".

Role-play

Ask the children to pair up and play the parts of Eddy and Walter. Walter starts to splash, but Eddy raises his trunk before Walter gets a chance. Walter wipes his face and says "**Ew, you.**" Swap roles and repeat.

Phonemic awareness and language development

Explore the **ew** scene in the *Story Phonics* software and/or *Beyond ABC* book. Ask the children to hunt for items in the scene that include the **ew** sound. (The full list is at the back of the book.)

Eddy and Walter in
Beyond ABC

Group activities

Blending with Picture Code Cards

The words below come from the **ew** song that is the next activity below. Make the words below with the picture side for **ew** only. Children blend each word using the Roller Coaster Trick. Discuss the different meanings of **new** and **knew**. Also talk about the meaning of **shrewd** and **shrewdest**. Point out that the letter **i** in **view** is silent.

PCCs for 'Guess Who?' plus **ew**

Words: **new, knew, view, shrewd, shrewdest** (shrewd est)

Song

Display the lyrics for the song (*TGCD*). Read through the words for the children and then all sing along. The children should not be expected to read or decode all the words.

Segmenting with Picture Code Cards

Call out each word for children to repeat. Then ask them to stretch and segment it and decide on the letters needed. Let children come forward to help build the words (with the picture side for **ew** only). Discuss the meaning of the words, especially those that have homonyms (e.g. **threw/through**, **blew/blue**)

PCCs for 'Guess Who?' plus **b, l, ew**

Words: **chew, drew, stew, flew, threw, blew**

Word Detectives

Ask the children to come to the board and Picture Code or underline each **ew**. Then read the sentence a few times together.

Eddy knew a few new tricks.

Reading and fluency

'Tricky' words

Phonics Readers 4d: *Harry Hat Man's new roof*

Teach the 'tricky' words **should** and **friends**, then read the story together.

Fluency List S *(TGCD)*

Introduce this new list by echo reading each line or by choral reading. Later ask partners to re-read to each other.

Phonics Readers 4d

Blending and segmenting

You'll need
- ✓ *PCCs for 'Quick Dash' plus* **b, c, d, k, l, p, r**
- ✓ *Magnetic Word Builders or other letter sets*
- ✓ *Phonics Readers 4e*
- ✓ *Fluency List S (TGCD)*
- ✓ Gather 'Tricky' Word Cards for review
- ✓ Make a 'Tricky' Word Card: **laugh**

Review previously learned letters and sounds
'Quick Dash' *PCCs*: Silent Magic **e, s, s/z/, t, aw, au, ew, ll, oo, oo, u/oo/**

Blending

Revise the story logic
Display the **aw, au, ew, oo, oo, u**/oo/ *PCCs*. Ask the children to help retell the story logic for each *PCC*. You may want to ask the children to quickly role-play some of these stories again.

'Live Reading'
Arrange children with the *PCCs* to form the first word. Use picture sides for the **aw, au, ew, oo, oo, u**/oo/ *PCCs* only. Ask the class to do the **Roller Coaster Trick** to read the word. Provide an oral sentence with the word or ask the children to provide one. Then quickly make the changes to form the next one. Keep the activity fast-paced to maintain engagement.

Use the *PCCs* from 'Quick Dash' above plus **b, c, d, k, l, p, r**

> Words: **cool, claw, crew, crook, pull, pool, paw, pew, pause, stew, stood, stool, straw, saw**

Segmenting

Provide children with *Magnetic Word Builders* or other letter sets. Words are listed in two sets to avoid putting two spellings for the same sound together. Display the *PCC*'s as listed below. Call out each word for children to repeat, segment and spell with their own letters. For multi-syllable words children say the whole word, then each syllable separately. Then they segment and spell one syllable at a time as usual.

Magnetic Word Builder

Letters: **a, b, c, d, e, f, g, h, i, k, l, l, n, o, o, m, n, p, u, r, s, t, w, y**

> Set 1   Display the *PCCs*: **aw, ew, oo** (foot)
>
> Words: **awful** (aw ful), **stood, grew, shook, yawn, chew**
>
> Set 2   Display the *PCCs*: **au, oo** (boot), **u** /oo/(push)
>
> Words: **pulling, mood, cause, bull, launch, smooth**

Reading and fluency

New 'tricky' word for this lesson: **laugh.**
Review previous 'tricky' words as required.

'Tricky' word

Phonics Readers 4e: *Who will help?*
Continue discussing the theme of cooperation with this story.

Fluency List S *(TGCD)*
Review this list with children and then ask partners to re-read to each other.

Phonics Readers 4e

ow, ou as in how and out

You'll need

✓ *PCCs for 'Guess Who?' plus c, d, Silent Magic e, f, g, n, p, r, s, t, ow/ou/, ou*

✓ *Beyond ABC or Story Phonics software*

✓ *Blends & Digraphs Songs CD*

✓ *Phonics Readers 4e*

✓ *Fluency List S (TGCD)*

✓ Make a 'Tricky' Word Card: **their**

Review previously learned letters and sounds

'**Guess Who?**' *PCCs:* aw, au, ch, er, ew, igh, oo, oo, ow/ō/, u/oo/

Oscar Orange and Walter Walrus

Display the picture side of the **ow** *PCC.* Ask the children to examine the picture and talk about the characters and what they are doing.

We know that Mr O sometimes stops Walter Walrus from splashing Oscar Orange. But Mr O is not always around. Then Walter splashes salty water that gets in Oscar eyes. What Walter forgets is that when you tease someone, you can also hurt yourself. He slips and bumps his chin. So they both howl "**Ow!**" at the same time.

Turn to the plain letter side of **ow**. Ask the children to say the sound each time you push the plain letters forward: "/**ow**/… /**ow**/…".

Picture Code Cards

Role-play

Ask the children to pair up and role-play the parts of Oscar Orange and Walter Walrus. Walter splashes and bumps his chin and Oscar puts his hands to his eyes and they both howl, "**Ow!**". Swap roles and repeat.

Phonemic awareness and language development

Explore the **ow** scene in the *Story Phonics* software and/or *Beyond ABC* book. Ask the children to hunt for items in the scene that include the **ow** sound.

Oscar and Walter in *Beyond ABC*

Walter Walrus in Uppy Umbrella's letter

Show the picture side of the **ou** *PCC.* As we know, Walter Walrus sometimes sneaks into Uppy Umbrella's letter when she's away. He likes her letter because it can hold lots of water that he can splash on Oscar Orange. Once again Oscar gets his eyes full of salt water and Walter Walrus bumps his chin, so once again they both say "**Ou!**" (Same sound, different spelling.)

Turn to the plain letter side of **ou**. Ask the children to say the sound each time you push the plain letters forward: "/**ou**/… /**ou**/…".

Picture Code Cards

Phonemic awareness and language development

Explore the **ou** scene in the *Story Phonics* software and/or *Beyond ABC* book. Ask the children to hunt for items in the scene that include the **ou** sound.

Oscar and Walter in *Beyond ABC*

Group activities

Blending ow and ou words

Make the words below with the picture side for **ow** and **ou** only. Children blend each word. Then you or one of the children says a sentence with the word.

PCCs for Guess Who?' plus c, d, Silent Magic e, f, g, n, p, r, s, t, ow/ou/, ou

Words: **now, frown, power, crowd, out, ouch, grouch, house, sound**

Song

Display the lyrics for the **ow** and **ou** song (*TGCD*). Read through the words for the children for phonemic awareness and then play the songs for everyone to sing along with the *Blends & Digraphs Songs CD* or *Story Phonics* software.

Word Detectives

Ask the children to come to the board and Picture Code or underline each **ow** and **ou**. Then read the sentence a few times together.

The bells in the tower made a loud sound all over town.

ow / ou words	
now	out
down	about
owl	cloud
cow	sound
town	loud

Reading and fluency

Phonics Readers 4e: *What big flippers you have!*
Teach the 'tricky' word **their** and enjoy the story with the children.
Discuss the ways that this story is like and unlike Little Red Riding Hood.

their
'Tricky' word

Phonics Readers 4e

Fluency List S *(TGCD)*
Ask the children to practise with partner. You may want to use some of the words or sentences for dictation.

Lesson 86: A boy called Roy
oy, oi as in boy and coin

You'll need

- ✓ *PCCs for 'Quick Dash' +* **b, ĕ, l, j, n, r, s/z/, t, oi, oy**
- ✓ *Far Beyond ABC or Story Phonics software*
- ✓ *Blends & Digraphs Songs CD*
- ✓ *Phonics Readers 4e*
- ✓ *Fluency List S (TGCD)*

Review previously learned letters and sounds

'Quick Dash' *PCCs:* **ar, or, ea, ai, oa, ue, aw, au, ew, oo, oo, ow/ō/, ow/ou/, ou, u/oo/**

A boy called Roy

Display the plain letter side of the **oy** *PCC*.

We are going to meet a new Letterlander today. Show the picture side. This boy is called Roy. He has a special game he likes to play. He likes to leapfrog over that **o** and jump into Yellow Yo-yo Man's sack. Does that look like fun? When he jumps he shouts, **"Oy!"**. Yellow Yo-yo Man pretends to be ann**oy**ed and he shouts, **"Oy!"** at exactly the same time.

Turn to the plain letter side of **oy**. Ask the children to say the sound each time you push the plain letters forward: "/**oy**/, /**oy**/...".

Picture Code Cards

Role-play

Ask the children to pair up and role-play the story logic. One partner is Roy, who stands behind Yellow Yo-yo Man. Roy, put your hands on Yellow Yo-yo Man's shoulders and jump up in your place. Both of you say **"Oy!"**. Let's do it three times: **"Oy!...oy!...oy!"**.

Phonemic awareness and language development

Explore the **oy** scene in the *Story Phonics* software and/or *Far Beyond ABC* book. Ask the children to hunt for items in the scene that include the **oy** sound.

Far Beyond ABC

Roy and Mr I

Sometimes Roy plays his game with Mr I instead of Yellow Yo-yo Man. Show the picture side of the **oi** *PCC*. They still say the same sound "Oi!".

Picture Code Cards

Plain letters oi and sound

Turn to the plain letter side of **oi**. Ask the children to say the sound each time you push the plain letters forward: "/**oi**/, /**oi**/...".

Phonemic awareness and language development

Ask the children to listen for words and hunt for items in the illustration that include the **oi** sound. (The full list is at the back of the book.)

Far Beyond ABC

Group activities

PCCs: **b, c, ĕ, l, j, n, r, s/z/, t, oi, oy**

Words: **Roy, toy, coin, noise, boil, boi, boy, join, joi, joy, enjoy**

'Live Reading'

Distribute the *PCCs* listed below. Let two children hold **oi** and two more hold **oy**. Guide the children in forming the words above for the class to do the **Roller Coaster Trick**. After they read **boil**, take off the **l** and ask the children to blend the non-word **boi** to discover that it is pronounced, "**boy**". But as you have already learned, Mr I doesn't like being on the end of a word, does he? Why doesn't Mr I like being on the end? "**He gets dizzy.**" Then ask the children with the **oy** card to take the place of those with **oi**. The class blends the new word. Follow similar steps with **join**, (non-word) **joi**, **joy**.

Song

Enjoy the song *Roy and the Yo-yo Man* on the *Blends & Digraphs Songs CD* or the *Story Phonics* software. You may want to read through the lyrics (*TGCD*) for the children but they should not be expected to decode all the words at this stage.

Word Detectives

Ask the children to come to the board and Picture Code or underline each **oy** and **oi**. Then read the sentence a few times together.

Roy likes to join his friends to enjoy noisy toys.

Individual activities

Introduce the relevant page from the *Blends & Digraph Copymasters* for children to work on independently or in small groups.
Ask the children to fill some **oy** words in their *Word Bank Copymasters* from the board. Add a few distractors to make this more of a challenge. Individual activities.
Ask the children to complete the **oy/oi** page in their *Workbooks*.

oy / oi words	
boy	oil
toy	boil
joy	coin
enjoy	soil
annoy	foil

Reading and fluency

Phonics Readers 4e: *Nick's noisy new toy*

Enjoy the story with the children. Use one or two sentences from the story for dictation.

Fluency List S *(TGCD)*

Children practise reading the list to a partner.

Phonics Readers 4e

Blending and segmenting

You'll need
- ✓ *PCCs for 'Guess Who?'* + **c, ĕ**, Silent **e, f, j, l, n, p, s**
- ✓ *Magnetic Word Builders* or other letter sets
- ✓ *Phonics Readers 4e*
- ✓ *Fluency List S* and *Reading Racer Chart (TGCD)*
- ✓ Make a 'Tricky' Word Card: **people**
- ✓ Gather 'Tricky' Word Cards for review

Review previously learned letters and sounds
'Guess Who?' *PCCs*: **ch, ee, er, ou, ow/ou/, oi, oy, sh, th, ue**

Blending
Display the **ou, ow/ou/, oi,** and **oy** *PCCs*. Ask the children to help retell the story logic for each *PCC*. You may want to ask the children to quickly role-play these stories again.

'Live Reading'
PCCs from 'Guess Who?' above plus **c, ĕ**, Silent Magic **e, f, j, l, n, p**

Words: **clown, power, south, couch, found, soil, noise, joy, enjoy**

Arrange children with the *PCCs* to form the first word. Use picture sides for the **ou, ow/ou/, oi,** and **oy** *PCCs* only. Children do the **Roller Coaster Trick** to read the word. Provide an oral sentence with the word or ask the children to provide one. Then quickly make the changes to form the next one. Make the activity fast-paced to keep children engaged.

Segmenting

Spelling with Magnetic Word Builders
Provide the children with the *Magnetic Word Builder* or other letter sets. Words are listed in two sets to avoid putting two spellings for the same sound together. Display the *PCCs* as listed below. Call out each word for the children to repeat, segment and spell with their own letters. For the multi-syllable word **power**, the children say the whole word, then each syllable separately (**pow er**). Then they segment and spell one syllable at a time as usual.

Magnetic Word Builder

Letters needed: **a, b, c, d, e, f, g, h, i, k, l, l, n, o, o, m, n, p, u, r, s, t, w, y**

Set 1	Display the *PCCs*: **oi, ou**
	Words: **point, shout, sound, noisy, mouse, boil**
Set 2	Display the *PCCs*: **oy, ow**
	Words: **crowd, boy, town, toy, power**

Reading and fluency

'Tricky' word

'Tricky' word review
Use the cards you have made for recent 'tricky' words. Ask the children to read them. Move a little faster as children read the words a second time. Suggested 'tricky' words for this review: **their, friend, does, what, water, one, there**.

Phonics Readers 4e: *Squeaks, the house mouse*
Teach the 'tricky' word **people**. Enjoy the story with the children.

Phonics Readers 4e

Fluency List S *(TGCD)*
Time the children on this list. They can record scores on *Reading Racer Charts*.

air, ear as in fair and year

You'll need

- ✓ PCCs for 'Quick Dash' plus **h, l, n, p, p, air, ear**
- ✓ *Far Beyond ABC* or *Story Phonics* software
- ✓ Materials for spelling
- ✓ *Phonics Readers 4e*
- ✓ *Fluency List T (TGCD)*
- ✓ Make a 'Tricky' Word Card: **through**

Review previously learned letters and sounds

'Quick Dash' *PCCs*: **au, aw, ch, ew, ow/ō/, oi, ou, ow/ou/, oy**

Capturing two Vowel Men - Mr A and Mr I

Display the Vowels Out Walking Poster. Do you remember the story about when two Vowel Men go out walking? The first man does the talking and the second man is silent. Do you remember why? Yes, he is too busy looking out for vowel stealing robots. The trouble is, sometimes he doesn't spot a lurking robot in time. Then that Vowel Stealer captures both Vowel Men! When that happens, don't expect the Vowel Men to be behaving as usual – not when they have just been tossed into a robot's sack! They are too startled to shout!

Show the picture side of *PCC* **air**. Here you can see it. The robot has captured Mr A and Mr I! They are such a heavy load that the robot puffs out, "**Air, I need air! I've caught a pair!**" So what is the new sound? /**air**/!

Push the plain letters forward, children say : "/**air**/, /**air**/...".

Vowels Out Walking Poster

Picture Code Cards

Role-play

Ask the children to pretend to have a heavy load on their backs and then repeat what the robot says when he captures Mr A and Mr I.

Phonemic awareness and language development

Explore the **air** scene in the *Story Phonics* software and/or *Far Beyond ABC* book. Ask the children to hunt for items in the scene that include the **air** sound.

Far Beyond ABC

Capturing two Vowel Men - Mr E and Mr A

Show the *PCC* **ear**. Sometimes other Vowel Men get caught out, too. Exactly the same thing can happen when Mr E and Mr A go out walking!

A different robot has captured Mr E and Mr A! They are very upset and complain loudly about being captured. But the robot pretends that he can't hear them, as he says, "**Oh, dear! I fear my ear can't hear you.**" So what is the new sound? /**ear**/!

Push the plain letters forward, children say : "/**ear**/.../**ear**/...".

Picture Code Cards

Role-play

Ask the children to pretend to have these two different protesting Vowel Men in their robber sacks while they repeat the robot's words.

Phonemic awareness and language development

Explore the **ear** scene in the *Story Phonics* software and/or *Far Beyond ABC* book. Ask the children to hunt for items in the scene that include the **ear** sound.

Far Beyond ABC

Group activities

Blending air and ear words

Make the words below for children to do the **Roller Coaster Trick**. Use the plain letter ā (saying /ŭ/) for the first letter **a** in **appear**.

PCCs: ā, c, Silent Magic e, h, l, n, p, p, ch, air, ear

Words: **air, hair, chair, ear, hear, clear, appear**

Spelling with Magnetic Word Builders

Provide the children with the *Magnetic Word Builder* or other letter sets. Call out each word for children to repeat, segment and spell with their own letters.

Words: **pair, fear, spear, stairs, fair**

Word Detectives

Ask the children to come to the board and Picture Code or underline each **air** and **ear**. Then read the sentence a few times together.

We could clearly hear the pair on the stairs before they appeared.

air / ear words	
air	ear
chair	dear
fair	hear
hair	bear
pair	year

Individual activities

Introduce the relevant page from the *Blends & Digraph Copymasters* for children to work on independently or in small groups or look at *Workbook 6*.

Reading and fluency

Phonics Readers 4e: *Lily and the fairies*

There is a bonus story *'Missing at the fair'* which you can use to review many of the sounds taught in Section 5.

Fluency List T *(TGCD)*

Introduce this new list to the children by echo reading each line or by choral reading. Later ask partners to re-read to each other.

Phonics Readers 4e

Home link

Make copies of the Section 5 *Take-Home Booklets* from the *TGCD* for children to read in class and then take home to read to their parents.

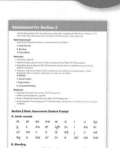

Take-Home Booklet

Assessment - Refer to your TGCD

Use the Section 5 assessments a few days to two weeks after completing the final lesson in Section 5. All assessment material including full instructions and Assessment forms are on the *TGCD*.

Assessments for Sections 2-5

We have provided thorough assessment tools. You may not need all of them for every child. Choose only those that will be useful for your teaching.

Section 6 :
Appendix

This Appendix provides you with all the Letterland strategies that can be used again and again in your teaching. You will be referred to specific strategies in the lesson plans, but you can also visit this section as a central resource. Reviewing the strategies and the many variations suggested will help keep your teaching sharply focused and fresh.

The Letterland Tricks

This is a summary of the six main strategies for children to learn. Present them as 'tricks' that the Letterlanders have thought up to help them become better readers and writers. They are called 'tricks' because once children know them, they can use them independently whenever they are reading and writing. The tricks are referenced within the Lesson Plans and are explained in detail on the pages indicated below.

To see videos of these tricks please visit our website: www.letterland.com/training

Sound Trick
Just say the Letterlander's name and start to say it again, but this time stop with just the first sound. That is exactly the sound this letter makes in words.

.... 181

Action Trick
Each Letterlander has made up an action for you, to help you remember the sound. Just do the action and say the sound.

.... 182

Alliteration Trick
The Letterlanders have a trick so you can predict what they like by listening for their sounds at the beginning of words. Lucy Lamp Light especially likes animals like lions, lambs, llamas, and lizards etc.

.... 184

Uppercase Trick
The Letterlanders help us remember their uppercase shapes even when they don't look at all like their lowercase shapes. Each one has a special trick they do whenever they get a chance to start an important word like a name or the beginning of a sentence. Here is Eddy Elephant's 'Elephant on End' trick.

.... 186

Roller Coaster Trick (blending)
Even when we know each Letterlander's sound, blending letter sounds smoothly can be a challenge. Imagine that your outstretched arm is a roller coaster hill. Place the sounds on it, then slide your hand down the roller coaster as you blend the sounds to read the word.

.... 188

Rubber Band Trick (segmenting)
Hearing each letter sound in a word isn't easy. It helps to pretend you are stretching a big rubber band as you slowly say the word. As you stretch a word, it is far easier to segment each sound. Use this trick whenever you need to segment a word and spell it.

.... 190

Strategies for teachers

The **strategies for teachers** summarised below are organised from the smallest units of language, phonemes, then word level strategies, to the largest units, fluent reading of stories.

Letter sounds

Children practise responding with the sounds instantly when they see the plain letter, and to recall the letter on hearing the sound.

Letter shapes

Children learn to form the letters correctly, to recognise both lowercase and uppercase letters and to avoid reversals in reading and spelling.

Reading and spelling words

Reading stories

Mmm

Sound Trick (initial phoneme segmenting)

Objectives

For children to learn to:
- learn simple recall routes to the **a-z** letter sounds..

Resources

- *Picture Code Cards* of new or recently learned letters.

Explanation for children

Let's learn a new trick that will help us discover the sound that the Letterlanders make in words.

Hold up the **m**, picture side. Who is this? **"Munching Mike."** Yes, it is Munching Mike, and here's the special way to discover his sound. It's called the Sound Trick. You say his name and then just **start** to say his name again, but **stop** just as the name starts to come out of your mouth, like this, **Mmm...** Don't say too much, just that very first sound in his name. Let's do the Sound Trick together. First we say his whole name very slowly, and then just **start** to say it, but only the very first sound, **"Mmmmuuuunnnching Mmmmiiiike, mmmm."** Yes, that's the sound he makes in words: /mmm/.

Procedure

Step	Description	Example
1	**Teacher** shows the picture side of the *PCC*.	
2	**Children** say the Letterlander's name.	Clever Cat
3	**Teacher** shows the plain letter side.	
4	**Children** start to say the name again but stop on the first sound.	/c/

Clever Cat   /**c**/

When to use

- Use the Sound Trick when introducing a new sound in Section 1, or revisiting the letter in Section 2 of this *Teacher's Guide*.
- Use the Sound Trick in revising letter sounds that some children are unsure of.
- Encourage children to use the Sound Trick on their own if they need it to recall a letter sound.

Development over time

Once children know the letter sounds, move on to children saying only the sound in response to the plain letter.

Variations

For children finding difficulty in isolating the beginning sound in the Letterlander's names and in other words, try adding this kinaesthetic support. The child says the character's name while pretending to stretch an imaginary rubber band wrapped around their hands. The child starts to say the name again while stretching the rubber band, but stop just as his hands begin to pull apart. The best letters for learning this process are the easily prolonged sounds: **f, m, n, r, s, v, z** (see page 192).

"Mmmunching Mmmike"

"Mmm"

Action Trick (VAK phoneme cues)

Objectives
- To develop multisensory (kinaesthetic-auditory-oral-visual) memory cues for letter sounds
- To provide a movement to keep children engaged and alert.

Resources
- *Action Tricks Poster* and *Picture Code Cards*.

Explanation for children
Each Letterlander has made up an action to help us remember his or her sound. They call them the **Action Tricks**.

When to use
- Action Tricks are taught for each letter when it is introduced.
- Action Tricks are used with the 'Quick Dash' activity (page 194) to revise letter sounds. They can also be used with the 'Guess Who?' activity (page 196).
- At first, ask the children to make the actions at the same time as saying the letter sound. Once they know them well, try some of the activities below.

Variations
- **Get the wiggles out** When you notice children getting restless and in need of a change of pace and some movement, try this: Go through the alphabet **a** to **z** with everyone making the actions as they say the sounds. Action Tricks can be used sitting or standing. As an option, ask everyone to repeat each sound and action three times before moving on to the next letter.
- **Follow the leader** Ask one child to silently do an action and everyone else respond with the action and add the sound.
- **Action spelling** Show one child a regular word. That child silently does the actions for each letter in the word. The other children write the word or make it with a *Magnetic Word Builder* or in the word building section of the *Story Phonics* software. Then everyone reads the word.

Action Tricks

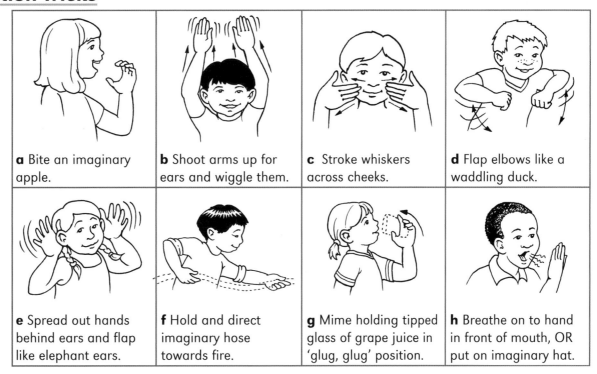

a Bite an imaginary apple.	**b** Shoot arms up for ears and wiggle them.	**c** Stroke whiskers across cheeks.	**d** Flap elbows like a waddling duck.
e Spread out hands behind ears and flap like elephant ears.	**f** Hold and direct imaginary hose towards fire.	**g** Mime holding tipped glass of grape juice in 'glug, glug' position.	**h** Breathe on to hand in front of mouth, OR put on imaginary hat.

 **i** Touch fingers to thumb on the same hand as if sticky with ink and make an 'icky' face.

 **j** Juggle imaginary balls.

 **k** Lift one arm and one foot in a k-shape. If sitting, use arms only.

 **l** Touch finger tips above head to suggest Lucy's lamp-shade hat.

 **m** Rub tummy.

 **n** Bang one fist on the other, as if hammering a nail.

 **o** Form round shapes with both mouth and hand and adopt a surprised look.

 **p** Stroke down long imaginary ears.

 **q** Point index finger up as if ordering 'Quiet!', while saying 'qu…'.

 **r** Make a robot-like running movement with arms.

 **s** Make snake movements with hand and arm.

 **t** Lift arms horizontally at shoulder height in T-shape.

 **u** Hold up imaginary umbrella with one hand low and the other above the head.

 **v** Hold hands together in v-shape.

 **w** Flick both hands up and away as if splashing water, ending with arms in a w-shape.

 **x** Cross arms on chest in x-shape.

 **y** Move hand up and down as if controlling a yo-yo.

 **z** Tilt head and rest against hands to mime falling asleep.

Long vowel action
Each Vowel Man punches the air with his right hand as he calls out his name enthusiastically.

Initial sounds in spoken words

Many children will have learnt to listen for beginning sounds in words and match them to letters in an Early Years programme. For them the Alliteration Trick and the game below will be a good revision of this skill. For other children who have not fully developed their abilities in this vital area, the Activity Bank (pages 232-238) provides several excellent activities to use with the whole class or in small groups. You can also use alliterative words at any time, with the Letterlanders naturally attracting image-rich language and verbal associations to themselves.

Alliteration Trick (phonemic awareness)

Objective
- To develop phonemic awareness of initial sounds.

Resources
- Display a *PCC* of the character.

Explanation for children

Every Letterlander likes things that begin with his or her sound. So if we want to know what foods Peter Puppy likes to eat, we just start to say his sound and think of a food, like ... p-p-pears, p-p-potatoes. When we use words that begin with the same sound we call that alliteration. We can use this Alliteration Trick to discover all sorts of things about the Letterlanders.*

*For example, you won't be surprised that **P**eter **P**uppy likes to **p**lay **p**ing **p**ong. He **p**lays his favourite game to **p**erfection, often with **T**alking **T**ess, who is also **t**errific at the game, but she insists on calling it **t**able **t**ennis!

Procedure for the Alliteration Game

The teacher displays the *PCC* for a Letterlander.

Step	Description	Example
1	**Teacher** suggests categories to help children think of things the Letterlander would like because they start with his or her sound.	*Let's think of places Peter Puppy likes to play.*
2	**Children** name things that start with the Letterlander's sound. Teacher writes their suggestions on the board in categories.	**"the park" "the pool" "a playground"**
3	**Teacher** gives the child clues to help them think of a suitable alternative if a child says a word that doesn't begin with the target sound.	Child: **"At my house."** *That's a great idea, but we need to think of something that starts with his sound, like this, /p/. If it is raining, do you think Peter Puppy might like to play in a muddy /p/.....?* Child: **"puddle!"** *Perfect!*

At this stage the children are not expected to read the words on the board. As a concluding activity, the teacher can re-read the categories and the words. *Look how many words you thought of that name things that Peter Puppy likes because they start with his sound! Let's count all our words.*

Things in your pocket
pad of paper, pen, pencil,
peppermints, a pebble, a
penny, pine cone

Favourite characters
Puss in Boots, Peppa Pig, Pooh, Peter
Rabbit, Harry Potter, Peter Pan

Food
pancake, parsnip, pasta, peach,
pear, peas, pie, pizza, plum,
popcorn, pork, potato, prune

Actions/verbs
paint, pant, pedal, peel, pick,
plant, point, poke, press, pull,
punch, push

Places
park, pool, playground,
puddles

Animals
panda, parrot, penguin, platypus,
pony, poodle, porpoise, puppy

When to use

- The Alliteration Trick can be used with the *ABC* book or *Living ABC* software when children look for items beginning with the character's sound. Some children may need lots of practice at listening for initial sounds in words. Several initial sound games based on the Alliteration Trick can be found in the Activity Bank, such as the Eyes Shut Riddle Game and Knock, Knock (pages 237-238).

- The full Alliteration Game as shown above with Peter Puppy can be used when teaching a letter in **Section 2: a-z Word Building**. It works best with letters that start many words.

- Whenever you have a few minutes of time to fill, you and the children can verbally play with alliterative ideas. For example, you might ask, I like lemon drops and lime lollipops, who am I? Then let the children ask classmates some similar questions of their own.

Development over time

- In the early stages, the Alliteration Trick helps children focus on and enjoy listening for the sounds in words – the very essence of phonemic awareness. As they advance beyond initial sounds they enjoy knowing that they can anticipate what each character will like through alliteration. They also enjoy finding alliterative strings coming naturally out of their own mouths as, for example, when they describe details in a underwater scene in *Alphabet Adventures* with, "**I can see a crab and a clam by Clever Cat,**" or "**There's Sammy Snake swimming with a swordfish.**"

Uppercase Trick (upper and lowercase link)

Objective

- To help children associate lowercase and uppercase forms of the same letter even when they are dissimilar.

Resources

- *Picture Code Cards* and *Big Picture Code Cards - Uppercase*.
- Optional: *Living ABC* software.

Explanation for children

When a Letterlander gets a chance to start an important word like your name or the name of a street or city or the beginning of a sentence, they get so excited that they do a special trick. Some just take a deep breath and get bigger to show that they start an important word. But other Letterlanders do a trick that makes their letter shape look really different.

Procedure for introducing an uppercase letter

Step	Description	Example
1	**Teacher** shows the picture side of the lowercase *PCC* with the *Big Picture Code Card - Uppercase* hidden behind them.	When Golden Girl is needed to start an important word, she gets out of her garden swing, gets into her go-cart, and drives in the Reading Direction.
2	**Teacher** reveals the *Big Picture Code Card - Uppercase* picture side while explaining the change.	
3	**Teacher** repeats the Uppercase Trick explanation and has each child retell the story to a partner. Encourage them to talk about the Uppercase Trick at home.	

When to use

- The Uppercase Trick is introduced in the Section 2 lesson for each letter.
- When children are having difficulty with a uppercase letter form, give them a hint that will help them remember the Uppercase Trick, e.g. Let's think about the trick that Golden Girl does when she starts an important word?
- Revise previously taught uppercase letters by asking the children to retell the Letterlanders' tricks.

Variations

- Other resources to teach and practise uppercase letters: *Class Train Frieze*, *A-Z Copymasters*, *Handwriting Practice 1*, *Handwriting Practice 2*.

See next page for all Uppercase Tricks

To see the Letterland Tricks, please visit our website:
www.letterland.com/training

Uppercase Trick

 In Letterland, the apples sit on an Applestand to start names and sentences.

 Ben proudly balances his blue ball on his head to start names and sentences.

 Clever Cat takes a deep breath and makes herself bigger at the start of a sentence or name.

 This is Dippy Duck's door. She opens names and other important words with it.

 Every time Eddy Elephant starts an important word or sentence, he does his 'Elephant-on-End' trick.

 Firefighter Fred takes a deep breath and gets bigger and straighter at the start of a name or sentence.

 Golden Girl goes and parks her Go-cart right at the start of important words.

 When Harry has a chance to start a name, he is so happy, he does a handstand with his hat on!

 Impy Ink starts important words with his long, thin ink pen.

 When Jumping Jim starts an important word, he does a big jump, and his head and ball disappear in the clouds!

 When Kicking King starts an important word, he takes a deep breath, so his arm and kicking leg get longer.

 When Lucy Lamp Light starts important words, her legs grow so long that she has to kneel on the line.

 Munching Mike may look big, but he's really only a little monster, so his much bigger Mum starts words for him.

 Nick starts important words with three big nails, like in Noisy Nick's name.

 Oscar Orange takes a deep breath and makes himself look bigger at the start of a sentence or name.

 When Peter Puppy has a chance to start an important word he is so pleased that he pops up on to the line.

 This is Quarrelsome Queen's Quiet Room. She likes to sit quietly in it to start important words like her own name!

 When he starts a name, Red Robot gets bigger. But the rascal also changes shape, so he's harder to recognise.

 Sammy Snake takes a deep breath and makes himself look bigger at the start of a sentence or name.

 When Tess starts her name or a sentence, she takes a deep breath and grows so tall that her head is in the clouds.

 Uppy Umbrella takes a deep breath and looks bigger at the start of a sentence or name.

 Vicky Violet can make her very own valuable Vase of Violets get bigger just by taking a deep breath herself!

 Walter Walrus takes a deep breath and makes himself look bigger at the start of a sentence or name.

 Fix-it Max takes a deep breath and makes himself look bigger on signs like EXIT.

 To start an important word, Yo-yo Man empties some yo-yos from his sack so he can step up on to the line.

 Zig Zag Zebra takes a deep breath and makes herself look bigger at the start a sentence or name.

Multisensory blending and segmenting

The reversible processes of blending and segmenting the individual phonemes of words are abstract ideas that do not come naturally to the uninitiated child. The use of hand and arm movements provides a way to make these abstract processes into visible, physical acts that enable children to understand and gain control of them. These movements also help you to know if everyone is participating, and give you and the child a visual and kinaesthetic way to deal with any difficulties with blending and segmenting. The two multisensory strategies that follow (**Roller Coaster Trick** and **Rubber Band Trick**) will support all the word building activities. Encourage children to use them in their independent reading and writing whenever the need arises.

Roller Coaster Trick (blending to read)

Objective
- To blend sounds (phonemes) to read words.

Resources
- The **Roller Coaster Trick** is usually used in 'Live Reading' and to read words made with *Picture Code Cards* and magnetic letters. (This practice prepares children to use the trick when needed with written and printed words.)

Explanation for children
Did you know you can make an imaginary roller coaster with your hands and arms? It can help you read words! Here's how to do it. Pretend that your left arm is a steep hill on a roller coaster. Hold it out like this. Now your right hand is the car that you ride on going down the hill.
Ask the children to try whizzing their hands down their roller coaster from shoulder to wrist.

Now, here's how we use our roller coaster to help us blend the sounds to read a word...

Procedure Display a word. (e.g. sip)

Step	Description	Example	
1	**Children and teacher**: With your right hand, touch your left shoulder, mid-arm, and wrist in sequence, and say the sounds.	/s/ /i/ /p/	/sss/ /ĭ/ /p/
2	Touch again and repeat the first two sounds.	/s/ / ĭ /	/sss/ /ĭ/
3	Slide your right hand from your left shoulder to mid-arm as you prolong the first sound and begin the second without a pause between.	ssssiii	sssiii
4	Say the first two sounds together as you slide your hand from shoulder to mid-arm again. Then lift your hand and touch your wrist as you say the last sound.	si /p/	si /p/
5	Slide your hand down your whole arm. Say the three sounds without stopping.	sssiiip	sssiiip
6	Slide your hand faster down your arm and say the word.	sip	sip

When to use
- Your children will vary in how long they will need to use this trick. Since some of the group will continue to need this support for quite a while, use it regularly with at least some words in word building activities such as 'Live Reading' and Blending with *PCCs*, etc.
- When reading words in stories or in lists, ask the children to read them without obvious blending if they are able to. Use arm-blending in these contexts only when they need it to slowly blend a word.

Development over time

- When first teaching children to blend, use initial letter sounds that can be prolonged (**f, h, l, m, n, r, s, v, w** and **z**) because children can sustain the first sound until they say the second sound.

- As children become able to handle three sounds at once, you will be able to skip Steps 2-4 and go directly from saying the three sounds separately (Step 1) to sliding them all together (Step 5).

- As they begin to blend words with four sounds, teach them to place their hands at four points along the arm. Later do the same with five sounds.

- As children continue to progress, you may find that they are able to blend words without first saying each sound separately. You may only need to use Steps 5 and 6 above. Using only these steps will also be helpful for children who are having difficulty sounding 'all through the word' without pausing.

Variation

- **Blending Leader** Once you have taught children to arm blend, let them take turns as the Blending Leader. Before the other children blend a word, the Leader blends it as the rest observe. Then everyone follows suit. Children enjoy being leader and it enables you to observe how individuals are progressing with the vital strategy of blending. If the leader has difficultly, just do the Roller Coaster Trick with the child.

Blending words with a suffix

Step	Description	Example
7	**Teacher** builds or writes the whole word.	rained
8	**Teacher** asks the children if they see a suffix.	Does this word look like it might have a suffix added on the end?
9	**Children** identify the suffix and one of them separates it from the word (or covers the written suffix).	"Yes, the e-d is a suffix."
10	**Teacher** and children arm-blend the base word.	/r/ /ā/ /n/, rain
11	**Teacher** or a child replaces the suffix.	
12	**Children** read the word with the suffix.	"rained"
13	**Teacher or a child** says a sentence with the word.	"It rained and rained yesterday."

Blending multi-syllable words

Step	Description	Example
1	**Teacher** builds or writes the whole word.	contest
2	**Teacher** makes a space between the syllables (or covers the second written syllable).	This word has two syllables.
3	**Teacher and children** arm-blend the first syllable.	/c/ /ō/ /n/, con
4	**Teacher and children** arm-blend the next syllable.	/t/ /ĕ/ /s/ /t/, test
5	**Teacher or a child** pushes the syllables back together.	
6	**Children** read the whole word.	contest

Rubber Band Trick (segmenting to spell)

Objectives
- To segment the sounds in words to develop phonemic awareness and spelling.
- To reinforce blending skills.

Resources
- Word stretching is used for 'Live Spelling' and when children are spelling words with *Picture Code Cards*, *Magnetic Word Builder* or other letter sets, or when writing words.

Explanation for children

Let's learn a new trick that can help us hear all the sounds in words so we know just what letters to use to spell them. Put your hands together in front of you like this. Pretend that there is a strong rubber band wrapped around your hands holding them together. Now we can stretch out that rubber band but only very slowly. Children try slowly stretching their rubber bands by pulling their hands farther and farther apart.

Now, let's use our rubber bands to stretch out some words. Let's try it with the word **map**. Listen and watch while I 'slow speak' the word map just as I stretch out my rubber band: **mmmmmaaaaaaaaap.** Begin the /mmm/ with your hands together and end with /p/ as your hands reach about body width apart. Ask the children to do the same with you the second time.

Procedure

Step	Description	Example
1	**Teacher** says the word, says a brief sentence with the word, and repeats the word.	Our town is on the map.
2	**Children** repeat the word normally.	"map"
3	**Teacher and children** prolong the word or 'slow speak' it as everyone pretends to stretch a rubber band with their hands.	"mmmaaap"
4	Start to 'stretch' the word again, saying only the first sound while moving hands slightly apart.	/mmm/
5	**Children** name the Letterlander (or letter). **Teacher or a child** places the *PCC* or writes the first letter.	"Munching Mike"
6	**Teacher and children** start to stretch the word again, saying the first two sounds. Move your hands back and forth as you repeat the vowel sound. **Children** name the Letterlander. **Teacher** places or writes the second letter.	"mmaaa - /ă/ /ă/"
7	**All** stretch the whole word again moving your hands as you repeat the last sound. (**Children** name the Letterlander.) Place or write the final letter.	"mmaap -/p/ /p/"
8	**Children** roller coaster (arm-blend) the word to check the spelling.	"mmmaaap, map"

mmmaap

mmmaa - /ă /ă/

mmmaap - /p/ /p/

When to use word stretching
- **Segmenting and spelling** Use the Rubber Band Trick to focus everyone's attention on listening for each sound and choosing the letters. Use with 'Live Spelling', spelling with *PCCs*, *Magnetic Word Builder*, writing words on the board or with individual writing resources.
- **Writing** Whether children are writing to dictation or composing their own stories, encourage them to use this trick to help themselves as needed.

- **'Tricky' words** Stretching and segmenting of 'tricky' words is a part of your initial teaching of each word. After children have segmented the sounds, they decide which letters are making their usual sounds and which are not. The 'tricky' letters (often marked with a wavy line below) will have to be memorised.

'Tricky' word

Development over time

- **Fewer steps** As children become adept at segmenting words, you can simplify the steps in the Rubber Band Trick at times. Rather than placing letters one at a time and then stretching the word again for the next letter, your children may follow Steps 1 and 2, and then segment out all three sounds before they 'Live Spell' the word. This will require them to hold the three sounds in their memory as they build the word. They can always stretch all or part of the word again if they forget a sound or letter.

- **More sounds** To spell regular words with four or five sounds, practise stretching and segmenting some longer sequences.

Variations

- **Stretching Leader** Once children 'catch on' to word stretching, ask them to take turns being the Stretching Leader. The Stretching Leader demonstrates stretching and segmenting the word before everyone else tries it. Change leaders after one or two words. The children like being the leader. Meanwhile you can check on each child's development in this vital skill of segmenting words. If a Leader has difficulty stretching the word, simply do it with them.

- **Catch and stretch** To quickly get children ready to stretch a word and segment it, use the 'catch and stretch' method. You 'throw' the word to the children on an imaginary ball as you say it. They pretend to catch the ball and repeat the word at the same time. Just saying, Put your hands up to catch a word, will quickly tell you by their show of hands whether everyone is listening and ready to participate.

Word stretching for words with a suffix

Description	Example

Teacher says and children repeat:
    Whole word
    Base word
	jumping
	jump

Teacher and children:
    Stretch the base word
    Segment the sounds
    Build or write the base word
    Add the suffix
	jump
	juuummmp
	/j/ /u/ /m/ /p/
	jumping

Word stretching for multi-syllable words

Description	Example

Teacher says and children repeat:
    Whole word
    Pause between syllables
    Repeat first syllable
	picnic
	pic nic
	pic

Teacher and children:
    Stretch the syllable
    Segment the syllable
    Build or write the syllable
    Do the same with each syllable
	piiiiic
	/p/ /i/ /c/
	nic, /nnn/ /iiic/
	/n/ /i/ /c/

Teacher Strategies - letter sounds

Use the activities below to help children move from learning the Letterlanders' names to instantly and automatically responding to the plain letter with the **correct sound.**

Pronunciation guide

Children need to pronounce letter sounds correctly in order to use them effectively for reading and spelling. When saying consonant phonemes in isolation, they tend to put a vowel sound after them, leading to "buh, mmmuh, puh, suh" etc. instead of the pure /**b**/, /**mmm**/, /**d**/ and /**sss**/sounds. The 'uh' sounds then distort children's blending, so, for example, sip becomes "sssuhipuh" .

To avoid the extra 'uh' sound, the three categories of consonant sounds set out below are helpful. Useful tips for helping children pronounce each group are provided. Some sounds fall into more than one category. That just means you have more ways to help children get the sound right.

Whispered sounds are spoken without the voice box. We just whisper them.

Prolonged sound can be extended or 'stretched.' We can continue the sounds of 'sssss' or 'mmmm' until our breath runs out. Tell children to stop the sound before dropping their jaws to avoid 'ssssuh' and '**mmmuh.**'

Almost closed mouth sounds are the hardest to say without adding an '**uh**' sound. Tell children to keep their mouths almost closed and say these sounds both quietly and quickly.

To listen to the correct pronunciation of a-z sounds, short and long vowels, you can refer to:
- www.letterland.com/letter-sounds
- *Living ABC* software
- *Alphabet Songs CD.*

For consonant blends, consonant digraphs and vowel digraph sounds:
- *Blends & Digraphs Songs CD*
- *Story Phonics* software.

Picture Coding (grapheme-phoneme practice)

Objective

- To fuse the association of letter sound, shape and spatial orientation in an imaginative, creative activity.

Resources

- Optional: Copies of large plain letter(s) from the *TGCD*.
- Pencils, crayons, markers or paints.
- A *Picture Code Card* or other example to use as a model. Sample Picture Coding below.

Procedure

Step	Description	Example
1	**Teacher** draws a plain letter on the board. Then draws in the Letterlander in a simple form as she describes how she does it. (Drawing with simple lines and shapes will reassure children that they can do it, too.)	Clever Cat: Let's see. I can make two pointy ears sort of like triangles up here on top of her letter. Then two almond-shaped eyes with black dots inside. Add her nose and mouth. She has some whiskers on both cheeks....
2	**Children** Picture Code their letters and perhaps draw things that begin with the letter sound around the edges. They could also write words or a sentence as well.	

Development over time

- As children become accustomed to Picture Coding, they will not need printed letters. Instead they can write or paint a large letter for themselves and then Picture Code it.
- As children begin to blend and segment words, ask them to Picture Code whole words.
- As they begin to learn more than one sound for the same letter, Picture Coding gives them a way to consolidate and display their learning.

Variations

- Children can enjoy making the Letterlanders out of clay or plasticine.
- One creative teacher asked older children, who needed to work on digraph sounds, to make clay figures of the Letterlanders. These children then used a video camera and the stop motion technique to animate the letters and explain the Letterland story logic for the new sounds. They shared the videos with younger children and improved their own literacy skills and self-confidence.

'Quick Dash' (grapheme to phoneme practice)

Objectives
- To revise and consolidate letter shapes and letter sounds.
- To work towards a quick and automatic letter sound response to the plain letter.
- (Optional) To revise letter names – best deferred as long as possible (see page 239).

Resources
- *Picture Code Cards* or *Story Phonics* software.

Explanation for children
When you see the Letterlanders' pictures, say their names. When you see only the plain letter, remember to quickly say only their sound. The sounds are the most important because that's how the Letterlanders help us learn to read.

Procedure: Letterlanders' names and sounds
Use about 10-16 previously introduced *Picture Code Cards* (*PCCs*)

Step	Description	Example
1	**Teacher** shows the picture side of the *PCC* and says:	Who is this?
2	**Children** say the character's name.	"Annie Apple"
3	**Teacher** shows the plain letter side and says:	What's her sound?
4	**Children** say the sound. (Option: do the Action Trick with the sound.)	/a/

Procedure: Sounds Race (sounds only)

Step	Description	Example
1	**Teacher** shows plain letter sides one after the other.	
2	**Children** say the sounds. (Option: do the Action Trick with the sound.)	/t/, /m/, /ă/, /sh/, /aw/...
3	**Teacher** goes through the *PCCs* more quickly, showing only the plain letters.	
4	**Children** say the sounds quickly. (Option: do the Action Trick with the sound.)	/f/, /s/, /aw/, /sh/, /ō/...

When to use
- The 'Quick Dash' is used for revision to begin every other lesson - alternating with the 'Guess Who?' activity. You may also want to include these letter sound reviews in small group sessions if children need more practice.

Development over time
- As children internalise the letter sounds, you will only need to use the picture sides and Letterlander names for recently introduced *PCCs*. You will want to move on to using primarily the Sounds Race which is done with plain letters only.

Variations
- **Pocket chart/shelf** As an alternative to the above steps for the Sounds Race, display all the *PCCs* that you plan to revise on a pocket chart or spread along a shelf (using plain letter sides). After using this plan a few times, you could have a child lead the Sounds Race in this way, while you observe responses or take a moment to get ready for the rest of the lesson.

- **Letter names** Once children are confident and quick with using the letter sounds to blend words, you may want to include letter names as another step in the 'Quick Dash' after the character names and letter sounds. If you choose to do so, add the steps below after Step 4 above.

Optional procedure for adding letter names to your 'Quick Dash'

Add the following steps after 1-4 above.

Step	Description	Example
5	**Teacher** traces the letter shape using proper handwriting strokes and says:	What's the letter name?
6	**Children** say the letter name.	"Tee."

On screen 'Quick Dash'

You can create your own card revision 'Quick Dash' with the *Story Phonics* software. Display the cards on screen at the front of the class. You can choose the order (options include: alphabetical, Letterland teaching order, **satpin**, create your own). Point to each letter in turn as children quickly respond with the sound. The display allows you to show the cards:

- with or without the characters
- in a straight or precursive (Sassoon) font
- with key words
- with sounds.

'Guess Who?' (phoneme to grapheme practice)

Objectives

- To review letter sounds by starting with the sound and recalling the letter shape.
- To prepare for spelling words using the letter sounds.

Resources

- 8 to 16 *Picture Code Cards* (*PCCs*).
- A box or sack decorated to look special perhaps with question marks.

Explanation for children

> The Letterlanders like to play a game with us called 'Guess Who?' I have hidden several of the *Picture Code Cards* in this box. I am going to say one of the Letterlander's sounds. You listen and then repeat the sound together a few times as you trace the letter in the air. Then I'll say 'Guess Who?' That's when you all say the Letterlander's name. Then I'll take out the *Picture Code Card* from the box and show you the picture side so you can see if you are correct. This will help us when we need to spell a word. Are you ready to try the 'Guess Who' game.

Procedure

Step	Description	Example
1	**Teacher** keeps the *PCC* hidden and says the sound.	/p/
2	**Children** trace the letter in the air as they repeat the sound.	/p/, /p/, /p/...
3	**Teacher** says:	Guess Who?
4	**Children** say the name of the Letterlander(s).	"Peter Puppy"
5	**Teacher** shows the picture side to confirm the children's answer.	

When to use

- 'Guess Who' is used in every other lesson alternating with 'Quick Dash'. If some children need more practice, use it in small groups as well.

Development over time

- In Section 1, Fast Track, and early in Section 2, children may not yet have learned letter formation. In that case, leave out the letter-tracing. Just ask them to repeat the sound before you say, "Guess Who?"
- If there are two letters that make the same sound, (e.g. **k** and **c**), children should air-trace or write both and respond orally with both Letterlander names (e.g. **"Clever Cat and Kicking King"**). The letter names can be used as children begin to learn digraphs and more alternative spellings. For example, soon after learning that **c** and **k** both say /k/, they learn that at the end of words the same sound is often spelled **ck**. At that point when you say /k/ in a 'Guess Who' exercise, they learn to respond orally with letter names, **"c , or k, or c-k."**
  Spelling tip: Which to use for the hard **c** sound, **c** or **k**? Always choose **k** before **e, i** or **y**.

Variations

- Rather than tracing the letter in the air, children can write their response to the sound on whiteboards or paper.
- Children can learn to lead this 'Guess Who?' activity themselves, giving you a moment for any last minute preparations.

Letter shapes

With the activities below, children learn to form the letters correctly, to avoid reversals in reading and spelling, and to recognise both lowercase and uppercase versions of all 26 letters.

Handwriting Songs (letter formation)

Objectives
- To train correct letter formation.
- To consolidate recognition of each letter shape.
- To associate each letter shape with its correct letter sound.

Resources
- *Handwriting Songs CD*,
- and/or *Living ABC* software.

Explanation for children
The Letterlanders always like to be helpful. They have made up songs to help us write their letters. Each letter has a song that tells us where to start the letter and how to go about writing it.

Procedure for introducing letter formation

Step	Description	Example
1	**Teacher** shows the *PCC* and traces the picture side of the letter while saying the handwriting verse.*	Draw Dippy Duck's back. Go round her tum. Go up to her head. Then down you come.
2	**Teacher** says the verse again and traces the plain letter.	
3	**Teacher** writes a huge version of the letter on the board. (If using *Living ABC*, project the handwriting screen instead).	
4	**Children** air-trace the letter with straight arms and wrists, and two fingers extended (see page 199). Ask them to sing as they trace.	

* Here's a helpful hint when you or the children want to remember the words of the handwriting verse. The first word in every song begins with the Letterlander's sound (e.g. 'Hurry from the Hat Man's head...').
Song lyrics on *TGCD*.

When to use
- Chant or sing the verse to practise handwriting with air-tracing, on paper and with other resources such as the *A-Z Copymasters* or *Early Years Handwriting Copymasters*.

Development over time
- Children soon internalise the handwriting strokes and many will no longer need the verses. For others the words can still be a useful reminder where to start the letter stroke (e.g. at Ed's headband) .

Reading Direction (letter formation)

Reading Direction

Objectives

- To avoid confusion between letters such as **b**, **d**, **p** and **q** and others that children tend to write backwards.
- To support 'Live Reading' and 'Live Spelling' activities, reminding children to always read, write and build words from left to right.

Resources

- Prepare a large Reading Direction sign with arrows and put it up on a wall behind the area where children will be building 'Live Reading' and 'Live Spelling' words. A chalked arrow line on the floor in front of their feet can also be helpful at first. You can also download a sign from our website: www.letterland.com/information/downloads

Teaching letter shapes

- Point to the Reading Direction sign, when you are introducing a letter, explain that most of the Letterlanders like to look, bounce, walk, hop, jump, etc. in the Reading Direction, because they always want to see who is going to be the next Letterlander in the word.
- Only three Letterlanders don't face in the Reading Direction and there are good Letterland reasons for each (explained below and in the lessons for each of these letters).

Why don't these three Letterlanders face in the Reading Direction?

Golden Girl gets giddy in her garden swing so she forgets which way she is facing.

Quarrelsome Queen is just too quarrelsome to face in the Reading Direction.

Zig Zag Zebra is too shy. She likes to be at the end of the alphabet where she can look back at all her friends.

- Refer to the Reading Direction when you show children how to air-trace a new letter. Be sure that you face in the same direction as the class. If you face the children, they will see you making a letter in reverse.

Teaching Word Building

- Use the Reading Direction sign during 'Live Reading' and 'Live Spelling' to remind children to blend and spell from left to right.
- When children are writing on paper, you might teach them to look up at the Reading Direction sign and make a small arrow on the left side of their paper pointing to the right. It will remind them where to start and which way to go.

Handwriting practice suggestions

Objectives

- To develop comfortable, fluid, readable handwriting.
- To consolidate letter shapes.

Teaching points

- Handwriting is best scheduled separately from the main Letterland lesson. Approximately ten minutes is recommended each day for doing all or part of the activities below.
- It is important that children learn to form letters in a consistent fashion. This contributes to their overall knowledge of the letters and also to more efficient and fluent writing.
- It is important for children to say the sounds of the letters often as they write. Once they know the correct starting point and direction, ask them to repeat the sounds as they air-trace or write.
- Emphasise standard pencil grip with children. Also, note that our hands work best if we slant our paper so that the corner of the paper points toward us.

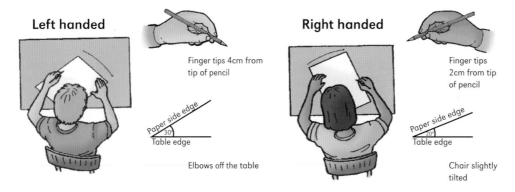

Air-tracing to pencil writing

Objective

- To consolidate handwriting for new and previously introduced letters.

Resources

- Whiteboard for you to make a huge letter. Paper and pencils or other writing resources for children.
- Optional: *Handwriting Songs CD* or the same songs in *Living ABC* software.

Procedure for air-tracing

Teaching children to air-trace as follows will ensure they use their large, gross motor muscles, and will also make it easier for you to observe and correct their letter strokes.

- Children should hold their arms out straight without bending at the elbows, wrist or fingers. (They may want to support their writing arm with the other hand to add control and prevent fatigue.)
- Point to the large letter on display and air-trace with two fingers extended.
- Make a very large version of the letter to be practised (perhaps 60-90 cms tall) on the board, or show the *Living ABC* handwriting screen for the chosen letter.

Step	Description
1	**Teacher** plays the *Handwriting Song* or says the verse, or describes the letter formation in other terms with each step below.
2	**Children** air-trace the large letter, pretending that their arms extend to the board and they can touch the letter as they trace. They repeat the letter sound as they trace.
3	**Children** close their eyes and air-trace again repeating the sound. They try to imagine writing their own giant letter in whatever colour they wish.

Procedure for paper and pencil

Children may use pencils, crayons, markers on whiteboards or any other writing resources. Use unlined paper until later in the year.

Step	Description
1	**Children** write the letter two to four times. They all repeat the sound as they write (e.g. "/fff/, /fff/, /fff/").
2	**Teacher** observes. If a child is starting in the wrong place or moving in the wrong direction, ask them to air-trace with you as you say the handwriting verse (or other instructions). Then ask the child return to paper and pencil as you repeat the verse.
3	**Children** repeat air-tracing the letter two to five times.
4	**Teacher** gives children a few minutes to write whatever they want to.

Variations

- Ask the children to trace a letter on a friend's back. Let the friend guess the letter.
- Trace in a special media: sand, rice, lentils, etc.
- Write with different resources: chalk, paint and brush, finger paint, on a chalkboard with water and a brush.

Using the Fluency Lists for handwriting practice

- **Fluency Lists** for copying are provided on the *TGCD*. Each one is used over the course of four or five lessons to review previously learned information. They consist of letter sounds (graphemes), words and sentences for children to practise as a revision of recent learning. You may want to assign a row of words on the list or one of the sentences for children to copy for handwriting practice. After they write, they ask a partner to read it aloud.

Using other Letterland resources for handwriting

- **Rainbow writing** The *A-Z Copymasters* have large 'hollow letters'.
  Ask the children to trace over the hollow letter with their fingers a few times using correct strokes.
  Then show them how to rainbow write in these letters. You could say or sing the *Handwriting Song* while they make the letter, first in one colour and then in another. Or just ask them to repeat the sound over and over as they write.

- *Handwriting Practice Books 1-3* provide practice with handwriting as well as letter sounds, spelling and more. There are larger letters to trace with a finger and plenty of practice writing letters, words and sentences.

Words: Reading and spelling

The strategies that help children blend sounds into words and segment words into sounds are explained in this section. Beyond decoding and encoding words, children need to practise reading those same words until they recognise them instantly. In addition, they need to learn common exception words that have unusual or unique spellings but are needed to read even the simplest stories. Eventually, they need to deal with structural concepts such as base words and suffixes, compound words, multi-syllable words and contractions.

'Live Reading' (blending)

Objective
- To actively develop children's understanding of how to blend phonemes to read words.

Resources
- *PCCs* or *BPCCs*.
- A Reading Direction sign is helpful. www.letterland.com/information/downloads

Explanation for children
All the Letterlanders like to build words so they can help you to read them. They always line up in the Reading Direction so we know where to start and which way to go. Let's pretend that these three children are Noisy Nick, Uppy Umbrella and Talking Tess. Imagine that the wall behind them is a great big page in a book. They are going to say their sounds, starting with Noisy Nick, in the Reading Direction. Then the rest of us will use the **Roller Coaster Trick** to discover the word they are making.

Procedure
Distribute the *PCCs* for the words you plan to build. When not helping to form a word, ask the children to put down their *PCCs* to avoid distraction and to free their hands for the **Roller Coaster Trick** (page 188).

Step	Description	Example
1	**Children** 'in the word' push their *PCCs* forward as they say their sounds in order.	/n/ /ŭ/ /t/
2	**Teacher** and class say the sounds and blend them using the **Roller Coaster Trick** (page 188).	/n/ /ŭ/ /t/ **nnnuuuttt, nut**
3	**Teacher** uses the word in a brief sentence.	I ate a nut.
4	**Teacher** rearranges children with PCCs to make a new word (e.g. hut).	Harry Hat Man, please take Noisy Nick's place.

When to use
- **Learning to blend** 'Live Reading' is used from the first lesson on blending (page 41). It draws children into the idea of saying each letter's sound and the blending of those sounds into words. At times you may want to only do a few of the words in the lesson with 'Live Reading' and the rest using just the *Picture Code Cards* set out for all to see (page 204).
- **Introducing new sounds** Some lessons recommend that children briefly dramatise the story logic that explains a new sound as a part of 'Live Reading'. Others suggest variations on 'Live Reading'. For example, when 'Live Reading' with **ar**, Arthur Ar and his captured apple, stand to the left of the class. When they are needed in a word, they rush into place with Arthur Ar calling out his last name /**ar**/. These adaptations help keep 'Live Reading' interesting and help children remember the grapheme / phoneme connection.

Development over time

- As you begin blending three sound words with 'Live Reading', ask the first two children with *PCCs* to stand close together and the third one to stand a bit apart. Ask the children to blend the first two sounds using the Roller Coaster Trick. Then the third child moves in closer. The class 'reads' the first two sounds blended together, then the last sound. Finally they blend all the sounds on their arms. Move on, when children are ready, to saying all the sounds in the word and then blend them all at once.

Variations

- **Blending Leader** Choose a child to demonstrate blending of the word. Then the rest of the class 'follows the leader'. Frequent use of Blending Leaders will help keep children's interest high and allow you to observe individual children's development of blending ability.

- **List the words** As each word is formed by the children with *PCCs*, ask another child to write them down on a whiteboard. This will provide a useful list for a quick review after 'Live Reading'.

- **Other ways to use the word** After children read the word, ask one or two children to volunteer to make up an oral sentence with the word. They could make up sentences that are about a particular Letterlander, perhaps the one that is featured in the current lesson. Another way to make a meaningful response to the word, is to ask the children to think up and do an action that relates to the word's meaning (e.g. making a digging motion after reading the word **dig**).

- **Costumes and props** are not necessary for 'Live Reading' or 'Live Spelling', but when children are beginning to blend sounds, a few simple ones can help keep their attention (e.g. a wand for Silent Magic **e**) and make these activities more engaging and memorable. The props can create photo opportunities, too, leading to a photo display of 'live words' which the children enjoy re-reading since they're in them!

- **Vowels-go-round** is suggested in the lessons as a fun strategy for revision. In Vowels-go-round, two or three children with consonant *PCCs* stand in place with a space for a vowel (e.g. **h_ t**). Each child with a vowel takes a turn amongst the consonants, and the class decides whether they have made a real word or a nonsense word (e.g. **hat, het, hit, hot, hut**).

'Live Spelling' (segmenting)

Objective

- To actively engage children in listening for the phonemes in a word by personally behaving like letters.

Resources

- *Picture Code Cards*
- A Reading Direction sign is helpful (see page 198). www.letterland.com/information/downloads

Explanation for children

I have given *Picture Code Cards* to some of you so that you can be the Letterlanders. The rest of us are going to help listen for your sounds in words. Then together we can decide which Letterlanders we need to spell the words. We call it 'Live Spelling'.

Procedure

Distribute the *PCCs* for the words you plan to spell. When not helping to form a word, ask the children to put down their *PCCs* to avoid distraction and to free their hands for the **Rubber Band Trick** (page 190).

Step	Description	Example
1	**Teacher** says the word, a sentence with the word, and repeats the word.	tag. We like to play tag outdoors. tag

2	**Children** say the word in a normal way.	**tag**
3	**Teacher and children** stretch imaginary rubber bands as they Slow Speak the word, and then segment out each sound.	**taaaaag, /t/ /a/ /g/**
4	**Teacher** elicits from **children** which Letterlanders (or letters) are needed. **Children** with the needed *PCCs* line up to form the word.	
5	The **remaining children** blend the word to check the spelling using the Roller Coaster Trick.	**/t/ /a/ /g/, tag**

- If the next word differs by only one letter (or two in longer words), leave the children in the first word in place as their classmates stretch the next word (Steps 1-3) and then decide who needs to sit down and who needs to take their place in the new word. If the next word differs by several letters, ask all the children to sit down and start from scratch.

When to use

- **Learning to segment** 'Live Spelling' is used early on to help children develop the ability to pull a spoken word apart to isolate the individual sounds. By pretending to be the Letterlanders and making their sounds, they feel a personal involvement in this otherwise strange and abstract process.

- **Recently introduced sounds** 'Live Spelling' is often in the lesson on the day after a new sound or spelling is introduced. Children read the words with the new sound one day and spell the words the next day, using 'Live Spelling' or one of the other activities for spelling below. Just as with with 'Live Reading', certain props or variations may be helpful to bring home the story logic in a dramatic way that will remind them to use the new spelling when they write.

Development over time

- At first, when children are just learning to segment, stretch the whole word and then start to stretch it again to get the initial sound. Then ask the child with the *PCC* to stand in the first position to start the word. Then stretch the word again for the second sound, ask the next child to stand next to the first. Finally stretch the word again for the final sound.

- Later, when children are more skilled at segmenting they can segment out all the sounds first, and then decide who is needed in the word.

Variations

- **Segmenting Leader** Use a Segmenting Leader often to maintain children's engagement and build confidence. This will also allow you to see individual children's progress in the vital phonemic awareness skill of segmentation.

- **List the words** As each word is 'Live Spelled' by the children, ask another child to write them down to provide a list for a quick reading review after 'Live Spelling'.

  Costumes and props, again, while not essential, can be very helpful in drawing the children into an activity that may be quite challenging at first. Later, using a few props and a bit of action for new digraphs or other word elements, can enhance children's enjoyment and strengthen their memories.

Blending with Picture Code Cards

Objective
- To guide children in blending sounds to read words.

Resources
- *PCCs* or *Story Phonics* software.

Explanation for children
The Letterlanders are hiding behind their letters, but they have made a word here for us. Let's see if we can blend their sounds to read the word.

Procedure
This activity can be done on screen, on a pocket chart or on your whiteboard shelf. Make a word with the plain letter sides of the *PCCs*. (At times you may want to use the picture sides of one or two newly introduced letters or digraphs while using plain letters for the rest.)

Step	Description	Example
1	**Teacher and children** blend the word on your arm.	/p/ /ar/ /k/
2	**Teacher or children** use the word in a sentence.	We had a picnic in the park.
3	**Teacher** changes the letters to make a new word.	dark

When to use
- **New and review** Use this blending activity when first building words with a newly introduced sound or concept. It allows you to quickly make a number of words for children to practise blending. It is also a good way to revise words from previous lessons.

Variations
- **Small group** With a small group, you can make the words on the table or carpet. To manage the *PCCs*, you can ask each child to place a few of the cards in front of themselves. Then ask for the letters by sound as you need them in a word. (For example, We need /s/ /k/ /i/ /p/ to make our next word.) The children place the *PCCs* in order, and then blend the word using the **Roller Coaster Trick**.
- **Predict the vowel** Once you have introduced a new pattern such as the Vowel Men Out Walking (e.g. **ai**), make a word with only plain letters (e.g. **trail**). Ask the children to predict what the vowels will say. They can also quickly revise the story logic as needed. Flip the *PCC* to check their prediction. Then ask them to blend the word on their arms.
- **Blending Leader** Let several children take it in turns to be Blending Leader.

Segmenting with Picture Code Cards

Objective
- To actively engage children in listening for the phonemes in a word to spell it.

Resources
- *PCCs* or *Story Phonics* software (word building section).

Explanation for children
Let's listen for the sounds in this word and decide on how to build it.

Procedure

Step	Description	Example
1	**Teacher** says the word, a sentence with the word, and repeats the word.	moon. The moon was full last night. moon

2	**Children** repeat the word in a normal way.	"moon"
3	**Teacher and children** stretch imaginary rubber bands as they slowly say the word, and then segment out each sound.	mmmooooonnn, /m/ /oo/ /n/
4	**Teacher** elicits from **children** which *PCC's* are needed to form the word.	Munching Mike, The Boot Twins, Noisy Nick
5	**Teacher** or **child** places the *PCC's* to form the word.	
6	**Children** blend the word and check their spelling.	/m/ /oo/ /n/, moon

When to use

- **New and review** Use this segmenting activity when first segmenting words with a newly introduced sound or concept. It allows you to quickly spell a number of words together. It is a good way to revise previous learning and to prepare children for spelling on their own.

Variations

- **Stretching Leader** Let several children take it in turns to be Stretching Leader.

Whiteboard reading (blending)

Objective

- To guide children in blending sounds to read words.

Resources

- Whiteboard.

Explanation for children

I'll write some words on the board. Then we'll say the sounds and blend them.

Procedure

Step	Description	Example
1	**Teacher and children** blend the word on the arm.	/w/ /i/ /sh/
2	**Teacher or children** use the word in a sentence.	Blow out the candles and make a wish.
3	**Teacher** changes the letters to make a new word.	with

When to use

- **Quick practice** You have just a few minutes and you want children to practise blending some of the new sounds they have been learning. No special resources are required, just write a word on the board.

Development over time

- **Blend two letters, then three** When children are just learning to blend, this activity can be adapted to provide additional support. First, ask the children to put all three sounds on their arm roller coaster. Then ask them to blend just the first two sounds as you underline the first two letters. Ask them to repeat those two sounds and blend the third as you underline the whole word. You could ask individual children to come up and do this type of underlining while they blend as well.

- **Smoother blending** Once children become quick at giving each sound and then blending, they can begin to blend without saying each sound separately first. As they slide their hand down their arm roller coaster, you make a continuous line under the word, maybe going slowly on a first try. Then underline it again more quickly as children say the word in the normal way.

Variations

- **To erase or not to erase** If going from the word **wish** to the word **with**, as in the example above, you may want to just erase **sh** and write **th** in its place to quickly show that only one sound is changing. Alternatively, at times you may want to write **wish** and then write **with** below it and continue to add to the list. Then you end up with several words on the board for children to revise by reading the list.

Whiteboard spelling (segmenting)

Objective
- To guide children in segmenting sounds to spell words.

Resources
Whiteboard.

Explanation for children
Listen for the sounds in this word and tell me how to spell it.

Procedure

Step	Description	Example
1	**Teacher** says the word, a sentence with the word, and repeats the word.	fly, Many birds fly south in winter. fly
2	**Children** repeat the word in a normal way.	"fly"
3	**Teacher and children** use the Rubber Band Trick (page 190).	ffffllllyyy, /f/ /l/ / ī/
4	**Teacher** elicits from **children** which letters are needed to spell the word.	"f l y"*
5	**Teacher** or **child** writes the word on the board.	fly
6	**Children** blend the word and check their spelling.	/f/ /l/ / ī/

* Teachable moment: It sounds like / ī /, so why can't we write **i** at the end of this word? Children: **"Because Mr I gets dizzy on the end and Yellow Yo-yo Man takes his place."** Yes, and what does Yellow Yo-yo Man get for being so helpful? **"Mr I gives him an ice cream."**

When to use
- **New and review** This is a quick way to provide children with segmenting and spelling practice that requires no gathering of resources or preparation.

Development over time
- Early on when children are just learning to blend, you may need to stop after getting the first sound and ask the children to tell you what to write. Then stretch the word again, write the second letter, etc.
- Later when children are confident about segmenting, they will be able to segment all the sounds before you begin to write the word. When a new challenge is introduced such as words with four sounds or five sounds, you may want to revert for a time to segmenting and writing one letter sound at a time.

Variations
- **Stretching Leader** As in any segmenting/spelling activity, it is usually a good idea to ask the children to take a turn at being the Stretching Leader.

Magnetic Word Builder
Reading with Magnetic Word Builders

Magnetic Word Builder

Objectives
- To engage each child directly in blending sounds to read words in a small or large group setting.
- Children learn to slide their fingers under their own letters as they blend.

Resources
- *Magnetic Word Builder* or other letter sets.
- A set of letters for the teacher (visible to the children) or a board to write the words.

Explanation for children
I am going to say some sounds (or letters) for you to line up on your *Magnetic Word Builder*. Build your word in the Reading Direction in the order I say the sounds. Then we will blend the word together. Listen carefully because you know some of our sounds are very quiet and quick.

Procedure
Each child has their own set of letters.

Step	Description	Example
1	**Teacher** says each sound (or letter) that is needed in order.	/b/ /ĕ/ /s/ /t/
2	**Children** place their own letters in order.	**best**
3	**Children** touch their letters as they say each sound.	/b/ /ĕ/ /s/ /t/
4	**Children** slide their finger below the letters as they blend the sounds.	"beeeessssst"
5	**Children** slide their finger quickly as they say the word normally.	"best"

If the next letter differs by only one letter sound (e.g. **best** to **nest**), ask the children to replace the letter and blend the new word as above.

When to use
- **Hands on** Usually, new letter sounds are introduced with *Picture Code Cards* rather than with *Magnetic Word Builder*. But once children are exposed to new phonic information, using letter sets provides an excellent way to practise blending. By asking the children to change one letter or sound at a time, you can go over a lot of words quickly. More importantly, each child is placing their own letters, touching them and sliding a finger under them, ensuring close attention to the blending process.

Development over time
- **Blend two letters, then three** When children are just learning to blend, you can provide additional support by having them slide their fingers under the first two letters and blending these first. Then they start with the two sounds again and blend all three.
- Later they can skip to Step 3 above (saying separate sounds) and just slide their finger beneath and blend all the sounds.
- **Sounds or letter names?** As you teach Sections 2 and 3 of this *Teacher's Guide*, it is useful to use letter sounds, reinforcing them, as you tell children which letters to place in their words. Beginning in Section 4, there will be more than one way to spell many of the sounds and there will be silent letters as well. So at this point using letter names will be more useful.

Spelling with Magnetic Word Builders

Objectives
- To engage each child in segmenting and spelling words in a small or large group setting.
- Give children blending practice as they check their spellings.

Magnetic Word Builder

Resources
- *Magnetic Word Builder* or other letter sets.
- A set of letters for the teacher (visible to the children) or a board to write the words.

Explanation for children
We are going to spell some words with your *Magnetic Word Builder*. Listen closely as we pull the words apart with word stretching so you can hear each sound and make the word.

Procedure
Each child has their own set of letters.

Step	Description	Example
1	**Teacher** says the word, a sentence with the word, and repeats the word.	week. Every week has seven days. week.
2	**Children** repeat the word in a normal way.	"week"
3	**Teacher and children** stretch imaginary rubber bands as they slowly say the word, and then segment out each sound.	wwweeeek, /w/ /ē/ / k/
4	**Children** build the word with their own letters. When most children are finished, the **teacher** makes the word or writes it for all to compare. **Children** make corrections as needed.	
5	**Children** touch each letter or letters as they say the sounds, and then slide their fingers below the letters as they blend.	/w/ /ē/ /k/ "week"

When to use
- **Hands on** You will usually use *PCCs* the first time you spell words with a new letter sound. After that the *Magnetic Word Builder* provides a great way for children to consolidate what you have taught. (There is no erasing - children like that). By changing only one sound at a time, they can spell a number of words very quickly, and because each child is placing their own letters, this activity leads them effectively toward independent spelling.

Development over time
- **One sound/several spellings** Once children begin learning the long vowels and other vowel sounds (in Sections 4 and 5 of this *Teacher's Guide*), they will often know more than one way to spell the same sound (e.g. **she, sea, neat, these**). In these situations it helps to display the *PCCs* for the relevant vowel spellings. For example, if you are spelling words with long **a**, long **e** and long **o**, you could display the **ai**, **ea** and **oa** *PCCs*, and explain that every word will include one of these three spellings.
- **Cover and spell** Once children are regularly using letter names as well as letter sounds, you can add this step to the *Magnetic Word Builder* routine after Step 5: Children cover their word with their hand, and spell the word aloud together using letter names (e.g. "**coin, c-o-i-n, coin**").

Written spelling (segmenting to spell)

Objective
- To segment and write words.
- Children also practise blending as they check their spellings.

Resources
- Writing resources: whiteboards, paper, copies of *Spelling Boxes TGCD* laminated or in plastic page protectors with erasable markers.

Explanation for children
You are going to write some words that include some of the sounds that we have been learning. Listen closely as we stretch the words. Write the letters for each sound in the order you hear them.

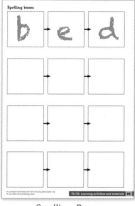

Spelling Boxes

Procedure

Step	Description	Example
1	**Teacher** says the word, a sentence with the word, and repeats the word.	bed. I have a comfortable bed. bed
2	**Children** repeat the word in a normal way.	"bed"
3	**Teacher and children** stretch imaginary rubber bands as they slowly say the word, and then segment out each sound.	bed, /b/ /ĕ/ /d/
4	**Children** write the word. When most children are finished, the **teacher** writes the word on the board for all to compare. **Children** make corrections as needed.	bed
5	**Children** blend the word and check their spelling.	/b/ /ĕ/ /d/ "bed"

When to use
- **More challenging practice** Written spelling is usually more challenging than building words with *PCC*s or magnetic letters. For most children, handwriting is still a somewhat slow and arduous task that requires their full mental attention. Correcting errors with pencil and paper can be a chore. So when teaching a new letter sound, ask the children to practise word building before word writing. Written spelling then becomes an important part of the writing process, helping to consolidate words in children's memories and gradually creating automatic neuromotor patterns between hand and brain.

Variations
- **Spelling Boxes** There are three versions of *Spelling Boxes* on your *TGCD* (for 3, 4 and 5 sounds). Children write each sound in the word in a separate box, so the two letters of a digraph (e.g. **th, ea, ow**) go in one box since they stand for one sound (likewise a trigraph e.g. **igh** goes in one box). The boxes focus attention on the number of sounds in relation to the letters. When children have filled the page with words, ask them to read their words to a partner and listen to the partner read theirs.

'Tricky' words

Objective

- To read and spell the most common words in our language that have irregular or unusual spellings.

About 'tricky' words

With the lessons in this *Teacher's Guide* you will introduce a few common exception words each week. Over the course of more than 100 lessons your children will learn the 100 most common words in English. Some of these are regular, so not a problem. The less regular ones will be introduced as 'tricky' words. Some of these will become decodable later on as children learn more spelling patterns (e.g. **see, for, look**). The remainder will remain 'tricky' due to their unique spellings (e.g. **said, one, people**).

Children will have opportunities to read new 'tricky' words in the *Phonics Reader* story that follows the lesson, and again in subsequent *Phonics Readers*. To spell them they learn to use the traditional alphabet names.

Resources

- Teacher-made 'Tricky' Word Cards (as indicated in this *Teacher's Guide* lesson plans).

Explanation for children

In some words, some of the letters don't make the sounds that we have learned from the Letterlanders. We call these 'tricky' words because we can't blend them like we do most words. We have to remember those letters with different sounds so they won't trick us. Let's see if you can discover the tricky parts in this word...

Procedure for introducing a 'tricky' word

Prior to or during the lesson, write the 'tricky' word on a card (or on the board as well).

Step	Description	Example
1	**Teacher** points to the word and says it, says a sentence or two with the word, and then repeats it	This word is **was**. It was raining when we came to school. was
2	**Children** say the word.	"was"
3	**Teacher and children** stretch imaginary rubber bands as they slowly say the word, and then segment out each sound.	wwwooozzzz, /w/ / o / /z/
4	**Children** decide which letters are not making their usual sounds.	"The **a** is not making Annie Apple's sound or Mr A's name. It needs a wavy line. The **s** is a Sleepy Sammy, saying /zzz/ so it's not tricky."
5	**Teacher** adds a wavy line over the letters that have tricky sounds.	
6	**Children** practise reading the word along with several other recently learned 'Tricky' Word Cards.	

Procedure for learning to spell a 'tricky' word: The 3-by-3 Strategy

Resources

- Children will need writing resources (whiteboards and markers, pencil and paper etc).
- A 'Tricky' Word Card previously marked with a wavy line(s).

Step	Description	Example
1	**Teacher** writes a word in large letters on the board.	was
2	**Air-tracing: Children** say the word, then air-trace the letters as they say each letter name. Finally they repeat the word. They do this three times a) with a normal voice, b) whispering, c) silently mouthing the word and letters.	"was, w...a...s, was" "was, w...a...s, was" "was, w...a...s, was"
3	**Teacher** erases the word.	
4	**Invisible writing: Children** repeat Step 2 a-c, but this time they write invisible letters with their finger on their desks, the carpet or other surface.	"was, w...a...s, was" "was, w...a...s, was" "was, w...a...s, was"
5	**Visible writing: Children** repeat Step 2 a-c, but this time they write the word three times on a whiteboard or paper. They cover the word after each time they write it.	"was, w...a...s, was" "was, w...a...s, was" "was, w...a...s, was"

Follow-up

- On day two of spelling a 'tricky' word you might ask the children to re-read three to five 'Tricky' Word Cards. Then practise spelling two or three of them as above but only using Steps 4 and 5.

- On days three and four you may ask the children to re-read a few 'Tricky' Word Cards and practise spelling two or three words using only Step 5.

- On day five you might dictate several 'tricky' words or a sentence which includes a few of them. If children misspell some words, do more practice over several days with some of the steps above. Even if children spell them correctly, do continue to revise them from time to time to make sure they are retained.

Reading words quickly and accurately

Once children have sounded out a word a few times, the next step is to recognise that word quickly without having to overtly blend the sounds. This type of instant word recognition is essential for fluent reading and comprehension. Use the following activities to help develop this speed and accuracy.

Tractors, Trains, Planes and Helicopters (reading automacity)

Objective
- To build toward automatic word recognition of decodable words.

Resources
- A list of words (on the board or a chart) with recently taught sounds and review sounds.
- A pointer or ruler.

Explanation for children

We are going to read these words in a special way with a game called **Tractors, Trains, Planes and Helicopters**. Can you say the name of the game with me? **"Tractors, Trains, Planes and Helicopters."** Think about the purpose of all those things in the name of the game. What can we do in all of them?... Yes, we can travel in them. Which one do you think goes the fastest? Yes, planes usually fly faster than the rest. Which one is the slowest? That's right, tractors go pretty slowly, especially if they are ploughing up a field to get ready to plant a farmer's crops.

So, we are going to start reading our words like **tractors**, slowly and carefully sounding through the words. Are you ready? Start up your tractor! (Children can make engine starting sounds and read the words as described below.)

Trains go a little bit faster than tractors. And now that we have ploughed through our words once, we are ready to read them a bit faster, but not too fast, we don't want to come off the track. Let's hear some train sounds...

Planes can go even faster than trains, can't they? Are you ready to read the words even faster? Then let's put on our seat belts and start our jet engines...

Helicopters can take off straight up and turn quickly to go in a different direction and land almost anywhere. So we are going to skip around from one word to another like a helicopter. Can you make a helicopter's whirring sound before we start?

Procedure

Step	Description
Tractors	**Children** and **teachers** read slowly, sounding through the words as the teacher slides the pointer below each word.
Trains	**Teacher** points to the beginning of each word moving down the list at a steady pace. **Children** read without 'sounding out' the words.
Planes	**Teacher** points to each word and moves down the list at a bit faster pace as children read the words.
Helicopters	**Teacher** points to various words in the list in a random order for children to read.

When to use
- **With blending and decoding activities** While you and the children are 'Live Reading' or doing other word building activities, ask one of the children to make a list on the board of the words you build (or do so yourself). Then use Tractors, Trains... to practise reading the list of words more quickly.
- **Fluency List** You can project your current Fluency List (see next page), make an enlarged photocopy, or copy all or part of the list on the board or a chart. Then you can use Tractors, Trains... to add interest to

developing their speed.

Development over time

- **Reading speed** Adjust your rate, whether using Tractors or Planes etc., to one that most of the children can handle, but that still pushes or challenges them just a bit. Over several weeks or months of instruction, gradually increase your speed.

- **Taking turns** You can divide the class into groups and ask them to take turns reading the list. This is often done with a girl group and a boy group. But you can also come up with other ways to divide the class (e.g. children whose names begin with vowels versus consonants, names from a-m/n-z, children with birthdays in the first six months/last six months, and many other groupings.) You could also have individuals or pairs or groups of three take turns reading.

- **Voices** So long as the children keep in mind the goals of reading accurately and fluently, you can add variety by asking them to vary their voices, loud to very soft, deep voices like giants or squeaky voices like mice, etc.

Contractions

Contractions are first used in the *Phonics Reader* story *Ding dong*. The contraction used in that story is **it's**. Introduce the idea of contractions as set out below before reading the story.

Objective

- To read and understand common contractions.

Resources

- *PCCs*.
- A teacher-made apostrophe card as shown.

Explanation for children

Write this sentence on the board and ask the children to read it twice: It is Kicking King. There is a way we say this just a bit quicker. We can say, 'It's Kicking King.' Ask the children to repeat the sentence. Write 'It's' on the board just under 'It is". When we say 'it's' we leave out a sound. Which sound did we leave out? **"/ ĭ /"** That's right, we left out the / ĭ / sound in the words 'is'. And look here at 'It's'. Instead of a letter **i** there, we just see this little mark hanging in the air there, don't we? We are going to have Letterlanders help us find out what happens to that letter when we say 'it's' instead of 'it is.'

Make the words **it** and **is** with *PCCs*. Ask the children to read the two words. When the Letterlander's try to change 'it is' to the quicker way, 'it's', the Letterlanders all start to crowd together. Close the gap between the words. They squeeze in so close together that something has to give and... pow! One of the letters explodes! Replace the **i** in **is** with the explosion card. The letter **i** explodes! Can you all make little explosion noises? Turn the explosion card to the apostrophe side. When the explosion settles down, only one little piece of the exploded letter is left and it is right up near the top of the letters between the **t** and the **s**. It marks exactly the spot where its sound is missing. So now when we read this word, we don't make any sound for the exploded letter. We just read 'It's Kicking King.'

This shortened word is called a **contraction**. If something contracts it gets smaller. That's why we call this a contraction. This little piece of an exploded letter has a name too. It's called an **apostrophe**. Ask the children to practise saying and explaining these terms each time you teach a new contraction.

Development over time

More contractions are introduced in subsequent stories, one or two at a time. Before reading the story, build the two words that make the contraction with *PCCs* (e.g. **that is**, **has not**) for the children to read. Review the 'exploding letters' explanation and change the word to the contraction with your apostrophe card (**that's**, **hasn't**). Children will enjoy 'squeezing' the letters together themselves and telling about the explosion and making the explosion sounds.

Compound words and multi-syllabic words

Compound words are first introduced in Section 2 with the words **cannot**, **backpack** and **sunset**.

Objective
- To learn to read compound words.

Resources
PCCs, or your whiteboard

Explanation for children

Write the word **backpack** on the board. Underline **back** and **pack** separately as shown. This looks like one longer word than the other words we have been reading. But it is really two words put together. Cover **pack** and ask the children to arm-blend **back**. Then cover **back** and ask them to blend **pack**. Then ask them to say the whole word. Ask someone to say what the word means. Do the same with the other two compound words, **cannot** and **sunset**.

Just read one little word at a time and then put them together. When we have two words put together, it is called a compound word. Can you say that with me? **"Compound word!"**

As you teach more compound words and words of more than one syllable, you can help children read them in these ways:

- When building words with Picture Code Cards, leave a space between syllables, ask children to arm-blend each syllable, and then read the whole word.

- Write each syllable on a card. Children read each one, and then read them together.

- Write the word on your white board with each syllable underlined. Children read each syllable and then the whole word.

Fluency Lists

Objectives
- To build towards automatic word recognition of decodable words.
- To read previously taught 'tricky' words quickly (common exception words).
- To read sentences with expression and fluency.

Resources
- Fluency Lists from your *TGCD*. (There are 20 Fluency Lists A-T.) Each one is used with four or five lessons.)
- *Reading Racer Charts* (*TGCD*) for timing children reading the lists (optional).

Explanation for children

Here is a list with lots of words that you have been learning. It's called a Fluency List. Do you know what fluency means? Fluency means reading the words quickly just like when we talk. When we can read the words with fluency, it makes reading stories more fun and interesting. So, we are going to practise reading these words and sentences each day, so you can all be fluent readers.

If you are planning to use the option of timing children on reading the list, add the following: Then at the end of the week we will see how many words each of you can read in a minute. We'll do that twice and see if you can read more the second time. I bet you can. Show them a *Reading Racer Chart*. We will show how many words you read on your own *Reading Racer Chart*.

What's on the Fluency List?

The lists provide continuous, cumulative revision of previous phonics and vocabulary. Each Fluency List includes letter sounds, decodable words, 'tricky' words, sentences and nonsense words*. These items are chosen primarily from the preceding four to six lessons with some items from earlier lessons.

* The nonsense words are the last group of words on the page. You may omit these if you choose.

Procedure to introduce and practise a new Fluency List

The procedures below are suggestions. You will want to adjust these practices to fit the needs of your children and your classroom routines.

Day 1

- **Echo read** Read out the first line of phonemes as the children point to each one. If children have learned more than one sound for a letter, say both sounds (e.g. for letter **a** say /ă/, /ā/, for **s** say /s/ /z/). After you read the line, the children repeat the line in unison. Continue down the page echo reading each line of words and sentences.
- **Set a pace** that most children will be able to follow but that also provides a bit of challenge. As children read they should follow your pace. If they are reading too fast or too slow, you can guide them by reading with them, fading your voice in and out as needed.
- **Sentences** Read the sentences with a rhythm that suits the sentence and with slightly exaggerated expression. You may need to read a bit slower than normal speech but try to keep it sounding like natural expressive speech. Children follow your example as they echo read each sentence.
- **Choral read** You and the children read the whole list together at a steady pace. Children should point to the words as they read.
- **Pace** You can guide the pace again by fading your voice in and out as needed.
- **Action** To add a bit of action, you might all clap at the end of each line in the same rhythm as reading the words (e.g. "man, dig, can, tag, tin" CLAP. "hi, I, in, tan, him," CLAP, etc.).
- **Partner reading** Ask the children to read the list to a partner either just after choral reading or later in the day. See further suggestions for partner reading below.

Day 2

- Echo read or read chorally with all the children.
- Children partner read two times each.
- Listen to a few children read the list individually.

Day 3-5

- Echo read or read chorally with all the children. For variety, ask one child to read the first line and the class echo. Then another child reads line two and everyone echoes, etc. Or use different techniques for reading lists of words such as varying the rate, using different voices and having part of the class read and then another.
- Children read with partners.
- You may want to dictate some of the words or sentences from the list for children to write.

Additional list reading suggestions

- **Reading section titles** The headings 'Sounds, Decodable words, 'Tricky' words' are not meant to be decodable to children, but it may be a good idea to talk to children about what they mean. Children need to know that they should be able to sound out the 'Decodable words' using the phonics they have learned. And they need to know that, 'tricky' words will have some parts that they can't sound out.
- **Reading decodable words in columns** The decodable words make up the largest section of the Fluency List. Usually you will ask the children to read these words going across the rows of words. Alternatively you may sometimes want to ask the children to read these words down the columns to provide variety and avoid anyone memorising the order of words on the page.

Partner reading suggestions

- **Matching partners** Rather than match the highest reader with the lowest reader, which can lead to frustration for both partners, you might try this idea. For example, if you have 20 students, list them in order with the lowest reader as number 1 and the strongest reader as number 20. Then match number 20 with number 10, number 19 with number 9, on down the list to number 10 matched with number 1. This way each weaker reader has the support of a better reading partner but the gap is not so large. Of course you can adjust these match-ups based on children's personalities and change them from time to time them to provide variety.

- **Partners sign** each other's Fluency List to verify that the lists have been read. You could also ask each child to read to two different partners and have each one sign to provide more practice.
- **How to be a partner** Teach children some strategies that help make partner reading go smoothly. Perhaps make a poster entitled "How to be good partner reader." Strategies might include those shown on the poster here. Ask the children to demonstrate some of these partner strategies, and revise them often.
- **Partner echo reading** Ask one partner to read the first line, then the second partner read the *same* line. A second time through they may change which partner reads first.
- **Your line, my line** One partner reads the first line, the second partner reads the next line. After they are finished, they start again with the second partner reading the first line, etc.
- **Your section, my section** The first partner reads the Sounds, the second partner reads the Decodable Words, the first reads the 'tricky' words, etc. Then they read again with the second partner starting with Sounds, etc.
- **Whole page** Of course partners could each take a turn at reading the whole page. A variation on this would be for the two to first read the whole page in unison, and then each one read it to the other.

How to be a good partner
- *Find a place apart from others.*
- *Sit close and use quiet voices.*
- *Help by saying the word if your partner asks.*
- *If your partner misses a word, point to it. The reader tries it again.*
- *Encourage and praise your partner. Be a good friend.*

Timing children on the Fluency List (optional)

You may choose to begin timing children on the first Fluency List A or later in the lesson sequence.

Objectives
- To motivate children to practise the Fluency Lists.
- To build fluency with words and sentences.
- To provide information on children's progress over time.

Resources
- Copies of the current Fluency Lists (*TGCD*).
- *Reading Racer Charts* for each child (*TGCD*).

Procedure
Give all the children a copy of the Fluency List with their own name on it. Put the children in pairs. Pairs spread themselves around the room to reduce distraction. Pairs decide who will be the first Reader. The other child is called the Coach. The Coach holds the Reader's copy of the list and vice versa.

Step	Description
1	You give the signal to start reading, Go!
2	Each Reader begins reading the Decodable Words and continues to read rest the of the page until time is called. Each Coach puts a small x over any words read incorrectly.
3	After 60 seconds, say, Stop!
4	Each Coach marks a straight line and a number one (1) after the last word read by the Reader.

After the first reading, the Coach points to any words missed by the Reader and reads them out correctly. Then the first Readers all read again as you time them (Steps 1-4). This time the Coach marks words missed with a 0 above. After the last word read, the coach draws a line and a number two (2).

Then the Coach and Reader reverse roles. Follow Steps 1-4 again twice so that everyone will have two chances to be timed.

Reading Racer Charts

Take in the Fluency Lists from every child. When you have time calculate the number of words read in one minute by each child for each of the two attempts. Mark their total correct words on the *Reading Racer Chart* with a horizontal line. Later ask the children to colour in their charts up to the line you have drawn.

- Tell the children not to compare their charts with others. Most of them will get more words on the second try. Praise them for this and give encouragement.

- Compare children's word reading rates on the chart below. The chart shows the goal rates used in the assessments at the end of each Section (2-5) of this *Teacher's Guide*. Look for a trend of gradually increasing rates for each child over time.

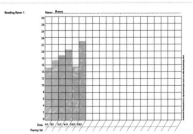

Section	Goal: Correct words per minute (cwpm)
2	15 cwpm
3	20 cwpm
4	25 cwpm
5	30 cwpm

Reading stories

Phonics Readers

Objectives
- To practise reading recently taught phonics and 'tricky' words in a meaningful context.
- To build accurate, fluent reading with good comprehension.
- To promote reading for meaning and enjoyment.

Resources
- *Phonics Readers* Sets 1-4.

Correlation to lessons
- The *Phonics Readers* include a decodable story for every lesson beginning with Lesson 8, Section 2 (a total of 83 stories). Lesson Charts at the start of each Section list the corresponding stories. The story title page is shown in each lesson.

- The first 31 stories include only words that contain the phonic elements taught thus far, along with a few 'tricky' words. In some of the later stories a few 'Story' words are used to make the stories more meaningful and interesting. These 'Story' words are listed on the title page of the story for you to preview with the children. Most 'Story' words will be partly decodable but if a child hesitates on reading any of these words, say the word for them.

Explanation for children
You've been doing such a good job of sounding out words and building words that now you are ready to read some real stories. In these books there are stories about children like you, families, animals and fun things to do. They are also about your Letterland friends. Who would you like to read about?

Teaching with Phonics Readers
The first stories that the children read are very simple and consist of just a few words. This is unavoidable since the children are just beginning to blend and have only learned a few letter sounds.

Below is a summary of suggested steps for introducing, discussing and revising a book.

Basic procedure

- **Teach** any new 'tricky' words (page 210). Read the 'story' words on the title page to the children and ask them to repeat them.
- **Predictions** Ask the children to look at the title page and the first page or two. Ask them to describe what they see and make predictions about the story.
- **First read** Ask the children to read a page or two at a time to themselves, decoding words by blending the sounds together from left to right, and checking that they understand the meaning.
- **Read together** Ask the children to read the story with you as they point to the words (choral reading). You can do this after they read each passage for themselves or after the whole story.
- **Partner read** Pair up the children and ask each child to read the story to a partner. This can be done immediately or later in the day during an independent work time.
- **Revision** Ask them to re-read the story several times over a few days. They may be reading a new story with you and revising several previous stories with a partner on the same day.
- **Check up** Ask several children to read to you each day in order to listen to everyone over the course of a week. Weaker readers should read to you more often.

Further suggestions

The suggestions below can replace some of the 'Basic' procedures or may be used in combination with them. Select combinations of strategies that fit a specific story and the children in your classroom.

Introducing a story

- **Ask a question** You may want to ask a question or two about the story title to activate children's thinking. For example, before reading *Fun in the mud* (*Phonics Readers* 2d), you could ask, What do you think Munching Mike would do if he saw a mud puddle? What do you think his Mum would have to say about it?

- **Hide the illustrations** You can hide an illustration by covering it as you project a page of the story. Children can read the text and then predict what they will see when you reveal the illustration. Alternatively, you could simply read the text to them before they see the illustration. For the brief early stories, you could write the text on the board.

Re-reading strategies

- **Choral reading** Ask the children to point to the words as they read aloud with you. Use your voice to keep everyone together by increasing your voice volume if they are getting out of synch. You can fade your voice out when children are reading together and walk about to hear how individuals are doing.
- **Echo reading** You read a passage and then the children read the same passage 'echoing' you. This is effective for building expression and fluency especially with verse or other unusual language.
- **Mumble reading** Sometimes you may want everyone to read with quiet voices at the same time but each at their own pace with no attempt to synchronise. Like choral reading, this allows you to walk about listening briefly to various children.
- **Partner reading** By pairing children to re-read a story, you are maximizing everyone's chance to read with someone to listen. If you use the suggestions for matching partners on page 216, you will have one reader who can support the other. Children can echo-read in pairs. See other suggestions for partner reading on pages 215-216.
- **Dramatise** This fun, optional strategy has learning benefits whether used by pairs of children, small groups or your whole class. Putting on a play is about reading dramatically. It can be done spontaneously or with preparation. It can be as simple as having half of the class read one page and the other half read the next. Or it can mean assigning children roles as characters who read the words in quotes and a narrator who reads the rest. Another strategy is to divide the class into groups and assign a page or more to each group. Ask them to practise reading their page together and then read to the whole class. After children have taken one role in a story, reassign roles and re-read.

Comprehension

Researchers have identified several strategies that good readers use to comprehend what they read. They have also shown that beginner readers can be taught to take ownership of these strategies as well. Much comprehension teaching for beginner readers is done with stories the teacher reads aloud because the only stories the children can read for themselves are necessarily fairly simple. However, the beginning texts in the Letterland *Phonics Readers* and *Take-Home Booklets* on your *TGCD* actually provide many such opportunities to supplement your comprehension teaching. The list below shows the research-based strategies that are recommended for teaching to five and six year olds.

Comprehension strategies for primary children

1. **Predictions** Look at the title and pictures and make predictions. Update your predictions as you read more.

2. **Questions** Ask what the story makes you wonder about as you read (e.g. Why did that character do that? What will happen next?). Answer the questions as you read more.

3. **Clarify** When something doesn't make sense to you, stop, re-read and think to try to clear it up. Sometimes reading further into the story will help clear up confusion as well.

4. **Images** Construct images in your mind that are expressed or implied in the text. Make a 'film in your head'.

5. **Story grammar** Look for the elements of the story as you read, the characters and setting. Look for problems that the characters face and their solutions.

6. **Connections** As you read, make connections with your own experience and other things you have learned or read about. But be careful to relate your own ideas to what you are reading—don't go off on a tangent.

7. **Summarise** Retell the important parts of the story.

In the activities that follow, the seven above comprehension strategies are identified in bold print.

Research has shown that how you teach and how children use these strategies are important. The emphasis should always be on the reader selecting strategies that help them get the meaning and that match their purpose for reading. One of the best ways to teach comprehension strategies is by modelling 'think-alouds' as you read to or with children. It is also important, once you have introduced a strategy, that you still incorporate previously taught strategies in your 'think-alouds' and discussions with children. Good readers use multiple strategies any time they are reading. Another important idea is to ask the children to describe how they are using various strategies in specific texts. And they should use the names of the strategies (e.g. **images**, **connections**) in these discussions. Not surprisingly, children gain more from small group comprehension instruction than large group because they have more opportunities to participate. Teachers can help build independent comprehension by circulating among children reading on their own and talking to individuals about their use of strategies.

*Block, C. and Pressley, M. (2007). Best practices in teaching comprehension. In L. Gambrell, L. Morrow, and M. Pressley (eds.), Best Practices in Literacy Instruction (pp 220-243). New York: Guilford.

Pre-reading discussion

Before reading most stories, you will want children to make **predictions** based on the title and just the first few illustrations so as not to 'give away' the ending. In some stories children can also use what they know about the Letterland characters to anticipate what might occur in the story.

Children benefit not only from making predictions but also from explaining their reasons for them. You and the children will naturally use some of the other comprehension strategies as well in your pre-reading discussion.

• Often predictions are based on children making **connections** to other stories they know or their own experiences.

• From the title and illustrations, children may recognise some of the **story grammar** elements such as setting and characters. They may be looking for what the problem might be and may speculate on a solution.

- They may have **questions** about the title.
- They may want to **clarify** something in the illustrations.
- They may form **mental images** about the rest of the story.

So, almost all of the strategies can be used *before children even begin to read*. You can model them as you combine your 'think-aloud' with the children's comments. These pre-reading discussions will not only help build comprehension, they will also motivate children to read and help prepare them for decoding and enjoying the story.

Teacher think-aloud

You can model any of the comprehension strategies by Thinking Aloud. As an example, you pick out something in the story that may make young readers wonder or ask a **question**, then talk about how you would think through that question. You might read another page or two and then talk about how you found the answer to your question. With the same story you might talk about how you would pick out key information to **summarise** the story.

Discussion during and after reading

You don't have to wait until the whole story has been read to have a brief discussion about it. If children make **predictions** before the story you will want to stop at a point in the story where you can discuss whether their predictions seem likely be accurate, or whether they may need to modify the prediction or even make a new one. You will also want to discuss **questions** that may arise or **clarify** confusions mid-story. After you have read the story, the discussion may focus on **summarising** the story. You may also want to ask more 'Why' questions at this point (e.g. Why did Sammy Snake look angry?). This type of question can help children make **connections** within the story and connections to their own background knowledge.

Constructing images

Help the children to realise that the illustrations do not show everything. Children still need to imagine what is *not* in the picture and what happens *between* picture one and two, etc. Children should still make 'a film in their head' that tells the whole story. One activity that encourages constructing images is 'Plan and Play' (page 222). Through discussion, you and the children plan out how the story could be dramatised and then take roles and act it out.

Another way to encourage image making is to read the story to children before showing the images. Then ask them to talk about what they imagine they will see in the illustration before you show it.

Similarly you can show just the text of a page or two on the board without illustrations, or by projection and let the children read the text and discuss their own images. After showing the actual illustrations, talk about how children's images and the artist's differ, including the possibility that the children's images are closer to the text or more complete than those on the page.

Story Stone (language development)

Objectives
- To motivate conversation.
- To encourage children to listen to their classmates.
- To aid learning how to summarise a story.

Resources
- An interesting pebble or small stone

Explanation for children
This little stone is called the Story Stone. The Story Stone likes to hear about stories but it cannot read because it is just a stone. When you hold it in your hand, it is your turn to talk about the story we just read. Tell us something important about the story. Everyone else will listen to you when you have the Story Stone. When you pass it on to another classmate, the Story Stone wants to hear something new about the story and not the same thing that someone else said. So listen closely and if you have something more to tell, then raise your hand when your classmate has finished talking.

Procedure

Step	Description
1	After **children** have read or listened to a story, hand the Story Stone to a child.
2	The **child** holding the Stone tells something important or interesting from the story as the other children listen carefully.
3	The first **child** or the **teacher** hands the Story Stone to another **child** who tells something different about the story.
4	If the **child** retells something already said, the **teacher** asks a question to elicit additional information.

Variations
- The Story Stone can be used to focus on any of the comprehension strategies discussed on page 219. For example, you might ask the children to make **connections** between the story and something that has happened to them, or links to another story they know.

Plan and Play (fluency and comprehension)

Objectives
- To encourage children to think actively as they read.
- To motivate re-reading of stories for fluency and comprehension.
- To increase enjoyment of reading.

Resources
- *Phonics Readers* or copies of other stories children have read.
- Objects from the classroom that with good imagination might serve as props for role-playing (e.g. a ruler might be a magic wand or a dog bone).

Explanation for children
That was a fun story to read, wasn't it? Would you like to pretend to be the characters in the story and act it out? Let's read a few pages again and then we'll talk about how we can act it out. After we have a plan for the first part, we'll act it out like a play.

Procedure
Read the story together then follow these steps.

Step	Description
1	**Children** and **teacher** re-read a page or a few pages of the story (in unison or perhaps with partners).
2	**Children** decide, guided by the teacher, what characters are needed, and what the characters will say and do to act out the story. Make ready any simple props that might help tell the story.
3	**Teacher** chooses children to play the roles in the story.
4	**Everyone** reads the page(s) of the story in unison.
5	**Children** chosen for the roles act out the story.
6	The class discusses any new ideas for the same part of the story and perhaps has another group of children re-enact it.

Then follow the same steps with the next part of the story.

Plan and Play provides unique opportunities for children to 'get inside' a story, and to learn to read all stories with deeper attention to their contents. Even simple stories are good candidates for Plan and Play. Discussing and acting out a story can help bring it to life and make it much more meaningful.

Development over time
- After many experiences with Plan and Play, you may divide your class into several groups. Let each group plan different parts of the story, and then present their part of the Play to the whole class. You can move from group to group to assist when you are needed, and children will have a chance to develop more self-management and cooperative skills.

Graphic organisers (comprehension)

Objectives

- To learn to collect and organise information.
- To build comprehension skills.

Resources

- A story or article that provides information that can be categorised/made clearer by organising visually.
- A chart tablet or the classroom board.

Explanation for children

Sometimes when we read or learn about something new, it helps us to understand it and remember it better if make a kind of map or chart.

Procedure

The steps below occur after the teacher and children have read a story or informational text. They have also already discussed it to some extent.

Step	Description
1	The **teacher** provides a framework to organise the information.
2	With further discussion, the **children** talk about information from the story and suggest where it fits on the framework.
3	The **teacher** and/or **children** write or draw on the framework.

Example of the use of a graphic organiser

This example is taken from one of the earliest stories in *Phonics Readers* 1a. In this story called *Sam*, Sammy Snake is shown in a rainy scene, a sunny one, wearing a sun hat, and finally with his hat being blown away. From the illustrations children can infer how Sammy feels in each scene. Below is the simple table that the teacher and children came up with to organise this information.

The teacher encourages children to think of additional describing words, even suggesting one or two. The teacher should not expect children to read all the words on the chart but with the story and illustrations, they should fully understand the information and how one column relates to the other.

Weather or situation	Sammy Snake's emotions
Rain	Sad, gloomy
Hot, boiling	Angry, unhappy
A big hat to shade him	Happy, pleased as punch
Windy, blustery	Upset, bewildered

Vocabulary

The children in your classroom will likely vary a great deal in the size of their 'meaning vocabulary.' This refers to the words that they can understand when they hear them and use accurately when they speak. Children with limited vocabularies are at a great disadvantage in becoming successful as readers and learners. Among these children even those who get a good start in beginning reading will falter later as they reach eight or nine years old. That is when most children begin to need to read many more words that are not in our day-to-day vocabulary. Children who have a deficit in vocabulary must begin to close that gap from the earliest possible age if they are to be successful in school and beyond.

Since beginning reading resources are necessarily composed of simple, everyday words, they do not help children build vocabulary. So it is important to teach the meanings of useful but less common words as a regular part of daily instruction.

Researchers have identified several principles that describe effective vocabulary instruction in primary classrooms. They include:

- regularly selecting 10-12 words to teach with child friendly definitions and interactive oral exercises from read-aloud books
- selecting words that are unknown to at least half of the children and that can be explained in ways that children can understand with direct, explicit instruction
- providing repeated exposure to new words in varied contexts in order to fully understand their meanings and be able to use them
- creating excitement about learning new words and discussing word meanings, so children become active seekers of new and interesting words.

Make use of quality children's literature and meaningful classroom experiences in addition to your Letterland lessons to ensure adequate vocabulary learning.

Teaching vocabulary with Letterland Phonics Readers

While the *Phonics Readers'* focus is on practising words with various phonic patterns, they can also be a source for learning new words and their meanings. Most of the words in the *Phonics Readers* will be familiar to children, but the characters and situations may suggest concepts and less familiar words.

For example, the story *Hugs* (2d), provides a clear example of a mother who is *distracted* and a child who is *frustrated*. Both are good words to know for children learning to manage their own behaviour, attention and feelings.

'Story' words

Some *Phonics Readers* include a few 'story' words listed on the title page. These are words that children are not expected to decode. They are included to make the story more meaningful and interesting. Children will readily understand most of these words, but a few will need explanation, leading to further vocabulary exploration.

Section 7 :
Activity Bank

Choose from the optional activities below to supplement the Strategies in the Appendix, and to provide variety while meeting the needs of your particular class. Each activity's focus and who it is for (individual, small group or whole class) is identified on the right. There are a number specifically aimed at small group teaching, including extra practice for children who need it. Some of these activities are designed to help you focus more closely on the needs of children who are struggling.

Summary of contents

Learning and practising letter sounds

Several of the activities below focus on increasing speed of response. Others provide fun games for ESL students and children who need more support for learning the Letterland characters and their sounds.

Action Trick Game

Objectives
- To strengthen the letter sound connections.
- To develop quicker responses.

Resources
- All *Picture Code Cards* (*PCCs*) **a–z** learned so far.
- *Action Tricks Poster* (actions illustrated and described on pages 182-183).

Procedure

Step	Description
1	**Teacher** shows the *PCCs* plain letter sides one after the other.
2	**Children** all do the actions and say the sounds.
3	**Teacher** goes through the *PCCs* a second time at a faster pace and perhaps a third time, still faster.

Sounds Box

Resources
- *Picture Code Cards* (*PCCs*).

Procedure

Step	Description
1	**Teacher** places several recently taught *PCCs* in a box labelled 'Sounds Box'.
2	Occasionally throughout the day **teacher** asks a different child to take a card and hold it up for the class to see.
3	**Teacher** invites the rest of the class to fill the classroom with the sound of the letter or digraph.

Sound Pops

Resources

• *Picture Code Cards* (PCCs).

Procedure

Distribute as many previously taught *PCCs* **a–z** as you like, one per child.

Step	Description	Example
1	**Teacher** says a letter sound.	**/fff/**
2	**Children** repeat it.	**/fff/**
3	**Child** with the corresponding *PCC* 'pops up' (stands) and says:	"I am Firefighter Fred and I say /**fff**/."

When to use

• Use Sound Pops to help children get used to listening for sounds. It will help prepare them for the 'Guess Who?' activity and for 'Live Reading' and 'Live Spelling'.

Development over time

• As children begin to learn consonant and vowel digraphs, this activity will still be valuable. Two children hold a digraph *PCC* together. Instead of naming the characters when they pop up, the children hold up their *PCC* and say, e.g. "**We say** /**sh**/."

• Once children learn more than one way to spell a sound, you may have several pairs stand up at a time. If you say the sound /ē/, the children with *PCCs* for **ee**, **ea**, and **Mr E** come to the front of the class, all hold up their *PCCs* and say, "**We all say** /ē/." The three children could ask other children to say a word that includes their spelling pattern. For example, the **ee** pair calls on a classmate who replies, "**tree**."

Where is...?

Objective

To support ESL children and others in learning the Letterlander names.

Resources

• *Picture Code Cards* (PCCs).

Procedure

Revise 4 to 6 character names showing the picture sides, then turn to revise their sounds on the plain letter sides. Then display all the picture sides.

Step	Description	Example
1	**Teacher** names a Letterlander.	Everyone say, 'Annie Apple'
2	**Children** repeat the Letterlander name.	"Annie Apple"
3	**Teacher** asks a volunteer to find the *PCC*.	Where is Annie Apple, Ryan?
4	**Child** holds picks up the *PCC*, shows the picture side and says:	"**My name is Annie Apple.**"
5	**Other children** say:	"**Hi, Annie Apple.**"
6	Steps 1-5 are repeated with each Letterlander. Everyone greets all the children holding *PCCs*.	"**Hi, Annie Apple. Hi, Talking Tess,**" etc.

Sound Trick Game

Objectives
To help children derive the letter sounds from the initial letter in the character names.

Resources
• *Picture Code Cards (PCCs).*

Procedure
Display four to eight *PCCs* picture side up on a table.

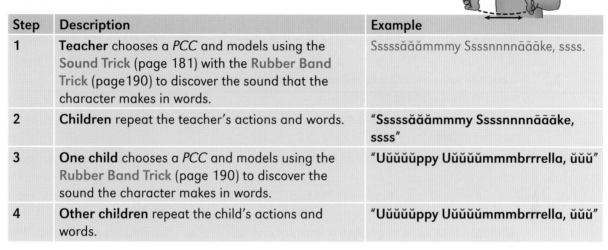

Step	Description	Example
1	**Teacher** chooses a *PCC* and models using the Sound Trick (page 181) with the Rubber Band Trick (page190) to discover the sound that the character makes in words.	Sssssăăămmmy Ssssnnnnāāāke, ssss.
2	**Children** repeat the teacher's actions and words.	"Sssssăăămmmy Ssssnnnnāāāke, ssss"
3	**One child** chooses a *PCC* and models using the Rubber Band Trick (page 190) to discover the sound the character makes in words.	"Uŭŭŭŭppy Uŭŭŭŭmmmbrrrella, ŭŭŭ"
4	**Other children** repeat the child's actions and words.	"Uŭŭŭŭppy Uŭŭŭŭmmmbrrrella, ŭŭŭ"

• Other children take turns with Steps 3 and 4.

Whose name starts with...?

Objectives
• To connect the letter sound to Letterlander's name.
• To move towards connecting the sound and the letter shape.

Resources
• *Picture Code Cards (PCCs).*

Procedure
Display the picture sides of four to eight *PCCs*.

Step	Description	Example
1	**Teacher** says a sound. (Prolong the sounds of **f, h, l, m, n, r, s, v, w, y**, e.g. /ffffff/. Repeat other letters' sounds three times, e.g. /t/ /t/ /t/).	/ssssss/ or /b/ /b/ /b/
2	**Children** repeat the sound.	"/ssssss/" or "/b/ /b/ /b/"
3	**Teacher** asks which Letterlander's name begins with the sound.	Whose name starts with /sss/?
4	**Children** prolong the sound or repeat it and then say the character's name.	"SSSSSSammy Snake" or "/b/ /b/ Bouncy Ben"

Development over time
• As they learn the sounds, children can take turns in the teacher's role doing Steps 1 and 2.
• As they make more progress, you can display just the plain letters. After Steps 1 and 2, you could call on individual children to point to the plain letter that matches the sound.

Hide and Seek

Resources

• *Picture Code Cards (PCCs).*

Procedure

Display the picture sides of four to eight *PCCs*.

Step	Description	Example
1	**Teacher** points to each one and says the Letterlander's name.	Clever Cat, Annie Apple, Firefighter Fred, Impy Ink, Talking Tess, etc.
2	**Teacher** points to each one again as the children name them.	**"Clever Cat, Annie Apple, Firefighter Fred, Impy Ink, Talking Tess,"** etc.
3	**Teacher** turns the *PCCs* to the plain letters, points to each one and says the sound.	/c/, /ă/, /f/, /ĭ/, /t/
4	**Teacher** points to each one again as the children say the sounds.	**"/c/, /ă/, /f/, /ĭ/, /t/"**
5	**Teacher** explains the Hide and Seek game.	The Letterlanders are hiding behind their letters. To make one come out, just point to it, say the correct sound and we'll turn it over to see who it is.
6	**Children** take turns to point to a letter, saying its sound and turning it to the picture side.	**"/t/"** (turns to the plain side). **"I found you, Talking Tess."**

Snails, Rabbits, Deer and Frogs

Objective

• To increase fluency of saying sounds in response to the plain letters.

Resources

• *Picture Code Cards (PCCs)*

Procedure

Display the plain letter side of eight to sixteen *PCCs*.

Step	Description	Example
1	**Teacher** explains the game and then points to each letter moving slowly from one to the next in order as children say the sounds.	Let's pretend to be snails crawling slowly from one letter to the next.
2	**Children** say each sound as the teacher points to the letter.	**"/m/, /p/, /l/, /ĕ/, /t/,"** etc.
3	**Teacher** explains the next step and points, in the same order, at a faster rate each time.	Lets pretend to be rabbits. They can hop from letter to letter very fast. Deer, with their long legs, can run even faster than rabbits.
4	**Teacher** likens hopping from word to word to behaving like frogs and points randomly from one letter to another with speed.	Frogs hop here and there. You never know where they might land.

Initial sounds in words

Just knowing the letter sounds is not enough for young readers. They need to be aware of those letter sounds within spoken words. Use these activities with any children who need more practice in isolating the beginning **sound** (e.g. "butter starts with /**b**/") or in matching spoken words or pictures to their initial letter shape.

Whole class

Listen and Jump Game

Resources
- *Picture Code Cards (PCCs).*

Procedure with one sound

Children stand in a large circle. They could be outside a circle formed by a rope or the circle can be imaginary. You could also ask them to stand on the outside edge of a mat or rug. Display the letter or *PCC* that stands for the target sound.

Step	Description
1	**Teacher** says a word and **children** repeat it.
2	If the word starts with the target sound, **children** jump into the circle. If not, they stay still.
3	When inside the circle, if the next word begins with the target sound they jump back out. If not, they stay still.

Development over time
- The game as described above is about initial sounds, but later in children's development it could used to listen for medial vowel sounds as well.

Variations
- Children can stand along one side of a real or imaginary line and play this game. On hearing a word beginning with the target sound they 'Jump the River.'
- You can also play 'Up and Down'. Children respond to the target sound in a word by standing up or if already standing, by sitting down.
- For a less active version, ask the children to put their hand to their ear if they hear the target sound. If not, they touch their tummies.

Procedure with two sounds

Children stand anywhere they have room to move to the left and right. Display the *PCC* (e.g. Annie Apple) for one sound on the class' left and the *PCC* (e.g. Mr A) for the second sound on the class' right.

Step	Description	Example
1	**Teacher** says a word that starts with one of the two target sounds.	acorn
2	**Children** repeat the word, then jump toward the *PCC* that matches the beginning sound they hear.	"acorn"

Small group

Clever Cat's Cup and games for every Letterlander

Resources
- *PCC* for Clever Cat.
- *Beginning Sound Pictures* for **c** and five to six for other letters (*TGCD*).
- A cup of some kind, perhaps labelled as 'Clever Cat's cup'.

Explanation for children
We have some pictures here and we need to decide which ones Clever Cat would like to put in her cup. She likes pictures of things that begin with her little /c/ sound.

Procedure
Display the picture side of the *PCC* for **c**. Combine the *Beginning Sound Pictures* into a mixed deck with plain sides up.

Step	Description	Example
1	**Child** starts off playing the role of Clever Cat and holds the cup.	
2	**Child** next to Clever Cat takes a *Beginning Sound Picture*, names the pictured item and says the initial sound. (If needed, the teacher helps the child use the Rubber Band Trick to isolate the initial sound. See below.)	"clock, /c/" Option, if needed: "cllllllooock, /c/"
3	If the initial sound is /c/, the child places the picture in Clever Cat's cup. If not, the card is placed face up beside the deck.*	
4	When a card is placed in Clever Cat's Cup, she thanks the other child. The first child responds.	"Thank you for the clock." "You're welcome."
5	**Child** that took the first *PCC* becomes Clever Cat. **Child** on his or her other side takes a picture, etc.	

* There are also cards with just a plain letter in Beginning Sound Pictures. When children pick up these, they say the sound and they get to draw another card. The plain **c** card can also go in Clever Cat's cup.

When to use
- Use with children who are just beginning to learn about initial sounds in words or those who need additional practice.

The Rubber Band Trick option
- If a child is having difficulty isolating the initial sound, use the Rubber Band Trick. First you and the child stretch the word. Then both start to stretch the word again but stop on the first sound.

Initial sound games for the rest of the Letterlanders
- You can adapt the above game for any of the Letterlanders. Use the suggestions below or make up your own game, perhaps with your children's help.

Apple's for Annie's Tree Draw a simple apple tree. Children place the /ă/ pictures on the tree.

Bouncy Ben's Six Brothers Ben wants to find a picture to give each of his six brothers. Include the plain letter **b** Beginning Sound Picture card in your deck. When children pick up the plain **b** or pictures that start with /b/, they put them in a row beside Ben's *PCC*. Everyone counts the pictures each time one more is placed. When you have found pictures for all six brothers, the game is over.

What's Behind the Duck Door Place Dippy's *BPCC - Uppercase* on the table, picture side up. When anyone finds a picture that starts with /d/, they 'open the duck door' and place the picture under it

Eddy Elephant's Water Spout Place Eddy's *PCC* on the table. As children find pictures of words that begin with /ĕ/, they line them outward and upward from Eddy's trunk like spouting water.

Fishing with Firefighter Fred Arrange the pictures face down on the table or on a large blue piece of paper cut in the shape of a pond. Children put /f/ pictures in a cup or basket labelled 'For Fred's Fish Fry.'

Give a Gift to Golden Girl Golden Girl holds a gift box or gift bag for children to put her /g/ pictures into. Children take turns being Golden Girl who always says, "Great, thank you," for the gifts.

Harry Hat Man's Hat Game Use a hat in the same way as Clever Cat's cup above.

Impy Ink's Drawings Pretend the Beginning Sound Pictures are Impy's own black ink drawings. Children place his / ĭ / words around Impy's *PCC*.

Jumping Jim's Jumbo Jet Place the j *PCC* picture side up on the table. When children pick cards from the deck that start with /j/, they place them around the *PCC*. Point to all the pictures that have been placed so far and ask the children to say these alliterative phrases for each picture: **jumbo jet**, **jiggly jelly**, **jerky jeep**, **jars** of **jam**, **jeans jacket**.

Kicking King's Crown Make a paper crown to put on the table. When a child gets a /k/ word, it goes inside the crown.

Lucy Lamp's Light Lucy's pictures have been lost in the dark. Place the /l/ pictures and others randomly on the table. Each child shines a torch on one of Lucy's pictures and asks, "Lucy, did you lose a _____?"

Munching Mike's Meal Children take turns using a sock puppet as Munching Mike or they can just use their hands as a puppet. If the puppet draws an /m/ word, he puts it in Mike's meal bowl. If it is not an /m/ word, the puppet spits it out.

Noisy Nick's Nice New Net Use a small butterfly net or a drawing of one. When a child picks up an /n/ picture, he or she says (e.g.), "**Here is nnn-newspaper for your nnn-nice nnn-new nnn-net, nnn-Noisy, nnn-Nick.**"

Oscar's Odd Pets Use the four animal pictures that start with /o/ and several other animals from the Beginning Sound Pictures. Oscar's odd pets have run off to play with other Letterland pets. The children help return Oscar's pets to him.

Peter Puppy's Pouch Peter Puppy puts his pictures in a pouch. When it is a child's turn to be Peter, the child says, "**Please pass Peter Puppy's pooch pouch.**"

Quarrelsome Queen's Quiet Room Place the Queen's *BPCC* - Uppercase on the table. Tell children that they must whisper throughout the game so as not to disturb the Queen in her quiet room. Each time they place a **q** picture beside the quiet room, ask them to all whisper the names of the pictures placed so far.

Red Robot's Robber Sack Red Robot holds a sack or bag. Place one /r/ picture and one other in front of the child beside Red Robot. The child names the two pictures and Red Robot robs the one that begins with /r/ and puts it in his sack. Then the next child gets to be Red Robot.

Sliding Snake's Game Place the Beginning Sound Pictures face down in a curving, snaky row. The Sammy Snake child holds his *PCC*. The next child picks a picture. If it starts with /s/, the child slides it over to Sammy.

Talking Tess's Telephone Place a /t/ picture and one that starts with another letter in front of a child. You pretend to be Talking Tess with a toy telephone or use your hand as a telephone. Ring up the child and ask if he or she has found a picture that belongs to you. (Children can be Tess after you have modelled the role.)

Under Uppy's Umbrella Draw a simple outline of an umbrella. Children place Uppy's pictures under her umbrella to keep them dry.

Vicky Violet's Extra Vase Vicky holds an empty vase. The child next to her has one **v** picture and one other. The child asks, (e.g.) "**Vicky Violet would you like a picture of a volcano or a moose?**" Vicky replies, "**I vote for the volcano,**" and places the picture in her vase.

Walter Walrus's Wiggles When Walter Walrus sees something that starts with his sound, he gets so excited that he wiggles all over. Show pictures one at a time for all to name. If the picture starts with **w**, all the children stand up and wiggle. For a calmer game, children could just wiggle their fingers.

Fix-it Max Place Fix-it Max's *PCC* picture side up on the table. Tell children that his sound doesn't come at the start of any words. For each picture card, they decide if the /**x**/ sound is heard in the middle or the end of the word, and place the pictures around the edges of the *PCC*.

Yellow Yo-yo Man Give each child a card with **Yes** written on it and another with **No**. Show each picture to the group. Children hold up their **Yes** cards for **y** pictures and their **No** cards for others. When you show the plain **y** card, they all stand up and do Yo-yo Man's Action Trick. Go through the deck a couple of times a bit faster each time.

Zig Zag Zebra Zooms Place the **Z** *BPCC - Uppercase* on the table picture side up. Tell children that Zig Zag Zebra likes to zoom fast wherever she goes and she often runs in a zig-zag pattern. When a child draws a card with a **z** picture, he or she slides the picture along Zig Zag's Z from nose to tail and then places it below the *PCC*.

Small group

Lost and Found Game

Resources
- *PCCs* for three Letterlanders.
- *Beginning Sound Pictures* (*TGCD*) that begin with the sounds of the three Letterlanders. There are five pictures for each letter **a–z**.

Explanation for children
A big wind came to Letterland and blew away these pictures that belong to three of our Letterland friends. It scattered these things all over Letterland. Now we need to help return them to their owners. How do you think we can tell which picture belongs to whom? Good idea, we can listen for their sounds at the beginning of the words.

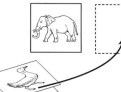

Procedure
Display the picture side (or plain letter) of three Letterlanders in a row. Shuffle the *Beginning Sound Pictures* for all three sounds together and place the deck within reach of the children.

Step	Description	Example
1	**Child** picks up a *Beginning Sound Pictures* card and names the picture.	"goose"
2	**Child** places the picture below the Letterlander whose name begins with the same sound.	Goose goes below **g** *PCC*
3	**Child** points to the *PCC* and everyone says the sound. Then **child** points to each picture below the *PCC* and everyone names them.	"/g/, **goal**, **goose**"

When to use
- Use with children who need additional practice listening for and isolating initial sounds in words and in matching the sound to the letter.

The Great Vowel Race

Objectives
- Initial Sounds: Listening for Vowel Sounds (short vowels) at the beginning of words.
- Medial Sounds: Listening for Vowel Sounds (short vowels) in the middle of words.

Resources for Initial Vowel Sounds
- *PCCs* for three to five of the Vowel Sounds (ă, ĕ, ĭ, ŏ, ŭ).
- *Beginning Sound Pictures* (*TGCD*) that begin with the sounds of the selected vowels. (There are five pictures for each vowel).

Explanation for children
The Vowel Sounds have decided to have a race to see who will get their five favourite pictures lined up first. They need us to help them.

Procedure for Initial Vowel Sounds
Display the *PCCs* (picture or plain letter sides) for three to five Vowel Sounds in a row. Select the five *Beginning Sounds Pictures* that go with each short vowel, shuffle them together and place the deck within the children's reach.

Step	Description	Example
1	**One child** picks up a *Beginning Sound Picture* and names the picture.	**"egg"**
2	**Child** places the picture under the vowel whose name begins with the same sound.	**"The egg goes beside Eddy Elephant."**
3	**Child** points to the *PCC* and everyone says the sound. Then the child points to the picture for all to name. As each next child adds a word, he/she points to each picture beside that *PCC* for everyone to read.	**"/ĕ/, egg, elbow, envelope"**
4	The race is won by the first vowel that has five pictures beside it. Option: play on to see which vowel comes second, third, etc.	

Resources for Medial Vowel Sounds
- *PCCs* for three to five of the Vowel Sounds (ă, ĕ, ĭ, ŏ, ŭ).
- *Beginning Sound Pictures* to match the vowels you are using: **yak, jam, rat, map, van; hen, jet, net, vet, web; fish, zip, wig, pin, lips; doll, log, sock, fox, box; cup, ducks, huts, pup, rug.**

Procedure for Medial Vowel Sounds
Display the *PCCs* (picture or plain letter sides) for three to five Vowel Sounds in a row. Shuffle the above *Beginning Sounds Pictures* and place the deck within the children's reach.

Step	Description	Example
1	**Child** picks up a *Beginning Sound Picture* and names the picture. Then the child stretches the word with the **Rubber Band Trick** and segments out the medial vowel (page 190).	**"net, nnnnee-e, /ĕ/"**
2	**Child** places the picture beside the vowel whose name begins with that middle sound.	**"I can hear Eddy Elephant."**
3	**Child** points to the *PCC* and everyone says the sound. Then the child points to each picture beside the *PCC* and everyone names them.	**"/ĕ/, hen, web, jet"**
4	The race is won by the first vowel that has five pictures below it first. Option: play on to see which Vowel comes second, third, etc.	

Memory Game

Objective

- To practise awareness of beginning sounds in words.

Resources

- *Beginning Sounds Pictures (TGCD)* four to six pairs of pictures (approx 20 cards in total).

Explanation for children

When it is your turn, turn over two of these pictures to see what they are. What are we looking for? Two pictures that start with the same sound. This is called the Memory Game because if the pictures don't match, you put them back face down and we all try to remember where they are for our next turn.

Procedure

Shuffle the pictures and then place them picture side down in rows.

Step	Description
1	First **child** turns two pictures over and names them. If they match the child collects them. If they do not match, the child returns them, face down, to the same place.
2	Each **child** in turn does the same.

Eyes Shut Riddle Game

Objectives

- To review letter sounds in a language-rich game-like activity.

Resources

- Optional: Make copies of each riddle below on a paper strip and place in a hat.

Explanation for children

The Letterlanders have all made up riddles about themselves. They would like you to listen closely to the riddle and see if you can tell which Letterlander it is about. And they have a tip for us – if you want to listen really well – keep your eyes shut!

Procedure

Step	Description
1	Each **child** in turn draws a riddle out of the hat. (Or the teacher simply reads them out in random order.)
2	**Children** all close their eyes as the teacher reads out a riddle.
3	**Children** raise their hands if they want to answer.
4	**Child** who drew out the riddle calls on a classmate to answer.

The Riddles

a	I like adding up apples. Who am I?
b	I like to balance my ball between my big, brown ears. Who am I?
c	I love eating cabbage and cucumbers and carrot cake. Who am I?

d	I think daisies and dandelions taste delicious. Who am I?
e	I eat lots of eggs for energy. Who am I?
f	I think it's fun to go fishing in my free time. Who am I?
g	I love playing games that I am good at, like guessing games. Guess who I am?
h	I like playing hopscotch and hide-and-seek. Who am I? (You could whisper this one.)
i	If you ask what my favourite colour is, it's indigo. Who am I?
j	I just love to travel by jeep or by jet. Who am I?
k	I keep a kangaroo and kittens and a kingfisher for pets. Who am I?
l	I love licking lemon-flavored lollipops. Who am I?
m	I love to munch on magnets mixed with mud sauce. Who am I?
n	I like to nibble nuts in my nut tree den. Who am I?
o	My best friends are an ostrich and an otter. Who am I?
p	I love playing the piano. Who am I?
q	I spend three quarters of my time quarrelling. Who am I?
r	I run off with other people's rulers and radios and rollerblades. Who am I?
s	I'm good at slithering and sliding in the sand. Who am I?
t	I love playing tennis and jumping on the trampoline. Who am I?
u	I always feel unhappy when I'm upside-down. Who am I?
v	We have lovely velvet petals and velvet leaves. Who looks after us?
w	I like to wallow in the water. Who am I?
x	I have a box of tools so I can fix things. Who am I?
y	One day, I hope to buy a yellow yacht. Who am I?
z	I love zipping around and around the Letterland zoo. Who am I?

Small group

Knock, Knock

Objectives
- To practise connecting initial sounds with their letters.
- Oral language development.

Explanation for children

The Letterlanders like knock, knock riddles. When you ask them, "Who's there?", they answer with a clue about something they like. Listen to the clue and you can tell who it is. Let's try a few.

Knock, knock!

"Who's there?"

I like to go fishing in my free time. Who am I?

"Firefighter Fred!"

Knock, knock!

"Who's there?"

I have a view of a volcano from my house? Who am I?

"Vicky Violet!"

- Ask the children to make up their own knock, knock riddles, on their own or in pairs, and then share them with the class.

Alphabet names

Letter names or letter sounds?

The traditional letter names ("aye, bee, cee") are not very helpful to children for reading words. To illustrate the point, consider a child trying to sound out the word **cat** using letter names: "ceeayetee". It is much more important that children learn to respond to the letter shapes with the sounds letter's make in words (/ă/, /b/, /c/). We suggest that these sounds are what you teach children first.

Many children may come into your classroom knowing only the names of some or all the letters and not the sounds. The good news is that this means they have learned to differentiate the letter shapes and that is a positive and important step. For learning to read, however, they will benefit from a de-emphasis on letter names since only five of them ever occur in reading (the five vowel names).

Trying to learn both letter sounds and letter names at the same time all too often leads to confusion between the two. Since not one of the 21 consonants ever says its name in words, and no less than 16 of them begin with another letter's sound, the traditional alphabet names (**aye, bee, cee**) are de-emphasised in early Letterland teaching in favour of the sounds that letters make in words (/ă/, /b/, /c/). The deliberate strategy of delaying the use of these traditional **a–z** names – ideally until children's blending skills are well in place, is one of the important ingredients in Letterland's early success.

When children have shown that they can read and spell simple words with three sounds, the timing is right for making sure they also know the letter names. These can come in handy when talking about letters that stand for more than one sound or for talking about how to spell words with digraphs (e.g. **th**, **ea**, **or**). There are a number of suggestions below for teaching letter names when children are ready.

Small group/whole class

Verses for traditional alphabet names

On the *TGCD*, you will find two pages with rhymes for practising every letter name. This first verse is a sample:

> **My name is Annie Apple, but some people say**
> **it's often quite handy to call me 'ay.'**

Suggestions for using the rhymes

- Share a few rhymes each day. Say the rhyme with a lively expression a few times and then ask the children to join in. Repeat all the rhymes each day and add a few more.
- You could ask the children to stand in front of the class holding *PCCs* for six or eight letters in alphabetical order (e.g. **a** to **h**, **i** to **p**). As the class chants each rhyme, the child with the relevant *PCC* shows the picture side in time with the character name (e.g. "Annie Apple"). Then as the class says the letter name, the child turns the card to the plain letter and traces it.
- Another option: Each child memorises a verse. All your children present to another class or to parents. Each child can say a verse and show both sides of the *PCC* as above.

Activities with the traditional alphabet song

Once letter sounds knowledge is fully in position you can use the alphabet song to help children attach letter names to the correct letter. Many children will already know the song, but they may not be able to connect the letter name to the right letter shape, especially if the letters are not in alphabetical order.

- Let children take turns pointing to the letters on the *Alphabet Frieze* as the class sings the song. Ensure you slow down when you get to "**l, m, n, o**" so the children hear and can point to each letter separately.
- You could also use *Alphabet Desk Strips*, the *Letterland Alphabet Poster* or other individual copies of the alphabet. Each child points to their own copy as everyone sings. Observe to see if their pointing is matching their singing.

Saying letter names in and out of order

- Ask the children to say rather than sing the letter names in alphabetical order as they do some of the same activities above. Vary the speed and use different voices, sometimes whispering, using deep giant voices, soft voices, spooky, staccato voices or slow stretched-out voices.
- Work on just part of the alphabet beginning with **a–j**. Write them on the board in order at wide intervals. Have everyone point from their seat at the letters as you all say them in order. Then you call out letters randomly and everyone points. Then point to letters at random for children to name. Do the same on other days with **k–s** and then **t–z**.
- The next step is reading random lists of letters (e.g. **h, p, l, a, t, d, u, c**...). A fun way to do this is to sing the letter names to the tune of a familiar song such as 'Mary Had a Little Lamb' or the 'Happy Birthday Song'. When you get to the end of the letters just start them again and keep singing to the end of the tune.

Incorporating letter names in other activities

The activities above allow you to keep your letter name teaching separate, as you continue generally working with letter sounds in words. When your syllabus requires alphabet naming proficiency, you can simply add practising them to the already familiar activities below.

'Quick Dash'

- The emphasis of the 'Quick Dash' should continue to be on children responding quickly to plain letters with the sound. To add letter names to this review activity, see 'Optional procedure for adding letter names to your 'Quick Dash'' on page 195.

'Guess Who?'

- For 'Guess Who?', the sound-to-letter review activity, the focus is on hearing the sound and matching it to the letter shape. As children advance, more and more of the sounds you will be reviewing will be digraphs or trigraphs (e.g. **ch, ai, or, igh**). At that point, responding with alphabet names becomes more practical. See the Steps that follow (left) and the alternative Steps (right) for using when your children are reviewing digraphs and trigraphs.

	Using Letterlanders' names	Example
1	**Teacher** keeps the *PCC* hidden and says the sound.	/p/
2	**Children** trace the letter in the air as they repeat the sound.	/p/, /p/, /p/...
3	**Teacher** says:	Guess Who?
4	**Children** say the name of the Letterlander(s).	**"Peter Puppy"**
5	**Teacher** shows the picture side to confirm the children's answer.	

	Using letter names	Example
1	**Teacher** keeps the *PCC* hidden and says the sound.	/or/
2	**Children** trace the letters in the air as they repeat the sound.	/or/, /or/, /or/...
3	**Teacher** says:	What letters
4	**Children** say the letter names	**"O-R"**
5	**Teacher** shows the picture side to confirm the children's answer.	

Word Building and Letter Names

- The emphasis on word building is always on matching sounds with the correct letters. But letter names begin to come into their own for learning to spell 'tricky' words and words with digraphs, split digraphs and trigraphs, as described below.

- **Reading/Blending activities** (e.g. 'Live Reading', Blending with *PCC*s) After children do the Roller Coaster Trick for the word and you use it in a sentence, ask the children to spell the word with letter names and then say the word (e.g. **"B-L-U-E, blue"**) as they look at the word. Then ask them to close their eyes and again spell the words with letter names and say it.

- **Segmenting /Spelling activities** (e.g. 'Live Spelling', *Spelling Boxes*) After children segment the word with the Rubber Band Trick and build it, they will usually be ready to close their eyes and spell it with letter names. After they spell it aloud ask them to repeat the word (e.g. **"S-H-I-N-E, shine"**). Similarly, when they are using *Magnetic Word Builder* or other letter sets for spelling, ask them to cover their word with their hand after they build it and then letter-name spell it and say the word.

Blending and segmenting words

The optional activities from this section provide variety to strengthen all your children's mastery of these key skills and help you support children who are struggling with blending and segmenting words.

Blending Clues

Sometimes children may need to practise blending orally without looking at letters. In this activity you give them the sounds orally. It allows the child to concentrate on the process of blending phonemes without being distracted by their spelling. Since it is entirely oral, you can use words with graphemes that have not yet been taught.

Objective
- To practise blending sounds smoothly into words.

Explanation for children
This is a listening and blending game. I am going to give you some sounds and then we'll blend them using the **Roller Coaster Trick.** Here's a clue: the word is the name of an animal.

Procedure

Step	Description	Example
1	**Teacher** gives a broad clue to the word.	It's an animal.
2	**Teacher** says the sounds as she touches her left shoulder with her right hand, then mid-arm and wrist.	/mmm/ /ou/ /sss/
3	**Children** say the sounds as they touch their left shoulders with their right hands, then mid-arms and wrists.	"/mmm/ /ou/ /sss/"
4	**Teacher** and **children** slide their right hands down their left arms as they say the sounds without stopping. They repeat more quickly.	"mmmousss, mouse"

Suggested categories and useful words for this game.

Animals	The body	Foods	Toys	At home	Activities
b-a-t	h-ea-d	b-u-n	d-o-ll	r-u-g	r-u-n
c-o-w	f-oo-t	m-ea-t	t-o-p	b-e-d	h-o-p
p-i-g	ch-i-n	j-ui-ce	k-i-te	b-a-th	s-i-t
f-o-x	kn-ee	ch-ee-se	b-a-ll	d-oor	l-au-gh
c-a-t	l-e-g	e-gg	b-oa-t	ph-o-ne	l-oo-k
d-o-g	m-ou-th	h-a-m	b-a-t	r-oo-m	s-i-ng
h-or-se	l-i-p	b-ee-f	b-i-ke	ch-air	j-o-g
ch-i-ck	ch-e-st	b-ea-n	g-a-me	r-oo-f	t-o-ss
b-ir-d	h-i-p	ch-i-p	h-oo-p	b-oo-k	c-a-tch
a-pe	n-o-se	r-i-ce	c-ar	t-a-p	h-u-m

Sammy Snake's Slide and Say

This activity lets you guide children in segmenting words without using letters. Sometimes with some children it can be helpful to just focus on the oral phonemic awareness task of segmenting. Once they can segment orally with ease, it is very important to do lots of segmenting and spelling activities with letters, as described throughout this *Teacher's Guide* (e.g. 'Live Spelling', Segmenting with *Picture Code Cards* and *Magnetic Word Builders*, Written Spelling (page 209)).

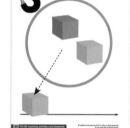

Objective

- To orally segment words into phonemes without letters.

Resources

- Copies of *Sammy Snake's Slide and Say* mat (*TGCD*).
- Three small cubes, counters, or pebbles for you and for each child.

Explanation for children

Sammy Snake likes to slip and slide as he says words. He has made a game to help us segment words into separate sounds.

Procedure

Everyone starts with the three cubes in the circle.

Step	Description	Example
1	**Teacher** says a word and the **children** repeat it.	rug "rug"
2	**Teacher** and **children** say the word using the Rubber Band Trick (page 190).	"rrrruuuuug"
3	**Teacher** and **children** each slide one cube from the circle down to the left side of the line as they say the first sound. Do the same with second and third sounds.	"rrrrrrrr" "uuuuuu" "g"
4	**Teacher** says: Touch and say **Children** touch each cube in the row in turn, from left to right, as they say each sound separately.	/r/ /u/ /g/
5	**Teacher** says: Blend **Children** slide their fingers under the cubes as they blend the sounds back together, and then say the word.	"rrrruuuuug, rug"

Everyone returns the cube to the circle to get ready for the next word.

When to use

- Use when children are just learning to segment – especially for those who find it difficult. Use in conjunction with the Rubber Band Trick to help children 'pull the words' apart and hear each sound.

Development over time

- Even after children have learned to segment CVC words, they may have difficulty when they begin segmenting four sound words with adjacent consonants. You may want to return to this exercise for a few days to help them focus on each adjacent consonant, as well as the other sounds.

Star Words

Objective
- To practise blending real and nonsense words.

Resources
- *PCC*s and a whiteboard or chart to write words on.

Explanation for children
In the Star Words game we are all on the same team. We take turns moving letters to try to make real words. Every time we move a letter we blend the sounds. If we have made a real word we colour in part of the star as our reward. When we fill up the whole star, we all win!

Procedure
Arrange *Picture Code Cards* in three stacks as shown to build three-sound CVC words. The list of letters below for each stack will help to ensure that more real words come up and also avoid letter patterns that the children have not yet learned. For more advanced words, see below.

CVC short vowel words	Initial consonants	Medial short vowels	Final consonants
	b, c, f, h, j, l, m, r, s	ă, ĕ, ĭ, ŏ, ŭ	d, g, n, p, t

Write the words **Real** and **Nonsense** across the top of the board.

Step	Description
1	**First child** reads first word, using the Roller Coaster Trick if needed.
2	**Group** decides if it is a real word or nonsense word.
3	**Teacher** writes the word under Real or Nonsense and the class reads the word from the board. If it is a real word the child colours in one section of the star.
4	**Second child** moves one card from any one of the three stacks to start a new stack just below (see illustration). Child reads the resulting new word.
5	**Group** decides where the teacher should write the word. If it is a real word, the child fills in a star section. When a word is added to either the Real or Nonsense list, the children read all the words in that column.
6	**Third child** follows the same Steps 4 and 5. After the third child, children have the option of putting a card back on the initial stack or moving one down to make a new word, but they cannot make a word that has been made before.
7	Game continues until the star is filled. Everyone can cheer and applaud.

Star Words: advanced spellings

Split digraphs	Initial consonant	Medial long vowels	Final consonants
	f, h, l, m, r, s	ā, ī, ō, ū	d, n, p, t (also Silent e)*

* Follow the same steps as above but in addition to moving one letter each time, the child can add or take away the Silent Magic **e** to make a word. Keep vowel letters on the plain side and explain that they can stand for the Vowel Sound or the Vowel Man's name, depending on Silent Magic **e**.

Vowels digraphs	Initial consonant	Medial vowel	Final consonants
	b, f, l, r, s, w	Long vowels: ai, ea, ee, oa*	k, l, n, p, t

* If children make a word that sounds like a real word but has a different spelling (e.g. **lait**, **roap**), write the correct spelling on the board and count it as a real word. This game also gives you an opportunity to talk about homonyms and their meanings such as **week** and **weak**.

Essential Words Phrase Game

Objectives

- To supplement your teaching of 'tricky' words.
- To build quick and accurate reading of the most common words including exception words and regular words.

Resources

Information for this game and instructions for how to play it can be printed from your *TGCD*. Easy to play independently in small groups or pairs, and more fun than one word flashcards, this game is a great way to improve children's speed and accuracy in mastering 60 of the 100 most high frequency words in the English language.

The game cards are divided into two levels. Once children master Set 1 they move on to Set 2.

Look-Say-Cover-Write-Check

Objective

- To learn and practise the correct spelling of words.

Resources

- *Look-Say-Cover-Write-Check* form (*TGCD*).

Procedure

To get started the child copies from the board or *Fluency List* to the first column. Alternatively the teacher fills in the first column and provides a copy to the child. Then the child follows the steps below with each word.

Step	Description
1	**Look-Say** Study and say the word aloud several times until ready to spell it.
2	**Cover** the word in the first column.
3	**Write** the word in the second column.
4	**Check** your spelling by comparing it to column one. If correct place a tick in column 3. Correct your spelling if wrong. Either way continue with Step 5.
5	**Write again** Cover column one and two and write the word again. Check and correct as before.

When to use

- This is a well-researched and time honoured method of learning to spell words. Use it to help children spell important irregular words and words with sounds that can be spelled more than one way.

Development over time

- At first you will need to closely guide the use of this method with the whole class or small group. In time, children will be able to use this method on their own or at home with parent supervision. Follow up by doing a spelling check-up test.

Phonics Teacher's Guide CD Contents

Assessment

Fluency Lists

Fluency Lists A-T
Reading Racer Charts

Letters for Picture Coding

Lower and uppercase **aA-zZ** letter shapes
Short and long vowel letter shapes
Double consonants and consonant digraph letter shapes

Take-Home Booklets

Section 2 - (A hat on a cat, Lost, Sam spots)
Section 3 - (The cat gets stuck, Handstands, Fantastic Fix-it Max)
Section 4 - (Name games, Trapped, Can Sammy see?)
Section 5 - (In the dark, A shrew on the loose, Look at me)

Song lyrics

Alphabet song lyrics
Handwriting song lyrics
Blends & Digraphs song lyrics

Learning activities and materials

Beginning Sounds Pictures
Essential Words Phrase Game
Look-Say-Cover-Write-Check
Sammy's Slide and Say
Spelling Boxes
Vowel Flip-overs
Alphabet names verses
b and d finger puppets

100 high-frequency words list

These are the most common words that children are expected to know by the end of their first year at school. The 26 words that are highlighted in grey are all 'decodable', that is, they can be sounded out using the first sounds children learn for **a-z**. As more sounds and spelling patterns are learned, more become decodable. Words highlighted in yellow indicate a long vowel sound. The irregular parts of each word have been underlined.

the	that	not	look	put
and	with	then	don't	could
a	all	were	come	house
to	we	go	will	old
said	can	little	into	too
in	are	as	back	by
he	up	no	from	day
I	had	mum	children	made
of	my	one	him	time
it	her	them	Mr	I'm
was	what	do	get	if
you	there	me	just	help
they	out	down	now	Mrs
on	this	dad	come	called
she	have	big	oh	here
is	went	when	about	off
for	be	it's	got	asked
at	like	see	their	saw
his	some	looked	people	make
but	so	very	your	an

Glossary of terms

adjacent consonants two or three letters with discrete sounds which are blended together: **sm**, **bl**, **cr**.

alliteration a phrase containing words beginning with the same initial sound: **C**lever **C**at **c**ollects **c**oins; **M**unching **M**ike loves to **m**unch **m**ushrooms in the **m**eadow.

base word a word minus any prefix or suffix added to it: un**concern**ed, **kind**ness, **goat**s, **snow**ing.

blending the process of sounding out each individual phoneme in a word and then blending them together to read the word. For example, /c/ /ă/ /t/ blended together is **cat**.

compound word a word which consists of two words put together with each retaining its meaning: **playground**, **roundabout**, **notebook**.

comprehension understanding the text being read.

consonant all alphabet letters except the vowels **a**, **e**, **i**, **o**, **u**.

contraction a word that combines two words with one or more sounds left out: **I'm**, **wasn't**, **we've**. An apostrophe is placed where one or more letters are left out.

decoding the process of going from printed or written words to verbal language whether reading aloud or silently.

digraph two letters representing one phoneme: **th**in, lu**ck**, **sh**op, gr**ow**, tr**ea**t, cl**ou**d.

grapheme a written representation of a single phoneme; may consist of one or more letters. For example the phoneme /s/ can be represented by the graphemes shown: **s**un, mou**se**, **c**ity, **sc**ience.

letter name the name commonly used when referring to letter shapes: **aye**, **bee**, **cee**, **dee**, **ee**, **eff**, **gee**.

letter shape the form of the letter.

letter sound the speech sound represented by a letter, often represented in print between back slashes: /t/ for the letter **t**.

multisensory the simultaneous use of visual, auditory and kinaesthetic senses (VAK) to enhance learning.

phoneme the smallest identifiable unit of sound in a word. A phoneme can be represented by one, two, three or four letters. The following words end in the same phoneme: t**o**, sh**oe**, thr**ough**.

phonemic awareness the ability to hear, identify and manipulate the individual sounds (phonemes) in spoken words. A child shows phonemic awareness when they can separate the phonemes in a word (**map**, /m/ /ă/ /p/).

phonics the teaching of the relationship between sounds and spellings (phonemes and graphemes).

pictogram a picture embedded in a letter or digraph that helps children remember the shapes and sounds even when they see the plain letters.

prefix a part added at the beginning of a base word that changes the meaning: **un**seen, **re**write, **dis**appear, **pre**view.

schwa an unstressed vowel phoneme. Any vowel can be pronounced as a schwa if the syllable is not stressed (shown underlined): m**a**n → workm**a**n.

segmenting the process of splitting up a spoken word into its individual phonemes in order to spell it: cat /c/ /ă/ /t/ → **cat**.

slow-speak a term used to describe stretching out a word by saying it slowly enough to identify each sound to aid spelling: **run, rrrrrruuuuuunnnn**.

split digraph two letters, split, making one sound, For example, **a_e** as in **make**.

suffix a part added to the end of a word that may change its tense, number, meaning, part of speech, or use in a sentence: reach**ed**, wish**ing**, bell**s**, care**less**, kind**ness**, think**s**.

syllable each 'beat' in a word is a syllable. Words with only one syllable (**cat**, **fright**) are called monosyllabic; words with more than one syllable (**super**, **superman**) are polysyllabic.

'tricky' words Frequently used words that cannot be decoded easily. They often have one or more unusual spelling patterns: **was**, **said**, **what**, **they**, **of**. Also called common exception words, sight words, irregular high-frequency words.

trigraph three letters representing one phoneme: h**igh**; h**ear**.

vowel the five vowel letters, **a**, **e**, **i**, **o**, **u**. They can represent short or long sounds (**cat**, **cake**). The letter **y** can also represent vowel sounds (fl**y**, ver**y**, bic**y**cle).

Index